NOVEL A FORUM ON FICTION

PUBLISHED IN MAY, AUGUST, AND NOVEMBER OF EACH YEAR

VOLUME 51   NUMBER 2   AUGUST 2018

NOVEL: A FORUM ON FICTION

NOVEL: A FORUM ON FICTION is published three times a year by Duke University Press, 905 W. Main St., Suite 18B, Durham, NC 27701, on behalf of Novel, Inc. A two-year individual membership ($90) or two-year student membership ($40) to the SNS includes a subscription to NOVEL. To obtain a membership, go to www.dukepress.edu/sns.

Submissions/Correspondence All manuscripts must conform to the most recent *MLA Handbook* guidelines, with in-text parenthetical documentation and a list of works cited. Manuscripts should be submitted electronically, along with a cover letter containing all relevant contact information (e-mail, mailing address). Electronic copies of the manuscript and cover letter should be sent in both Word and PDF format to **novel.forum @duke.edu.** Further information is available at **novel.trinity.duke.edu.** *N.B.* Presses seeking book reviews in NOVEL must send books to our Brown office: Brown University, Box 1984, 70 Brown Street, Providence, RI 02912.

World Wide Web Visit Duke University Press Journals at www.dukepress.edu/journals.

Contents

Introduction: How Do Novels Think about Neoliberalism?

JOHN MARX AND NANCY ARMSTRONG

The fourth biennial conference of the Society for Novel Studies was held at the University of Pittsburgh in May 2016 under the leadership of Jonathan Arac, then SNS vice president. *Novel* sponsored British novelist Tom McCarthy as the keynote speaker, and he agreed to let us publish both his talk and his provocative interview with Nicholas Huber. Members of the editorial board selected four additional papers from the conference that, in their view, shed new light on the relationship between the novel and neoliberalism. The remaining papers in this issue are based on invited talks from symposia held at Duke and Brown Universities that focused on the contemporary novel, critical theory, and the curious relationship these two modes of writing have taken up in the past half century. All the essays went through the journal's standard review process.

To introduce this special issue, we chose two essays that frame the largely unstated question that the collection as a whole addresses: McCarthy's keynote talk, "Vanity's Residue," which leans heavily on certain novels as a mode of critical theoretical writing, and Dierdra Reber's "A Tale of Two Marats," which leans just as heavily on the explanatory logic of political-economic theory as McCarthy does on that of novels. Together, these essays ask us to consider how major contemporary novelists have changed the novel's "partition of the sensible . . . which," according to Jacques Rancière, "allows (or does not allow) some data to appear" (11). Is this alteration of the reader's formal expectations a matter of course—an expression of the generic obligation of the novel to violate the established novel form, however one construes it? Or do the formal features that distinguish novels written in the last thirty years or so alter that obligation itself? Should we consider the variations that encourage us to identify certain novels with "neoliberalism" as variations of the novel as a genre—or do they amount to a different order of difference that in turn amounts to a different set of generic requirements? If the latter, then can we say that the novels now being written for a global audience are breaking with the novel form itself and dissolving the contract, which changes those expectations—including that of the element of surprise—that readers bring to novel reading?

Reber and McCarthy are of one mind that the turn in political and novel history now attributed to neoliberalism has actually been three centuries in the making. Reber begins with the concept of laissez-faire coined by the mid-eighteenth-century Physiocrats who argued that the economy should be free of regulations to develop according to its own natural law. She shows how that principle derives energy from its opposition ("abhorrence" is her word) to a form of vertical authority that describes itself as rational. Her account holds the vertical authority of empire responsible for curbing the horizontal drive of laissez-faire until the end of the Cold War period, when neoliberalism emerged from the collapse of vertical authority. She sees Trumpery as symptomatic of this collapse: "In a cultural climate dominated by laissez-faire logic, fact and truth and rational critique and judgment must cede . . . to opinion and affective preference."

McCarthy's keynote situates his work in a long history that goes back to the novels of Laurence Sterne and from there to Herman Melville, Lewis Carroll, and the quirkier works of modernism by Joseph Conrad, Virginia Woolf, Franz Kafka, and Samuel Beckett. These novelists all exceed the limitations of the generic form, and each does so in a sui generis style. McCarthy implies that some kind of leap separates his own fiction from that of Thomas Pynchon in terms of the novelist's inability to offer a future beyond the world of multinational capitalism. Having argued that the recent turn in the history of the novel was three centuries in the making, he ends up in much the same cul-de-sac as Reber. What is so new about their situation, aside from the fact that it takes a pair of revisionary histories to explain the relationship between the novel and the political-economic conditions that limit the possibilities of imagining a future?

According to Reber, both Left and Right have unleashed an abhorrence of vertical authority that formal hierarchies had for centuries contained and sublimated. Rather than expose the limitations of vertical authority, such unchecked antagonism has exposed the historical complicity of radical democracy and laissez-faire economic policy. The dissolution of the difference between the two means that the concept of radical democracy no longer provides a true alternative to government by multinational corporations.

The fact that McCarthy thinks with and through the novel would seem to put him at an advantage in this situation, were the endings of his novels, like that of his keynote address, not so "fucking weird" (*Satin Island* 203). Having discarded all possibility of a future beyond or outside what seems a limitless economic order, McCarthy's keynote ends with the baleful figure of the writer as a dying man "[s]et aside in one of the technical and secret zones (hospitals, prisons, refuse dumps) which relieve the living of everything that might hinder the chain of production and consumption" (Certeau 191). Borrowed from the conclusion of Michel de Certeau's *The Practice of Everyday Life*, this figure claims for writing something like the power that Raymond Williams ascribes to "the residual" and that McCarthy attributes to writing that can "in the darkness where no one wants to penetrate, repair and select what can be sent back up to the surface of progress." It seems to us that McCarthy uses this figure to reject the generic promise of the novel—just as Reber dismisses the promise of liberal democracy—on grounds that yearning for a more radical democratic future extends "the chain of production and consumption."

We find it interesting that both essays feature garbage pickers as surrogates for the contemporary artist: the anthropologist narrator of McCarthy's *Satin Island* (2015) collects bits of information from people's lives for a mysterious megacorporation, where Reber's protagonist, Vik Muniz, is a Brazilian-born and Brooklyn-based photographer of images composed of material from Latin America's biggest dump, the equivalent of no less than 244 American football fields. A team of *catadores*, garbage pickers who make a living by sorting out recyclable materials, assembles the images in Muniz's *Waste Land* series. Noting how the reproduction of *The Death of Marat* in this debris field exploits the radical horizontality captured in the luminous martyred body of the original, Reber balks at pronouncing Muniz's image a "redemptive portrait" simply because it pays tribute to Jacques-Louis David's revolutionary painting. The photograph's celebration of the *catadores'* entrepreneurial energy, in her view, has all too much in common with the argument of small-government advocates who link happiness to economic freedom.

Like McCarthy, Reber sees her task as penetrating the "partition of the sensible" for purposes of making visible some of the information that our master narratives have filtered out. Exposing this "waste" product of writing does not bring about some kind of transformation, in either view—much less one that points beyond writing. At best, both novelist and political theorist perform "a resurrection that does not restore to life" (Certeau 193). This raises a number of important questions about the relation of the novel to neoliberalism, which we pose and reflect on dialogically.

NANCY ARMSTRONG: If what we mean by *neoliberalism* is a culture marked by the collapse of the categories of liberalism (democracy/class hierarchy; democratic writing/literary genres; freedom/subjection), then does that collapse explain why post-WWII novels refuse to hold out "happy horizontality" as the resolution to the individual's struggle for self-recognition under dehumanizing conditions? A number of essays in this collection seem to be searching for something more: something in the way of an alternative to the opposition that has occasioned this struggle for more than two centuries, an opposition that might yield a new antithesis. Do you think any of these essays manages to formulate an alternative that allows us to think about recent novels in terms that can't be boiled down to the opposition between vertical authority and happy horizontality?

JOHN MARX: Well, Jane Elliott sure wants such an alternative. She thinks that in becoming universal, microeconomics has left us with no way to distinguish among different kinds of human actors and to privilege some as good and others as bad; terrorists and antiterrorists play the same kinds of microeconomic games. What do you think of the way these essays talk about tactics and strategy? Is that another kind of binary? I'm thinking of Rachel Greenwald Smith's suggestion that the novel today fetishizes stylistic and formal innovation without attention to the ideological big picture. Or Lily Saint's interest in how the contemporary novel conscripts its readers into networks of responsibility that are actually kind of irresponsible or that lack a strategic vision capable of providing a context for evaluating what it means to be responsible to this person rather than to that one. Does this sound different to you or like more of the same?

NA: I'm suspicious of the sudden overuse of "tactics" and "strategy," as formulated in Michel de Certeau's *Practices of Everyday Life* of thirty years ago. A number of the essays in our collection seem to be caught in the affective undertow of horizontality that Reber identifies with laissez-faire, and I find it telling that McCarthy concludes his argument not with a passage from the oft-quoted chapter "Walking in the City" but with a passage from the conclusion to Certeau's book titled "The Unnamable." If, as the earlier and more cheerful chapter suggests, tactics and strategy are mutually dependent sides of the opposition submission/domination, then, Certeau concludes, tactics can't very well unseat strategy without becoming exactly that. Would you say that in taking up this figure, McCarthy agrees with Reber that the collapse of strategy and tactics characterizes the present (neoliberal) moment? As for Elliott, when she calls attention to the upsurge of popular novels and films that turn the prisoner's dilemma game into a "microeconomic mode," can we say that she shows how this collapse occurs? The James Franco film *127 Hours* provides Elliott's bluntest example of how the collapse of strategy and tactics plays out at the level of the individual. Doesn't cutting off an arm save the individual's life by compromising the individual's autonomy? This would seem to eradicate the difference between tactics and strategy. Smith suggests that Rachel Kushner does the same thing in *The Flamethrowers*, when her photographer protagonist relinquishes her power of selective vision and embraces a "compromise aesthetics" that allows authoritarianism to flourish.

JM: If there is strategy in these examples, it operates at a scale seemingly beyond the reach of any individual actor even as, to follow Elliott, the "fierce determination" of the individual as microdecision maker takes center stage. Smith's compromise aesthetics is all tactics and no strategy, the victory of Francis Fukuyama's "endless solving of technical problems" (18). The formulation requires subjects capable of figuring out how to cut off their own arms but not how to run their own countries. As for how this dynamic came about, Smith wants us to note that strategy is still out there, even if it is not for us. "For a generation," she writes, "we have aspired to empty ourselves of collective forms of political ideology and intentional forms of authority." The result is that "we forget that there are authors" of the discourses that operate through us. Authors, but not novelists, at least not according to McCarthy, who locates himself as author in a situation comparable to the characters in the novels considered in this special issue. His novelist appears more adept at assessing and navigating the contemporary world than his readers, but no one is making claims for his novels' capacity to do very much to change it.

NA: I have to address that claim indirectly. I see McCarthy posing the Kafka problem in his bleak conclusion, which defines the writer's position as intolerable in the same way that solitary confinement is, with neither realistic possibilities of escape nor credible possibilities of transcendence. Why do twenty-first-century novelists put themselves in the same neither/nor position as that of Kafka? Sure, it lets them do a great job of turning the apparatuses confining them into the literary machinery of a monstrous government that authors them, but is that all there is to it? I realize, of course, that ours are very different times than Kafka's. Nevertheless, so many of the novelists who now interest me claim to descend from him and Beckett that there must be something for them in this state of being overpowered. I think they know that the bottom, so to speak, is more powerful than the top, because the top is actually not in charge. Matthew Hart's identification of the "extraordinary" event that cracks open the "enclave" form of J. G. Ballard's "late" novels is an obvious case in point. Jeanne-Marie Jackson's claim that the novels now coming out of Zimbabwe offer an "agonistic pluralism" strikes me as the counterpart to Hart's reading of the "extraordinary" event as a version of the same force-counterforce dynamic. If you buy that comparison, would it be all that much of a stretch to say that a novel like Dambudzo Marechera's *The House of Hunger* explains why it's impossible for novels aimed at global readership to achieve the unity, autonomy, and consensus that seem to provoke eruptions of apocalyptic violence in *Super-Cannes* and *Millennium People*? Would you say that Jackson and Emilio Sauri extend or overturn the postcolonial critique of European realism as informed by a wish for political autonomy and internal consensus? In focusing on the present moment, do Jackson and Sauri ask us to change the way we read the novels written in the former colonies?

JM: Yes and no. There's definitely something in Jackson and Sauri of the stock (and correct!) postcolonial literary critic's assertion that reading novels from outside the increasingly well-consecrated anglophone canon can provide a bracing reminder of the larger world. Jackson's essay might be read as doubling down on this rhetoric, inasmuch as it seeks a criticism capable of "digging deeper to grapple with locally and narratively emplaced structures of debate." Sauri, though, wants us to discern something abstract and global in Yuri Herrera's "attentiveness to setting," which "not only presupposes the existence of a society governed by abstract laws, structures, and functions but also signals the degree to which the novel is unthinkable without it." Neither critic is more confident than any of the other scholars in this issue that the contemporary novel is capable of acting on the world, however. Maybe it can help us imagine an alternate future (Sauri) or encourage us to keep several competing perspectives in our heads at the same time (Jackson). For all that these are accomplishments, they also seem like weak tea in comparison to the grand claims the novel was capable of sustaining in an earlier moment of postcolonial criticism.

NA: OK, I give, but know that it's my training in the great tradition of James and Conrad that makes me do so. What if we say that the material culture filtered out of classic political-economic and novelistic discourse as waste or garbage has something like an immanent vitalism—and that the jarring introduction of this material revitalizes a form and discourse stuck in a repetition compulsion (aka modernism). Gregor Samsa's bedroom/garbage dump serves as my own theoretical model for this formal behavior. Doesn't the rediscovery of incredible excess, or waste, produced by a form (the novel) at the heart of the discourse of "normal" modern life open up a space (the dump) where novels are relieved of the obligation to formulate an elsewhere?

JM: I like this formulation a good deal. If dumpster diving is what gives recent novels a sense of purpose, would you say it also gives them a politics? What you say could look truly like old-school bricolage—and Reber's second Marat suggests that—with all the theoretical sophistication and aesthetic pretension therein. But it could also look like the rather more ambivalent entrepreneurial practice that is colloquially associated with austerity, turning crises into opportunities, and the like. Maybe it's both? In which case, how do we tell the two apart?

NA: Point taken. I am a sucker for old-fashioned "bricolage," preferring it to the overused term "pastiche," or what often strikes me as parody without purpose. It seems to me that McCarthy rules out the possibility of such entrepreneurial recycling in *Satin Island*, when he makes his protagonist a belated Lévi-Strauss who halfheartedly collects endless amounts of information about consumer practices for a mysterious global corporation. Reber does the same in pointing out how Muniz unwittingly colludes with the neoliberal right (as Trump's base does with wealthy donors) by asking us to celebrate horizontality for its own sake. On the other hand, how do you deal with the fact that both she and McCarthy reject the redemptive or reparative possibilities of "dumpster diving" as the means of fulfilling the generic obligation to produce a moralized, healthy, or potentially normative (masculine?) alternative. Both seem to take a form of pleasure—at once infantile and sophisticated— in texts like this. I like to think of this as the emergence of a residual pleasure, the pleasure we gave up for the delayed gratification of mastering difficulty in classic works of modernism.

JM: Although it takes a weird form, this is the seductive pleasure of technical expertise, isn't it? Indulging it might offer another way of understanding these essays, inasmuch as they respond to horizontality by directing our attention to talent, however impotent or retro-modernist. We might imagine these essays as daring us to offer a hierarchical scheme worth supporting, once they have persuaded us that horizontality is a sham.

NA: Are you willing to see the contemporary novel as the emergence of a long tradition of novels that recycle "trash"? That would seem to explain why the novels McCarthy names are so different (sui generis) and nevertheless boil down to the same thing: that is, letting the novel be the novel. Do you have another way of explaining why our moment has experienced one of the great outbursts of formal innovation in the history of the novel? I haven't found contemporary economic theory especially helpful in explaining why a broad swath of these novels goes deliberately off the rails, but I think you're onto something with the concept of "talent," though talent that finds expression in and through technology versus a very different concept of talent as in "tradition and the individual talent." A very different virtuosity that brings some rigor to the term sui generis.

JM: Presume we buy it: there is a long tradition of "garbage novels" running back to the eighteenth century that acquires something like the status of a coherent genre in our present, or, as you put it, a broad swath of seemingly sui generis novels that seem to be doing the same thing. Isn't this what the history of genres looks like? In other words, scattered experiments in what will someday be the "garbage novel" that all of a sudden begin to cohere as a recognizable literary category. If that seems an apt amendment to the proposition, one follow-up question for me would be: What is the status of this genre among the full range of genres in our present? Is the "garbage novel" the one genre to rule them all? Is it to our moment as the bildungsroman was to the second half of the nineteenth century, or whatever? Or is this a minor fiction, the stuff of academic intrigue rather than the kind of novelistic power you, among others, have located in earlier centuries?

NA: For the sake of argument, I refuse to think of the tradition of "aberrant" or "garbage" novels as a generic innovation bent on revising readers' expectations for the purpose of dominating the global book market. I grant that what you say might very well come true someday, but I think we are in a position now to see that it's way more complicated—and interesting—than that. I have an abiding attachment to Williams's notion of an emergent form as a residual social formation to which "a structure of feeling," one that couldn't be formulated as such at an earlier moment in time, suddenly congeals stuff—extra material that doesn't feel like much of anything—so that it finds formal expression in fiction. Great traditions, like those of Ian Watt and F. R. Leavis, pretend to march forward in time, bringing past formulations up to date. You and I have done our bits to realign that kind of tradition for postcolonialism and feminism, respectively. But I have yet to hear of anyone, least of all McCarthy, who wants to line up Sterne, Carroll, Conrad's *Secret Agent*, or Pynchon in such a progressive history. I go along with Giorgio Agamben's definition of "the contemporary" in only one respect, that this concept snaps the spine of prevailing cultural historical narratives and forces us to search the not yet sensible areas of the past for makings of a history of the present. Williams would add that the novels of the day always look to certain past novels as the archive of residual material, material in excess of meaning. As for a minor literature, I completely buy the idea that Kafka's "minority" status as a novelist is not only the claim of so many novelists and philosophers (most notably Gilles Deleuze) who see him as their predecessor but also what Kafka was striving for. Don't you think, though, that sheer quantity changes everything? If the growing number of his successors displace the tradition that minoritized Kafka, then these novelists could not be major as opposed to minor but have (here we go again) invalidated that binary. Instead of one tradition, couldn't we say these novelists are restarting many different strands of history that have to be understood as more of a web than a road?

JM: I 100 percent agree that quantity changes everything. We could use someone with better computational chops than you or I possess to tell us how prevalent the "garbage novel" is, but knowing would not necessarily alter my assessment of how interesting it is. I even think I'd agree, although maybe grudgingly, that were we to discover that the "garbage novel" prevails mostly in academy-friendly global fiction, this fact would not make it any less intriguing. In short, I see no more advantage than you do in reinstalling a minor/major, core/periphery, margin/center schema. And yet, Kafka. I would be super happy to see a genealogy that did not rely so heavily on the Euro-American canon, including its minor figures. The gauntlet has been thrown: more non-Euro-American precedents for contemporary "garbage fiction" wanted.

NA: I can't say exactly when, much less why, I stopped imagining literary history as a discourse that claims to march forward irreversibly in time. I do know that it was about the same time that I became aware of a tendency I shared with my best students and closest colleagues. I was always getting sucked into the novel's drive for freedom (from generic restrictions, or whatever) and thus becoming subject to its emotional undertow: Reber's expanded definition of laissez-faire? Have the limits of the literary institution prompted novel criticism and theory to revise its historical and generic categories? Or can we blame "the novel" for recruiting us to look to horizontality as the political alternative to vertical authority? Are you suggesting that by way of taking me to task for my thing with Kafka?

JM: I think this is spot-on and invokes the question of politics I posed earlier. I would love to place the burden for this tendency of contemporary literary criticism on the novel form, although I hesitate to make us the victims of a plot from which we too might someday be free. I've always preferred formulations in which the question of freedom is less absolute, and I think that I've received a good deal of help in thinking about that from novels. I'll spare you my inclination to rattle off a list of novels that forgo absolutist terms for thinking about being free and being governed. Instead, let me ask you whether you think of this as primarily an aesthetic effect or a question of plot, to the extent that you'd be willing to differentiate between these two. In other words, is the freedom from genre invoking a high/low distinction? Fancy experimental novels are freer? Or is this a problem about the stories that novels tell?

NA: You certainly weaseled out of my previous question, but since you asked: for me the evidence suggests otherwise. I find Nathan K. Hensley persuasive when he shows how McCarthy's preoccupation with new forms of mediation finds expression in the same optical rhetoric that serves as the theater for cyberwarfare in popular "drone thrillers" or how Teju Cole does the same thing when he uses the Twitter platform to sabotage the conclusions of classic novels with 140-character "drone stories." Saint convinces me that Cole's *Open City* turns the self-righteous imperative "only connect" inside out and comes down on the side of distancing oneself from others as the more durable form of social relations. Paul Stasi boils down Walter Benn Michaels's influential definition of art in the age of neoliberalism to an effacement of "notions of relation and containment" that enables "a fluidity of experience" to transcend "the coherence of literary form and the determinations of social ground." Sound familiar? Stasi argues that James's *Golden Bowl* anticipates such a moment of transcendence, when "fortune and acquisition create an aesthetic power to see," a power to see that regards itself, as James does *not*, as "the emblem of all freedom." In each case, these essays imply that novels offer the lure of a freedom that proves to be anything but.

JM: Although these essays show how freedom functions as a lure, they do not appear interested in reinscribing it as a goal. I understand these essays as not particularly nostalgic for any pre-neoliberalism. It can seem as if the contemporary novel is more like a diagnostic tool than a fount of actionable information or a repository of instructions for conduct. I am not at all sure that our contributors are happy about that job description for the novel, however, and a look at their conclusions suggests cravings for other options. Vaughn Rasberry's essay is the perfect bookend for the collection, in part because of where he winds up: confirming via a reading of Francis Spufford's *Red Plenty* that the novel makes the past available as a resource. *Red Plenty* recalls a "road constructed but not traveled in the twentieth century," Rasberry explains, one "that could have precipitated what appears then and now as a hopelessly utopian prospect: a colorblind world order." Rasberry gives and takes away transcendence in the same gesture. I do not interpret this as a trick on his part so much as a confirmation: there are more interesting lost causes than liberalism's version of freedom buried in the garbage dump of history for novels to dig up.

* * *

Those readers who are keen to clarify these questions or redirect them in a way that would move the conversation forward should email commentary to novel .forum@duke.edu or tweet @novelforum. Please identify precisely where you would like to insert your comment and include your name and affiliation. Appropriate responses will be posted along with this introduction on the *Novel* website, novel .trinity.duke.edu, under "news."

* * *

NANCY ARMSTRONG is Gilbert, Louis, and Edward Lehrman Professor of Trinity College at Duke University and editor of the journal *Novel: A Forum on Fiction*. Her books include *Desire and Domestic Fiction: A Political History of the Novel* (1986), *The Imaginary Puritan: Literature, Intellectual Labor, and the Origins of Personal Life* (with Leonard Tennenhouse, 1992), *Fiction in the Age of Photography: The Legacy of British Realism* (1999), *How Novels Think: The Limits of Individualism, 1719–1900* (2005), and, most recently, *Novels in the Time of Democratic Writing: The American Example* (2017).

JOHN MARX is professor and chair of English at the University of California, Davis. He serves as an associate editor at *Novel* and has authored *Geopolitics and the Anglophone Novel, 1890– 2011* (2012) and *The Modernist Novel and the Decline of Empire* (2005, 2009). His book *Media U: A New History of the American University*, coauthored with Mark Garrett Cooper, is forthcoming in 2018.

Works Cited

de Certeau, Michel. *The Practice of Everyday Life*. Trans. Steven Rendall. Berkeley: U of California P, 1988.

Fukuyama, Francis. "The End of History?" *National Interest* 16 (1989): 3–18.

McCarthy, Tom. *Satin Island*. New York: Knopf, 2015.

Rancière, Jacques. "The Politics of Literature." *SubStance* 33.1 (2004): 10–24.

Williams, Raymond. *Marxism and Literature*. Oxford: Oxford, 1977.

Vanity's Residue

TOM MCCARTHY

Thank you for that generous introduction; and thank you for inviting me to contemplate, interrogate, or just divagate around this conference's wonderfully loaded title phrase, "The Novel in or against World Literature." It is, of course, a deliberately provocative formulation whose terms demand unpacking—and I've already been privileged to witness some expert unpacking today as I listened to some of the best minds in their respective fields advance and upgrade a set of critical practices that for some decades now have tracked the literary manifestations of empire and diaspora; championed the logic of hybridity and creolism over that of "natural" language or expression; plotted territory in terms of islands, archipelagos, dependencies, and zones of emergent autonomy. This work is important, indeed vital—politically, conceptually, and aesthetically—for any understanding of what literature is, has been, or might become. But it's not what I've been invited here to do. I've been kindly and indulgently given license to go a little off-road—and perhaps even to get a little lost. Which suits me fine. If I'm good for anything at all, it's getting lost. This, perhaps, is the prerogative of the novelist. It struck me recently that the relationship between the writer and the academic community is a bit like that between a Malaysian aeroplane and air traffic control: We get lost, you look for us, bringing an increasingly sophisticated array of hard- and software to bear in an attempt to get a lock, to pinpoint some location or event, even if what's ultimately revealed turns out to be not the finely crafted apogee of skill or *techné* but rather the chance movements of debris round global flows. So let me use the next forty minutes to send out, in the form of anecdotal summaries of a couple of projects I've been involved with over the last few years, a set of pings, or (if you like) distress signals—not, I hope, although vanity will be my subject, as a narcissistic demand to be gazed at and interpreted, but rather in the hope that, just as an object—any object, no matter how dull—over which a radar beam slides has the effect of illuminating the surrounding screen-surface, drawing latent vectors and terrains to visibility, so something of flow-space, of the grid itself, might glow and fizz, for a short while at least, while I speak.

Because, you see, it seems to me that this is where it all begins: with maps. For some time now I've been obsessed with the opening sequence of Aeschylus's *Agamemnon*. This play (which, we should note in passing, comes to us from a civilization that modern Western culture has placed at the top of its own genealogical tree but that, since geographically speaking it was spread around the entire Mediterranean basin, could equally be considered Middle Eastern or African)—this play begins with an elaborate act of mapping. The Argive watchman having spied the distant signal beacon announcing the fall of Troy, Clytemnestra appears before the palace and delivers a lengthy speech in which the message (Troy is finally ours) assumes

Originally delivered as the keynote address at the fourth biennial conference of the Society for Novel Studies, University of Pittsburgh, May 13, 2016.

Novel: A Forum on Fiction 51:2   DOI 10.1215/00295132-6846012   © 2018 by Tom McCarthy

only secondary importance to the *network* across which it has traveled. The visible signal beacon being merely the last in a long chain running between Troy and Argos, Clytemnestra names each other one, each post and its coordinates: Ida's summit, then the crag of Lemnos, then Mount Athos, then Macistus, onwards to the Plain of Aesopus, the Saronic Gulf, and so on. In her 1999 production at London's National Theatre, Katie Mitchell had the actress pull down a giant roller blind and give a PowerPoint presentation sketching the signal's route across an atlas page. It was an astute piece of directing, since not only this scene but also the entire Oresteian trilogy that grows from it follows a cartographic logic: measuring the relative positions of, distances between, and communication relays linking gods and humans, public and domestic space, divine justice and its corresponding fora in the civic realm—so much so that by the end of *The Eumenides*, democracy itself is born out of topography, an exercise in land division or ground demarcation: Athens will be where citizen-led, goddess-sanctioned law holds sway; the Furies' grotto tucked into its hillside the repository of older, cthonic orders.

The whole Hellenic corpus could be understood this way: the Greeks, seafarers, are always and foremost mapping, drawing charts up: marking off sanctioned and unsanctioned ground in *Antigone*; tracing the layout of the phone wires descending from Olympus to the Delphic switchboard and then on to Thebes and Corinth—plus, of course, the convergence of roads—in *Oedipus*; plotting the universe out as pure geometry in *Timmaeus*. And not just the Greeks. Isn't Dante's *Divine Comedy* also an epic work of cosmic mapping, a laying-out of metaphysics, history, and inner psychic space according to the geometry of spheres and circles? Doesn't Shakespeare's *Merchant of Venice* cast modernity itself along the latitudes and longitudes of the commercial orb, the far-flung geography—Tripoli, Mexico, the Indies, England—of which the *urb* of Venice is both the mirror and the marketplace? Isn't the Dublin of Joyce's novels also a kind of shadow globe, a surface on which all other places, epochs, currencies, and languages, incessantly migrating, scrawl their trajectories? So strong and so insistent is this mapping tendency that in the last decade of the twentieth century Thomas Pynchon is able to spin an eight-hundred-page novel around the simple act of two men, Mason and Dixon, drawing a line through space: the act, that is, of geo-graphy.

How do you put the world on paper? This is the basic cartographic question and the basic question of literature, of the novel. It's so basic that I think it's worth addressing at a basic level. Open any high school textbook on maps, and the first chapter will make the obvious but essential point that the earth is spherical but paper is flat. To quote J. A. Steers's 1927 primer *An Introduction to the Study of Map Projections*: "As it is impossible to make a sheet of paper rest smoothly on a sphere, so it is impossible to make a correct map on a sheet of paper." All maps deploy, like Mitchell's Clytemnestra, projections—and projections, being drafters' conventions, are both arbitrary and flawed. You can use zenithal, gnomonic, stereographic, orthographic, globular, conical, cylindrical, or sinusoidal projections—but you'll never get it *right*. In world maps drawn using Mercator's projection, the one that served as the standard in atlases for centuries, the equatorial areas pan out fine, but the map starts to distend as it nears the polar regions, stretching Greenland out until it looks bigger than Africa. The poles themselves cannot be represented at all: to depict these, you must rotate the image round through ninety degrees—the Transverse Mercator projection does this—only to find that another pair of points, on the equator, undergo infinite distortion and become invisible. And if you try to sidestep this by replacing Mercator's projection with a polar gnomonic one, the rest of the world just slips off the horizon.

Nor is this anamorphosis simply a formal problem. As [Hans] Holbein famously emphasized in 1553, cartography goes hand in hand with conquest and dominion; maps are not just navigational tools but also mirrors in which nations regard themselves, confirm and ratify their presumed status in the world. That's why the cartographic paraphernalia in his *Ambassadors*—globes, a torquetum, a quadrant—serve as props for the two statesmen, whose haughty demeanor is in turn undermined by the anamorphous blur between them, which in its turn, of course, resolves itself, when viewed from the painting's own border zone or unhallowed ground, into a *vanitas*, a skull. There's a direct genealogical line, I'd argue, between Holbein's subversive cartographic intervention and those of the twentieth-century vanguards—the Surrealists' 1929 one I'm showing you now, for example, which reallots to each country a size concomitant with its importance to the overall Surrealist project (you can see that both my country and yours—with the exception of Alaska—completely disappear, while Mexico, Peru, and Easter Island assume giant proportions); or the Situationists' maps throughout the 1950s and 1960s, which replace Parisian place names with those drawn from France's colonies or replot the city in line with the blueprint for Constant Nieuwenhuy's anticapitalist New Babylon; or as an assemblage of discrete yet co-reactive experiences and desires.

It was this history of interventionist cartography and the close relation with the skull that both mapmaking and the avant-garde maintain ("Time and space," Filippo Tommaso Marinetti tells us in the twentieth-century avant-garde's most gloriously bombastic statement, "died yesterday") that led me to found, in 1999—here's my first ping—the International Necronautical Society. After launching with a manifesto packed with stolen or recycled statements (our way of acknowledging that a contemporary avant-garde can only be, to borrow the critic Inke Arns's formulation, "post-historical"), the central one of which announced an intention to map the space of death, and after assembling a committee and a network of affiliates (one of whom, a coder at the BBC, would later help us hack the broadcaster's website, inserting into its source code INS statements and propaganda), the INS took up a residency in the Office of Antimatter in London's Austrian Cultural Institute, where over two weeks we interrogated some of London's leading novelists, philosophers, and artists. The depositions were transcribed and analyzed, and this in turn led to the general secretary's First Report to the First Committee, delivered in the Council Room of the Royal Geographical Society in 2001.

The Report revolved around three literary touchpoints, the first of which was Queequeg. Melville's Polynesian harpoonist, you'll recall, contracting a fever and convinced of his own imminent death, commissions from the ship's carpenter a coffin. But, making a complete recovery, Queequeg finds himself burdened with this redundant box, onto whose surface he passes the time copying the tattoos that cover his whole body. These tattoos, Ishmael informs us,

> had been the work of a departed prophet and seer of his island, who, by those hiero-glyphic marks, had written out on his body a complete theory of the heavens and the earth, and a mystical treatise on the art of attaining truth; so that Queequeg in his own proper person was a riddle to unfold; a wondrous work in one volume; but whose mysteries not even himself could read, though his own live heart beat against them; and these mysteries were therefore destined in the end to moulder away with the living parchment whereon they were inscribed, and so be unsolved to the last. And this thought it must have been that suggested to Ahab that wild exclamation of his, when one morning turning away from surveying poor Queequeg—"Oh devilish tantali-sation of the gods!"

Queequeg is a book, a "volume"; he is also a map, "a complete theory of the heavens and the earth." Yet being three-dimensional and thus unable to read himself on or as a parchment, a flat surface, he, too, must project himself—towards, again, the skull, or rather its correlative, the coffin. Why does this so shock Ahab the surveyor? Because he sees in Queequeg's enterprise, at some level or other, a distorting mirror of his own great mission: for isn't he, too, not only endlessly scru-tinizing charts but also trying to form the whole book's universe into a mirror-map of his own design, projecting himself onto the white screen of the whale, a surface on which he hopes to behold *his* image and *his* destiny as vengeful hero? The whale, of course, has other ideas. We could understand its final smashing of the *Pequod* as a form of radical and catastrophic anamorphosis. But what the INS Report emphasized was the material, rather than simply visual, aspect of this catastro-phe. Like some Hegelian factory, the *Pequod*'s work consists in turning all the world's cetacean matter, all the wide oceans' fat and sperm and bones, into quan-tified, exchangeable units, that is, into value, into signs, into abstracted, *Aufgehobte* meaning. As such, it stands as a symbol for the idealist version of all literature and art: consume the world, process it into truth. The catastrophe that *Moby-Dick* enacts, then, is precisely the catastrophe of idealism, its ruination on the rock of sheer material excess. If you continue all the way round to the side of *The Ambas-sadors*, you stop seeing even the skull; you just see mounds of oil and pleated canvas—like a Josef Beuys piece. *Moby-Dick*, in similar fashion, leads us to a limit beyond which the screen turns into blubber. At this point, this limit, one version of *techné*—that of skill or craft as global command vehicle—gives over to another, as Ishmael, sole survivor, clings to the same coffin we met earlier, and drifts, current-borne, until picked up. This degraded death-craft, this dented black box, thus becomes, quite literally, a narrative vehicle: in conveying the book's narrator back to safety, it carries *Moby-Dick*'s content to us. No longer volume-as-map but rather book-as-debris.

The Report's second touchpoint was *The Hunting of the Snark*. Lewis Carroll's "Agony in Eight Fits" also involves an epic sea voyage, as a motley crew set out to hunt a vague, uncanny quarry (the snark). The fact that one of them is a banker, another a barrister invites us, just as *Moby-Dick* does, to tune into the commercial and juridical allegories pulsing through the drama. And here, too, is pure, dazzling whiteness. The ship's captain ("the Bellman") dismisses out of hand conventional cartographic tools:

"What's the good of Mercator's North Poles and Equators,
Tropics, Zones, and Meridian Lines?"
So the Bellman would cry: and the crew would reply,
"They are merely conventional signs!"

Carroll continues:

"Other maps are such shapes, with their islands and capes!
But we've got our brave captain to thank"
(So the crew would protest) "that he's bought us the best—
A perfect and absolute blank!"

Henry Holiday's illustrations, accompanying the first, 1876, edition of the poem, reproduce this map: bordered by directional signage (Zenith, North, Meridian, Nadir, Torrid Zone), it's an unwritten page. Could we see it, still bearing Melville in mind, as a Bartlebean gesture, an act of writerly refusal (for Agamben, Bartleby, in not writing, becomes the writer par excellence, embodiment of the Arabic *Qualam* or Pen, angel of unfathomable potentiality)? Perhaps, so long as we don't lose sight, once more, of the materiality which overtakes Carroll's poem. As the ship, like the *Pequod*, becomes "snarked," its bowsprit getting mixed up with its rudder, one of the crew complains that "my heart is like nothing so much as a bowl / Brimming over with quivering curds!"

The heart, symbol of man's higher aspirations (courage, love), becomes a repository of what's lowliest and disgusting. Admittedly, these thoughts may well have been colored by the fact that the walls of the Royal Geographical Society's Council Room (in which this report was delivered) were hung with pictures of Ernest Shackleton's ill-fated *Endurance* mission. As the polar ice froze, Shackleton's boat, too, crumpled in on itself; he and his crew were reduced to eating first their dogs and then (according to some accounts) parts of their own frostbitten flesh, which they'd shave off and throw into the pot. [Gilles] Deleuze, contemplating the figure of the Eskimo in snow, sees the collapse not only of perspective but of an entire Western ideology of spatial domination, of the masterful gaze towards the horizon that furnishes (for example) Caspar David Friedrich's figures with their experience of the sublime; this idealist order's replacement by a haptic one in which space presses in, grows close-up, tactile. This, perhaps, best names the whiteness by which both Carroll's and Shackleton's figures find themselves surrounded: an expanse which is no longer blank and pliant but material, resistant, overwhelming in its excess.

Which leads to the Report's third touchpoint: Francis Ponge, whose 1942 prose poem "The Orange" perfectly illustrates what I'm getting at here. "As in the sponge," he writes, "there is in the orange an aspiration to gather itself together again after having undergone the ordeal of expression"—*l'épreuve de l'expression, expression* having in French, as in English, the dual sense of squeezing and representing.

Literature, once more, as pure cartography: how do you squeeze or flatten—express—a globe? "While the sponge always succeeds," he continues, "the orange never does, because its cells have burst, its tissues torn." But it still leaves a husk, *une écorce*—and, on the part of the "oppressor," the bitter awareness of a premature ejaculation of seeds. Derrida, in his reading of Ponge, picks up on the importance of the comparator sponge, five of whose six letters spell the name of Ponge himself. "The sponge," he writes, "expunges the proper name, puts it outside of itself, effaces it and loses it, soils it in order to make it into a common noun; it contaminates the proper name on contact with the most pitiful, the most unqualifiable object, which is made to retain every sort of dirt." At the same time, the sponge, in its absorbency (of both the name and dirt), its inexhaustible capacity to carry and re-excrete both, acts as a guarantor of the possibility of poetry. *L'éponge éponge*: sponge sponges, the sponge expunges, the sponge is Ponge. What Derrida's so brilliantly amplifying in Ponge is a vision of writing *not* as abstraction and refinement or distillation nor as any "authentic" form of self- or world-articulation, but rather as a messy, always incomplete engagement with material surplus, dirty spillage. As such, for me and my collaborators at the INS, Ponge, even more than Bartleby, stands as the writer of all writers.

If it seems my talk's been hovering round a certain scene of violence, deformation, and disintegration, that's because it has. The ping I want to put next on your screens is a project, an art installation, that I made in collaboration with Rod Dickinson—and showed in 2012 here in Pittsburgh, at Wood Street Galleries, before it traveled on to London's Hayward. *Greenwich Degree Zero* took its cue from an attempt, in 1894, on the part of Martial Bourdin, a French anarchist, to blow up the Royal Observatory in Greenwich—an attempt that failed when the bomb he was carrying detonated in his pocket yards from the building, scattering his flesh across the Prime Meridian. The episode was kept in the public consciousness for much of the twentieth century by Joseph Conrad's fictionalization of it in *The Secret Agent*; it was also revisited in the wake of 9/11 by historians who cited it as the first modern incident of terrorism against a symbolic rather than strategic target. The observatory served no military or judicial function: what it did was mark the world's main time line, in other words its central longitudinal axis, zero degrees, from and around which the globe was measured and partitioned in accordance with the demands of the British Empire. I grew up in Greenwich; what's most striking when you visit the observatory itself is that the line is actually inscribed into the ground: space itself, its arrangement, is already a result of writing—is already (we could almost say) a fiction. Like Rilke's Orpheus, what Bourdin was transgressing or trespassing against was a boundary; and, like Orpheus, or the *Pequod*, he ended up undergoing total anamorphosis. But Dickinson and I wanted to carry the event beyond this limit, to the absolute zero or negative zone at which the nonevent of the building's intended destruction actually *happens*. We decided to do this not by attacking the observatory all over again but rather by accessing, in the National Archives, the extensive 1894 newspaper reports of the event; modifying these; changing a word or phrase here and there, such that conditional became transitive and "attempted" became "successful"; then reprinting them in exactly the same format as that in which they first appeared. We also, on discovering that the

Lumiere Brothers unveiled their own device for reorganizing time and space the same year as Bourdin's death, found an early, hand-cranked camera on which to film the building's immolation, complete with (this is what you're watching here) period-costumed policeman racing past a frantically gesticulating top-hatted gentleman up the hill towards it.

Conrad's Bourdin is a simpleton, Stevie, who sits to the side of anarchist meetings drawing, like an autistic Dante or Timmaeus, "circles, circles; innumerable circles, concentric, eccentric, a coruscating whirl of circles that by their tangled multitude of repeated curves, uniformity of form, and confusion of intersecting lines suggested a rendering of cosmic chaos, the symbolism of a mad art attempting the inconceivable." Conrad deliberately daubs Stevie's activities with shades of the cultural avant-garde, for the good reason that a whole swath of vanguard artists and writers of the 1890s, from Georges Seurat to Félix Fénéon to Alfred Jarry, were also card-carrying political anarchists (*L'Avant Garde* was even the title of a journal advocating "propaganda by deed"—in other words, bomb throwing). Within a wider allegorical framework, if the Meridian line stands for the established way of surveying and inscribing or writing the world, then Stevie's intervention could be said to stand for an attack not just on global space, imperial cartography, but also on novelistic form. Stevie's attempt may fail, and Conrad may give the last word to his crazed nihilist The Professor, who mutters "Madness and Despair! Give me that for a lever, and I'll move the world," but in fact a consequential formal displacement of sorts does see itself through towards the end of *The Secret Agent*, as Conrad turns his attention (and this is where Dickinson and I took our cue from) to newspaper headlines, which his text, in a move that seems groundbreaking for its era, begins to sample, loop, and collage. The real Archimedian lever turns out to be not madness but media.

Effectively, Conrad is pioneering cut-ups, laying the ground for the experiments William Burroughs will conduct half a century later, first also with newspaper and then with other media forms. What's interesting about Burroughs's cut-ups in this context is that he understands what he's doing not simply as literary experimentation but also as a way of folding global space together, splicing Malmo into the Midwest, Tangier into Texas, crumpling all these far-flung scenes and their coordinates into a giant collaged "Interzone." And that he understands this—and here more direct bloodlines from Conrad could be traced—as a type of revolutionary sabotage or even terrorism. Media cut-ups, he tells us in "The Electronic Revolution," should be used "as a front-line weapon to produce and escalate riots. . . . So stir in news stories, TV plays, stock market quotations, adverts and put the altered mutter line out in the streets . . . Mexico City will do for a riot in Saigon and vice versa. For a riot in Santiago, Chile you can use the Londonderry pictures. Nobody knows the difference. Fires, earthquakes, plane crashes can be moved around." In his film *Towers Open Fire*, we see him doing just this from the back seat of a requisitioned limo: cutting, folding, sampling and remixing, sabotaging, commandeering the earth's signal beacon towers, turning the network and space against themselves. For all its multimedia supermodernity, this film vests enormous potential in the decidedly old-media format of the book: after the board meeting of the all-powerful controllers of the earth is invaded, its members liquidized and ledgers seized, pages covered in hieroglyphic writing are shown dancing on the breeze, as though they themselves had somehow brought about this whole turn of events. In this respect, it's interesting to note that the 1986 Paladin edition of *The Naked Lunch* carries on its front cover the blurb "The book that blew 'literature' apart."

Of course, there's also a deeply conservative aspect to Burroughs, whose reckless vanguard globe-trotting comfortably fits an older, khaki-clad colonial pattern. Even his prodigious drug taking could be seen in these terms. (Doesn't opium's trajectory perfectly follow that of a certain all-conquering idealism: you squeeze a poppy, like an orange, to extract its essence, which, once shipped around the vectors of the world, you then consume, thus altering your perception *of* the world? Is it a coincidence that Thomas De Quincey's opium visions, like Coleridge's, are so intensely *spatial*?) But that's a whole lecture in itself that someone else could do much better. What I want to home in on for the last few minutes here, in order to generate my final ping, is the subject Burroughs used his GI Bill funding to study, namely anthropology. The novel I published last year, *Satin Island*, has a corporate anthropologist as its narrator—an anthropology graduate, that is, who (like more than half of his contemporaries over the last two decades) puts his ethnographic wisdom in the service of consultancies, brand analysts, and governmental think tanks. I'm showing you the Knopf cover, with its gridded archipelagic look, here not just to advertise the book, but because Peter Mendelsund's inspired design perfectly illustrates Claude Lévi-Strauss's affirmation that the fundamental goal of anthropology should be to create a universal "grid" that, covering all the world, enables us "to establish a pattern of equivalences between the ways in which each society uses analogous human types to perform different social functions."

What so appeals to me, as a novelist, about Lévi-Strauss is the way he places writing at the center of his entire project—and, conversely (or not quite conversely), the way that writing, turning on its would-be master, twists the warp and weft of the very grid it should be helping sketch, its tropisms turning the tropics melancholic, triste. Not only are the problems Lévi-Strauss encounters in his charting of world culture—problems of misaligned temporality, of "lateness" and "too-soon-ness" or of perception's overcoding by culture's own archive—essentially identical to those that form the subject matter of Proust's *Récherche*, but the very mechanisms and technology of writing continually threaten to unravel the writing project itself. *Triste Tropique*'s central episode, in this respect, is the one in which Lévi-Strauss meets a tribe who don't know what writing is and witnesses the tribe's chief, wanting to maintain his elevated status, take up his, Lévi-Strauss's, pen and start to scribble on a sheet of paper, so as to trick his subjects into thinking that he's versed in this activity. Lévi-Strauss, aghast, sees himself mirrored in this dupery: isn't that just what he's doing with his "subjects," his readers? This episode is half-reflected in a later one, in which Lévi-Strauss, finding himself disappointed both by tribes whose rituals, too easily decoded, lose all their mystique and by ones so strange they remain quite illegible, fantasizes about perfectly "ambiguous instances" in which the balance of legibility and mystique would be just right. Yet, he continues, wouldn't these instances, too, be cons? Who's the real dupe, he wonders, of observations which are carried to the borderline of the intelligible, only to be stopped there? "Is it the reader who believes in us," he asks, "or we ourselves who have no right to be satisfied until we have succeeded in dissipating a residue which serves as a pretext for our vanity?"

The first commandment of [Bronislaw] Malinowski, the father of anthropology, was simply: "Write everything down." The smallest, most insignificant detail might turn out to hold the key to a whole culture as much as the most elaborate ritual, so capture it all, turn it all into data. By the time Michel de Certeau writes *The Practice of Everyday Life* half a century later, this commandment has both reached its end point *and*, in so doing, become redundant. Why? Because everything is already written down. With a nod to François Furet, Certeau claims that "[m]odernization, modernity itself, is writing." And with more than a nod to Kafka's Penal Colony, he envisages capitalism as a giant "scriptural enterprise," or writing machine, that both writes across and reads or scans all surfaces, not least human ones, such that all objects, subjects, spaces, or events "will thus be transformed into texts in conformity with the Western desire to read its products." This machine is not in the service of any operator; rather, "by an inversion that indicates that a threshold has been crossed, the scriptural system moves us forward on its own . . . it transforms the subjects that controlled it into operators of the writing machine that orders and uses them." If that was true in 1980, how much more so is it in the Google era? With iPhones archiving all our spatial transits, Facebook and Amazon mapping our structures of kinship and networks of exchange, the world-script writes itself and allots to human experience and "agency" roles no more significant than those of minor actions and commands in larger keychains.

Are all black boxes narrative vehicles? Yes and no. Who can read this one (the rectangular black building in the photo you're seeing is the NSA's headquarters, as captured from a helicopter by the artist Trevor Paglen)? Not even the NSA can decode—parse, trace back into the world, transform into a one-to-one efficient navigational tool with no glitches and blind spots—the hieroglyphics contained in its crypt. Has the role of the artist, or novelist, become simply to demonstrate the black box's existence, bring it to visibility, as Paglen does in this image (he too had to trespass, enter proscribed airspace, in order to reach the beyond-limit point from which he snapped it)? Or is this what writers—Melville, Conrad, Sophocles—were always doing anyway? Or is the artist-writer's role, as Burroughs might maintain, to open up the crypt and hack its source code? McKenzie Wark, in his *Hacker's Manifesto*, defines hacking as any cultural activity which breaches previously sealed or separated bodies of knowledge and crossbreeds their contents, producing "the plane upon which different things may enter into relation." But then Wark also points out that it isn't hackers who bring networks of surveillance or global finance or aviation crashing down, any more than it's terrorists who blow up nuclear power plants: they do this on their own. For Certeau, total revolution would be "a scriptural project at the level of an entire society seeking to constitute itself as a blank page with respect to the past, to write itself by itself"—the world redrawn, that is, as Carroll's map. Yet he too understands that nothing escapes the overall scriptural enterprise of power—not even bodies, since all bodies are, as he's already told us, seized hold of and written, transformed into code. But, he continues in a fascinating and poetic turn, when bodies grow obscene—that is another matter; then, bodily "reminiscences" become "lodged in ordinary language . . . incised into the prose of the passage from day to day, without any possible commentary or translation." These reminiscences, in turn, generate counterscriptural

> *resonances . . . cries breaking open the text that they make proliferate around them, enunciative gaps in a syntagmatic organization of statements . . . the linguistic analogues of an erection, or of a nameless pain, or of tears: voices without language, enunciations flowing from the remembering and opaque body . . . an aphasic enunciation of what appears without one's knowing where it came from (from what obscure debt or writing of the body), without one's knowing how it could be said except through the other's voice.*

The final section of *The Practice of Everyday Life* is titled, after Beckett, "The Unnameable"; and it takes as its subject the figure of someone—anyone—who is dying. "Set aside in one of the technical and secret zones (hospitals, prisons, refuse dumps) which relieve the living of everything that might hinder the chain of production and consumption, and which, in the darkness where no one wants to penetrate, repair and select what can be sent back up to the surface of progress," the dying figure finds their body transformed *from* a palimpsest on which the scriptural enterprise has stamped its law *into* a liminal, disgusting, and yet almost miraculous new space in which the binaries of life and death break down. And if the dying one "speaks" this death, their own, it is "to open within the language of interlocution a resurrection that does not restore to life."

Despite his borrowed title, Certeau does eventually give this dying figure a name: the writer, "a dying man who tries to speak." To write would be "to march through enemy territory . . . within the space of death," to inscribe death itself with footsteps on a page that Certeau, flipping Carroll's negative into yet another negative (which doesn't make a positive), calls "black, not blank." In what, for me, is the most astonishing and seductive formulation of all, he describes writ*ing*—the work—as the "waste product" borne out of this situation. Space's own excess, if you like; its toxic overflow. That's where I want to end. If the novel, through its many deaths, can somehow manage to embody that embodied space, to speak it—obscenely, opaquely, resonantly—that is indeed, each time, miraculous.

*   *   *

TOM MCCARTHY is a writer and the frontman, alongside Simon Critchley, of the International Necronautical Society. In addition to writing some of the most prominent novels of the twenty-first century—*Remainder* (2005), *Men in Space* (2007), *C* (2010), and *Satin Island* (2015)—he has also authored two critical works: *Tintin and the Secret of Literature* (2006, 2008) and *Typewriters, Bombs, Jellyfish: Essays* (2017).

Zero Degree Everything:
An Interview with Tom McCarthy

NICHOLAS HUBER

In this interview, Tom McCarthy considers his relationship to the novel and its history as a form, including the changing conditions of the contemporary literary world that have allowed for his existence within it. He provides a schematic for understanding the various modes of his own work and his interfacing with a set of "displacements" running through and around various "vanguards." Along the way, he discusses dead media, money, sound, post-Snowden politics as a literary problem, and the financial utility of *Finnegans Wake*.

NICHOLAS HUBER: *How did you approach composing the talk for the Society for Novel Studies?*[1]

TOM MCCARTHY: Well it's rather intimidating. I'm aware that I'll be in the company of people who dedicate their lives to thinking through questions around the novel in relation to global space, late capitalism, and colonial and postcolonial histories with an ever-increasingly sophisticated array of conceptual tools at their disposal. I really have nothing to tell them. I'm like a symptom, not the solution. So I thought I'd place a few symptoms on the table rather than offer any analyses; that's my approach.

NH: *The way you frame it there makes it sound like you think of yourself as strictly a "practitioner," and I'm not sure that's accurate.*

TM: No, you're right. We're part of the same language community, if you like. There is no pure practice that's separate from a critical reflection or theory or whatever you want to call it, and I don't think there ever has been. This is not a postmodern state of affairs. I mean, if you read Sterne, half of *Tristram Shandy* is critical reflection. But at the same time, I think maybe the psychoanalytic model is kind of interesting in this respect, because there is a difference between analysis, on the one hand, and the production of symptoms on the other, even if they're drawing on the same reserve of language and experience and allusion and the same conditions of possibility. I think there is a kind of modal difference.

NH: *What is it that writing a novel makes available for you that writing criticism or, for example, a long essay on Tintin doesn't?*

TM: Well, the book on Tintin I wrote at the same time I was working on my novel *C*, shortly after I'd written *Remainder* but in fact before I'd published it, and I was

---

[1] On May 13, 2016, McCarthy presented a talk titled "Vanity's Residue" at the 2016 Society for Novel Studies Biennial Conference at the University of Pittsburgh. That talk is published in this issue under the title "Vanity's Residue."

Novel: A Forum on Fiction 51:2   DOI 10.1215/00295132-6846030   © 2018 by Nicholas Huber and Tom McCarthy

coming at lots of the same issues, situations, themes that I'd worked through in those two books: trauma, family histories, technology, empire, politics, violence, and so on. The Tintin book is an analytical book even if it's playful, but you're right that these things blur into one another. I love Peter Mendelsund's cover design for the hardcover of my novel *Satin Island*, where he has not just the grid but all these words on it, like "A Memoir," "An Essay," "A Manifesto," and they're all crossed out, and the "A Novel" label is just one of those terms. It's not in larger or bolder print, it's just the only one that's not crossed out. So it doesn't mean the novel is the thing that that book positively is, rather that the novel is the thing that it least *isn't* among all those other terms. It's kind of a memoir, a manifesto, a confession, but it's not really any of those, and I suppose *the novel* is what you call that space of unresolved in-betweenness which is different from other types of in-betweenness, maybe.

NH: *I'm glad you mentioned the cover designs, because each one almost seems as if you've personally selected it. Is that the case?*

TM: No, I'm just very, very lucky to get Peter Mendelsund assigned to my books every single time, because the guy is a genius. This is someone who, in his spare time, is a concert-level pianist. And he's incredibly well-read. When he read the manuscript of *C*, he was virtually the only one who could see exactly what I'd been reading; he said, "OK, you've been reading Abraham and Torok, the Wolf Man, Virginia Woolf's *In Between the Acts* . . ." He saw where I'd stolen it all from instantly. And he's brilliant at distilling and framing whatever's going on in the books. I did actually want it to say, "A Manifesto," "A Confession," and so on, but I'd imagined it on the inside page, and he brought it up to the cover and did that wonderful kind of crossing out and laying it out on a map.

NH: *The manifesto is interesting, because it seems so tied to a particular historical moment and yet there has been a resurgence of more and less sincere manifestos in the last twenty years or so. In 1999 you released your own manifesto, for the International Necronautical Society, which you then proceeded to actually institute, appointing artists and philosophers to the First Committee and publishing other texts—proclamations, denunciations, and so on.*

TM: I'm really interested in dead media, like reel-to-reel tape or things like that. Crypts. I mean, all media are crypts, but dead media even more so since they don't work anymore. And the manifesto in a perhaps less material but equally kind of real way would be a wonderful example of dead media, since it so belongs to that early twentieth-century moment of political upheaval and artistic avant-gardes which align themselves either with the far Left or the far Right, in the case of Marinetti and so on; and that raises the question: what is the afterlife of the manifesto as a kind of defunct piece of media? That makes it doubly interesting for me. It's kind of like Duchamp's bicycle wheel, where it doesn't work as a bicycle wheel anymore, and by using it he triggers all these anxieties about meaning that wouldn't be triggered if the bicycle wheel were just doing its job and making a bicycle go 'round. It doesn't work, and that kind of dysfunction actually sets it to work in terms of generating anxieties towards meaning. Same with the manifesto.

NH: *There's a tension that emerges here between, on the one hand, an interest in under-standing modernism, for example, as a less restrained historical period and instead as something like a disposition, attitude, or a mode that is available from maybe Shake-speare's time to the present day, and, on the other hand, as the very real obsolescence of forms and media that are bound to material history. This is maybe an impossible question to answer . . .*

TM: Yes, it is an impossible question. I mean, you're right, and at the same time there is something patently ridiculous in distributing a manifesto in—well, 1999 is when I distributed the one for the International Necronautical Society—as though it were 1909. The context is not the same. By analogy: We could say we have always had technology and transport technology, but you'd look silly if in 1950 you turned up to a motorcar race with a horse. Nothing is categorically new; and yet, and yet . . . There is a kind of anachronism. In 1909 or even at the time of the Surrealist or Situationist manifestos, there is a direct, earnest engagement in politics that the manifesto is carrying out. The context in which I wrote that INS manifesto was late 1990s, end of communism, the rise of general neoliberal capitalism as the end of history and as the natural move beyond politics: history is over, politics is over, et cetera. And also the more direct influence was when I lived in Berlin in the 1990s, the group Neue Slowenische Kunst, who came out of Ljubljana in ex-Yugoslavia, and they were also this kind of semiparodic assemblage of an avant-garde with recognizable avant-garde tropes like manifestos and flags and uniforms, and they had their official philosopher, Slavoj Žižek, and their official rock band, Laibach, and they came and declared a state in Berlin, so to see them in the Volksbühne you had to go and get your passport stamped with a visa. So this is what really inspired me about them, that they were kind of playing out this idea of posthistory in a way that was absolutely saturated with irony, but in a way, it's no less political for that; it just has a different, less direct, more circuitous relationship with its political moment. Especially when its political moment is one of irony and subterfuge and nonpoliticalness. A more direct influence was the London-based group the AAA, the Association of Autonomous Astronauts, which, again—they would release all these manifestos about outer space, saying, "Why is NASA sending the military industrial complex, why isn't it sending poets, why aren't we doing sex research in space?" And they produced documentation that they'd squatted the MIR space station, they'd done sex experiments, and they meticulously produced this doc-umentation as though it were scientific reports. I mean of course it's silly, but they also had all come out of media degrees, they knew their media history and their history of the avant-gardes, but they were also involved in Reclaim the Streets, Women against Rape, Cyclists against Traffic—those kinds of political engage-ments in contemporary urban space. They'd organized three-sided football games in Greenwich Park, which is a move directly from the Situationist play-book. So I don't think irony and some kind of political consciousness are at all contradictory, especially not in our era.

NH: *In what way do you understand your own work—the novels, in particular—as ironic?*

TM: Well, I think it's ironic in the sense that Paul de Man understands irony. One version of irony would be the kind of smug, self-satisfied smirk that so much of Brit Art has. You know, a kind of twee little repetition of Duchamp for which you get a million from Saatchi which you then go and spend on cocaine. That's a version of irony that I don't find particularly appealing. The other version of irony is the type that de Man in that essay "The Rhetoric of Temporality" teases out of Baudelaire and Bergson, in which irony would name a total, radical *décalage* within experience: an unfixable split between action and consciousness, the subject and the world. Which is kind of subversive; it's utterly disruptive. Those things are both called irony, but it seems to me they're very different. I hadn't read that Paul de Man essay when I wrote *Remainder*, but I read it a couple of years later (when I was writing the Tintin book, actually), and thought, Yes! That's what I meant, that's what I was trying to do in *Remainder*.

NH: *This same kind of temporal opening that you're referring to in the latter form of irony is treated from a different angle in your essay published as "Recessional, or The Time of the Hammer." In that, recessionality is an alternative temporal mode that opens inside the dominant temporality, which is to say juridical clock time. And* Remainder, *from this perspective, I think stages a great political problem, which is that the recess from that dominant order of time—the rhythms of productive and reproductive labor—the recess is already accounted for by that dominant order . . .*

TM: Yes, like Google says, you've got to waste 20 percent of your time just day-dreaming and goofing around—because that's when you'll dream up something amazing, and we'll own it!

NH: *And that's what I think you get in the beginning of your recent introduction to Kafka's* Letter to the Father, *in which you point out that this recess is precisely the time when, for example, interest accumulates.*

TM: Right, that's what Naphta says in *The Magic Mountain* to Hans Castorp. You know, interest just means the monetization of the interval. It's what the *Merchant of Venice* is about also.

NH: *I was thinking that it's in this way that the reenactor/narrator of* Remainder *is a complete failure, again and again.*

TM: Because he never gets it right?

NH: *It's not that he never gets it right, it's that the excessive temporality he's working to open up is always anticipated and quashed by, for example, the volatile temporality of his financial investments, which spike and crash, or the procedural structuration of the bank at the end, which will have already had plans in place for the bank robbery scenario and will just carry on past the moment of violence. So maybe this opens onto a larger question about all your books, which is that even as they discreetly treat political questions, they remain suspicious of an outright political moment. Another example would be Madison's retraining and disillusionment in* Satin Island: *she starts out as a dissident, but after the demonstrations in Genoa and brutal police crackdown, she loses that radicalism.*

TM: Yes, this is true. The revolutionaries, the first thing they want to do is smash all the clocks and create a year zero, and in fact this afternoon I'm going to talk about the project Rod Dickinson and I did, blowing up the Royal Observatory in London's Greenwich Park, where all time in the world is measured from. We remade the event that Conrad's novel *The Secret Agent* is based on—this attempt to blow up the building and, by extension, time—by finding and reprinting and displaying all the newspapers from the weeks following the attempt in 1894. But we changed sentences in them here and there and inserted doctored photographs so as to remake the failed attempt into a success. In reality, the anarchist blew himself up ten feet from the observatory; but in our version, you see and read accounts of the building blazing to the ground. We made it that he *had* blown up the international time line. In documenting this event, we took this failure to the point where it succeeds. Revolution and time have this intimate closeness in creating this new year zero, an absolute now. And in *Remainder* that's what the hero wants—in fact, in all my books, there are all these characters in search of an absolute present tense that they can never quite find. They're always in the space of deferral. And I guess in one sense you could see that as a kind of political failure. Madison goes to Genoa to bring down capitalism and ends up entering this weird David Lynch, Kafka kind of labyrinth of weirdness.

NH: *Almost like fascist training camp.*

TM: It is. I was reading a lot of Sade. For that scene, but also for the whole of *Remainder*. But this is also the big political point in Kafka, and it's what [Gilles] Deleuze picks up on; it's not like in *Star Wars*, where you have the Death Star and there's this one point that if you can get the bomb there the whole thing blows up. In Kafka, the room is not the room, it's just the antechamber to the corridor to the other corridor beside the other atrium, waiting room, et cetera. And I love the way in Lynch, the films are always structured around this inner control room, and when you get to the control room there is always a telephone or a relay to somewhere else. So, the control room isn't a control room, it's just taking orders from somewhere else, and even if you got to that somewhere else there would always be somewhere *else*. What Madison's coming up against in that episode is that she's bringing an older model of political resistance, perhaps a slightly naive model, dare we say, and it just gets shipwrecked on networked supermodernity. I mean, there is no emperor within late capitalism. There is only the network. You kill the king, and it doesn't matter: it's not the king, it's the network. But at the end of *Satin Island*, U. is faced with this option that I lifted straight from Balzac's *Pere Goriot*. Balzac's character Rastignac stands on the hillside, and my guy stands at the port, but they're both at the edge of the city and could just go, "Fuck it, I'm going to leave it all behind and start again." But he doesn't; Rastignac turns back: "A nous deux" (me and you). He goes back into the machine and he carries all that unresolved anxiety back into the heart of it. He's like Dostoyevsky's underground man, whom Dostoyevsky describes as an insect in our system. I'm sure Kafka read that. You know, that idea of the bug, the glitch: the operator itself is a bug, a piece of a glitch software. If the right conditions presented themselves, it could just erupt and blow the whole thing up; but they never quite do . . .

NH: *They never erupt in the way that would be transformative but they erupt all the time in ways that are expected and predictable, ways that the order even relies upon. This is the story of 2008, among others.*

TM: Right, that's Naomi Klein's point about disaster capitalism, Katrina. Yeah, she's right, absolutely.

NH: *Could you speak a bit more to the connections between* Remainder *and* Satin Island? *The man in the labyrinthine basement with Madison in* Satin Island, *for example, reads as a resetting of* Remainder's *reenactor.*

TM: Well, Sade is really important to me, *One Hundred Twenty Days of Sodom* in particular. It seems so contemporary, especially after Abu Ghraib and the whole idea of the state of exception that [Giorgio] Agamben talks about. In Sade, they go extraterritorial; it's all about extraordinary rendition. They take these people out of the legal bounds of France in order to do these ritualized actions, and it's all about repetition; so the golden rule is nothing may be done unless it's already been done. They have some prostitute tell them, "One time I was screwing these three guys and one of them was on top of me," and then the people listening, the four guys who have paid for it, can go, "Oh that bit's good, let's redo it—but let's change it a little bit." So it's about modulating repetition, and they use all these kidnapped teenagers as extras in their endless movie. And they almost algorithmically run through all the possible combinations of perversity until everyone's dead. But it's also about the space of narrative, it's all about narrative; you're in this space of secondhandness, of something else being narrated. The prostitute does the talking, and within that space of narrative, for the privileged four libertines the game move is available to go, "That's good, let's do it," and then the others are just victims, they just get fucked and killed. That seems so contemporary and quite persuasive as a way of staging a conversation that's going on in global politics right now. Maybe that sounds a bit extreme. I mean, now I can say post–Abu Ghraib, Sade makes sense and reenactments and so on, and that's not untrue, but at the same time when I had the idea for *Remainder* I wasn't directly thinking about any of that stuff. I just had this idea: wouldn't it be fun if you could reconstruct this moment, where would you stop? Wouldn't it be fun if you could reconstruct the street and its events, but then continue scaling that upward, even to the point of everyone dying? It's kind of more intuitive.

And, of course, that logic of authority and repetition is something that, since being a child, I can identify with. You reenact the goal from the weekend football game, and you get your younger sibling to be the goalkeeper while you're Pelé or Kevin Keegan or Zidane. Or you reenact the scene from *Star Wars* where you're Luke Skywalker. Many kids can relate to that. And the kind of aesthetics of the action replay in sports, which I find absolutely fascinating. But a lot of this reasoning is quite post hoc. Which doesn't mean that those implicit structures aren't implicit when you do it, but you only come to realize it later. So, to answer your question, I started *Satin Island* with a delay in an airport caused by this plane doing the figure of eight, which is an obvious allusion to the end of *Remainder*, and I was stuck writing. I got that bit about the delay up and running, and then I found it incredibly difficult to write, didn't know where to go next and kept going down one avenue and it didn't work, writing something and it didn't work. It wanted to become a satire or something that I didn't want it to be. So, in terms of method, the method is you just intuit your way towards certain things. And then of course you read a lot to give structure to that as it starts actually getting some energy. But it's quite organic—or, not organic, but you make it up as you go along.

NH: *Is that true for publication as well? You've said somewhere that* C, *for example, is disguised in a particular way that you thought might allow you some kind of purchase in the publishing world while you were waiting for* Remainder *to be picked up.*

TM: That's true, when I started *C* I had not found a publisher for *Remainder*, nor had I found a publisher for *Men in Space*, a version of which I wrote before *Remainder*. And then because *C* on the surface of it looks like a nineteenth-century bildungs-roman, I thought *some* publisher's going to be fooled by this and agree to print it. But then by the time it was actually finished, things had changed, *Remainder* had opened everything up, and I could publish what I wanted. And writing *C*, I wasn't interested in writing a nineteenth-century bildungsroman; I was already sampling Marinetti and thinking about new media. So, it's a lot less strategic. After the books are written, it seems like there was a plan, but there really isn't; you just do what you can at the time. When I began *C*, I was doing this INS art project at the Institute of Contemporary Arts in London, where we had this radio transmission unit. It was modeled on [Jean] Cocteau's *Orphée*, it was modeled on William Burroughs's cut-ups, and I was reading a lot about the figure of the crypt and the relationship between new media and death and practices of mourning. This led me on this serendipitous route to think about [Howard] Carter, Egypt, and Tutankhamun, and then suddenly the idea for *C* came. But I could never have plotted that route, and I still find this is the case.

NH: *In your Tintin book there's a chapter organized around the flows of money. Money as a concept would seem to coordinate so many of your concerns: transmission, reception, encryption, problems of authenticity and deferral. And yet the only time money comes to the fore in your novels is in a few moments of* Remainder.

TM: Well, in *C*, Serge is tuning in to stock market prices when he's going through the radio dial, and I guess in *Satin Island*, U. is making money. He's making money for the man by repurposing critical theory and anthropology and Deleuze and everything else, but you're right. It's only in *Remainder* that it comes to the fore. The thing I'm just beginning to work on now is—I've just become interested in time and motion studies, but to cut a long story short, I haven't really properly begun it yet, but I'm looking at this correlation between the type of algorithms used in sports analysis and very similar ones used in developing financial derivatives. In fact, lots of hedge fund people go to work in sports analysis and vice versa. It's all about patterns of movement and analysis of data. And temporality.

NH: *You wrote that piece for the* Guardian *that said a figure like Joyce today, if one existed . . .*

TM: Would be working for Google! Right. The *Guardian*, they wanted a sensationalist line. That was maybe a bit overstated, overprovocative.

NH: *I actually thought, maybe it was sensational, but at the same time it was only almost there. It really should have been a hedge fund; they're writing the world.*

TM: Oh, totally. Here's a funny story. I have a friend called Finn Fordham who's a Joyce scholar. I bumped into him somewhere and he was tearing his hair out because in order to justify his department's funding he had to write a document for these idiots, the accountants that run the university, like, "Why is it useful to teach *Finnegans Wake*," and he was going, "What the fuck can I tell them? What possible use has it got?" But the next night or two days later, I'm having a drink with my brother-in-law, who works in a hedge fund, and he'd been moved to recruiting, and he said, "I will never hire someone who's done a business degree. They're useless because they think in series. I like hiring English graduates because they think in parallel, they can think in terms of constellated, correlative sequences and systems," which is exactly what *Finnegans Wake* is! It's exactly what *Finnegans Wake* trains you to do, so I wanted to connect them together, to say, hey, Finn, here's your argument, this is exactly what you need to say: read Joyce because you'll be a really good hedge fund manager afterward. Which, incidentally, Joyce is aware of. *Finnegans Wake* is infused with the language of stock markets as well as monetary appreciation, depreciation, credit, and debt.

NH: *In the introduction to* Letter to the Father, *you emphasize that Kafka insisted to his father that the time he spent writing was not redeemable to the latter's work ethic but was totally, shamefully unproductive. And I think what we've just agreed on is that this situation has now been reversed, that writing is one of the most economically productive activities you can do and everyone does it all the time. You're still filling out bureaucratic forms, doing your taxes, writing memos and reports and so on, but now as in* Satin Island, *production and consumption are slowly, historically, becoming enmeshed and confused— from this perspective of writing at least. Like a human centipede of textual, cultural, ideological regeneration.*

TM: I suppose people younger than us are just blogging fifteen hours a day. They're free content providers. Yes, absolutely. This is what really interests me about digital culture. Politics becomes a very literary problem, especially in the wake of Edward Snowden. Democratic life boils down to the fact that every single thing we do leaves a mark, it is inscribed on some surface, it creates an archive, a book. And then the question of politics becomes a question of who gets to read what and who doesn't get to read what. These are basic questions of legibility.

NH: *Speaking of legibility, I wanted to ask another question related to your talk here today, given that it is a keynote at the Society for Novel Studies conference. A few years ago, after* Remainder *had been passed on by a number of publishers, you quipped that it used to be that you had an art career that you didn't want and no literary career that you did want. It seems that you now emphatically have the literary career, and I'm wondering what you think are the conditions that have allowed for that change.*

TM: Good question. First, I'd separate the publishing world from academia. I think academia is a genuinely interesting space for critical reflection about literature, and I think that's a good thing and something that academia should hang onto. And beware the bloody creative writing program! I think the merging of English departments with creative writing departments threatens that criticality, given that most creative writing programs are just bringing writing in line with the demands of the market, trying to turn out something that is pliant and digestible. This should be quarantined away from a zone of critical reflection, which is always difficult and subversive, inherently by its very nature subversive. Even if you're studying Renaissance philology, it's still significant that this space is somehow configured differently than a market-driven space. But I was always surprised that I couldn't publish *Men in Space* and *Remainder* when I wrote them, because they seemed to me extremely literary novels in the sense that they're clearly plugging into a kind of literary gene pool. *Remainder* is so dependent on [Samuel] Beckett, [J. G.] Ballard, *Tristram Shandy,* and anything that involves reenactment, like Hamlet when he reenacts his father's death. Those things are so clearly pulsing through it that I thought this is just a straight-up novel. And then you interface with the contemporary publishing industry, which has become a very illiterate space in the sense that it's not actually a space in which literary history is resonating. It's become much more of a middlebrow, commercial market—the print wing of the entertainment industry. This was definitely the case in the UK in the late 1990s and early 2000s, and I think it still is, in the UK at least. The legacy of literary modernism and maybe of literary history tout court is being played out in the art world. Artists, they've all read Beckett and Stein, they've all read the *nouveau roman,* they've all read Burroughs, whereas most publishers haven't. So that was kind of odd. I found a complete stonewalling in the publishing world, and then all my friends who were artists were passing *Remainder* on to other people, and they just totally got it. And then the woman to whom I owe so much, Clémentine Deliss, published *Remainder* in her Metronome Press edition. She was doing a curating residency at the Cité Internationale des Arts in Paris, and she discovered Olympia Press, from the 1950s, which published Beckett and Burroughs and Nabokov and made its proceeds from porn. She wanted to kind of reenact this as a semi-ironic curatorial project by publishing unpublishable novels, distributing them through the art world, and commissioning porn as well. I don't know if you've ever seen the first edition of *Remainder,* but it looks exactly like an Olympia Press edition, typographically and everything. Full of typos as well. So, again, through this curatorial project, it was really the art world that became a home to me as a writer. And then it was America. Marty Asher at Vintage in New York read *Remainder* after Clémentine published it, because it was getting a lot of press as well. Marty got wind of it and decided to publish it in a mass-market edition, so then I was kind of slotted into the conventional publishing world too. But I think America's a bit different. Within big corporate publishers like the Random House Group, they're publishing not just my work but people like Ben Marcus, Ben Lerner, Shelley Jackson, and they're finding sizable audiences for them. The publishing world in America, for all its supercorporatism, is actually providing quite a healthy environment for—I don't want to say "avant-garde"—vanguard forms of literary endeavor to take place.

NH: *I'm curious about that appellation,* avant-gardist, *and the distinction you're making here between avant-garde and vanguard.*

TM: Well, this goes back to what we were saying about manifestos a few minutes ago. For me, *avant-garde* names a historical set of possibilities from the early twentieth century. But as Alain Robbe-Grillet said in the 1950s, the term *avant-garde* is now used by conservative journalists just to try and sideline writing that's not middlebrow. Robbe-Grillet's writing is utterly classical. It's where Sophocles ends up, in an Alain Robbe-Grillet novel, not in a Philip Roth novel or whatever. So in a strict intellectual sense, someone like Robbe-Grillet is actually totally the mainstream, he's the trunk inheritor of a literary tradition; but at the same time, I think it's legitimate to call someone like him vanguard because he's genuinely working out ways of—I don't want to say "new" because that inscribes it within this narrative of progress, which it's not—but I think he's finding dynamic forms of possibility that maybe have not yet been found, and there's something important about that. Which doesn't mean having fewer commas or fewer full stops and more breathless sentences. This is the problem with creative writing programs. They spend an afternoon teaching you Beckett as a style rather than as a whole ontological set of disturbances, and then people write rather boring novels, very conservative novels but breathless and with fewer full stops, and they think that's avant-garde. Avant-garde becomes a style. This is a very reactionary turn. Look at someone like Kafka: there's nothing particularly experimental—in the novels at least—in the prose. They're very conventional sentences. He doesn't experiment with words like Joyce does, and yet he's utterly vanguard; there's something absolutely radical about Kafka which I would call vanguard rather than avant-garde.

NH: *The most visible tendency in the contemporary novel right now, I think, is this kind of life-writing, memoir fiction. Is it surprising that the sensibility you're affirming as vanguard has a home in this climate?*

TM: I suppose if life-writing is wedded to an ideology of authenticity and self-expression, it's not interesting—but then look at Proust. That's life-writing, and it's totally about disjunctions within language, signs and representation, all that funky stuff that we're interested in. Or Michel Leiris, for example. Or Tao Lin, I think, is really interesting, or Ben Lerner, Sheila Heti. On the surface of it, they're just writing about "what I did last year," but they're actually writing about networks and capitalism and so on. I think the subject matter itself is almost secondary to what kind of ontological, epistemological, and ideological displacements are going on. That's what would make something interesting and dynamic—or vanguard—or not.

NH: *Let me finally ask you about sound, which comes at the question of materiality from a different direction in that sound seems not to leave a mark. But, to the contrary, your novels, in particular, register sound abundantly and self-consciously.*

TM: *C* is very much about sound. The protagonist spends a lot of time just listening to *sssssssskkkhhhhxxx*, just static on his headphones. But I see sound as writing. I'm a total materialist. So with Joyce there's a whole bunch of people, mainly who haven't read *Finnegans Wake*, who go, "Oh, to understand it, to appreciate it, you need to hear it. It's not about the text; it's all about the music," which is total bullshit. In fact it's all about textual process and reading and writing and hieroglyphics and decoding and transcribing material marks, and the sonority of it comes out of that. It's like this idea of the "grain of the voice," as in [Roland] Barthes. Rilke has this beautiful—I don't know whether to call it an essay or a prose poem—called "Primal Noise," "Ur-Geräusch." He remembers in school he had a good teacher who showed them that you can put a record needle on anything, you could put it on this table, and it would play. You could drag it down the street. Later, when he's a medical student and he sees a skull, he thinks of playing the groove of the skull. The point is that sound in that situation is the product of a trace, of a mark, of reading, of a stylus going through a groove, and I think even when we're talking about sound over the air or through headphones, the air has been marked. The air has been scored. This is not a metaphor, it has quite literally been scored into lines and waves. So I think there is a total, scriptural materiality about early radio, and for me, sound in its entirety is a subcategory of writing. I'm a total Derridean absolutist in that sense. Everything comes down to the trace.

NH: *Right, not only is sound the result of a trace but the traces it leaves are then . . .*

TM: Oh yeah, they inhabit space forever. There are aliens listening to 1930s radio broadcasts as we speak. It's this endless kind of archive to which schizophrenia corresponds very well. It's like what Caliban's describing in *The Tempest*: the air is full of sounds and sweet airs.

NH: *Which makes it very striking that each of your novels ends in silence.*

TM: Yes. A dribble out into silence. Sonic dribbles at the end of *C*. [Pauses to listen to the café radio.] AC/DC. Brilliant! "Highway to Hell." You should put this in the . . . somehow have a sidebar to say what tune is playing.

NH: *I'll request a hyperlink for the online version so people can listen to it as they read.*

TM: So, even at the end of *C*, when you've got this sonic explosion that kind of surges through him [Serge], that blows his circuitry, the very final image is the wake inscribed in the water that the boat makes and the detritus, the residue thrown into the water. It's about an inscription on the water. And in *Remainder* there's the vapor trail, which is moving and shifting and maybe disappearing. And all the wakes of the boats in *Satin Island* at the end. It's a tricky one. Silence would be a kind of degree zero of audibility, legibility, writability, everything. And then the book's over. Then you're done.

*   *   *

NICHOLAS HUBER is a PhD candidate in the Program in Literature at Duke University. He is finishing a dissertation on the mediation of money forms in contemporary fiction.

A Tale of Two Marats: On the Abhorrence of Verticality, from Laissez-Faire to Neoliberalism

DIERDRA REBER

At every turn, it seems, we hear that ours is a political and cultural moment witnessing a surge of "firsts" that break with all precedent. The vast majority of these commentaries revolve around the shape of American politics since the 2016 presidential election and such hot-button questions as the unchecked reach of executive powers into the judiciary branch, the oversized role of corporate interests in politics, and the imperilment of media independence from political and corporate influence. Wendy Brown's 2015 *Undoing the Demos: Neoliberalism's Stealth Revolution* offers an interpretive framework for these phenomena as the "transpos[ition] [of] constituent elements of democracy into an economic register," a process dictated by the "rationality" of "*homo oeconomicus*," with the effect of progressively undermining democracy: "The demos disintegrates into bits of human capital; concerns with justice bow to the mandates of growth rates, credit ratings, and investment climates; liberty submits to the imperative of human capital appreciation; equality dissolves into market competition; and popular sovereignty grows incoherent" ("Undoing the Demos").

Brown's is the negative inverse picture of what neoliberal proponents paint as the positive ideal of small government necessary for the liberation of capital and the maximization of happiness. In "Little House, Small Government," a title whose first term references Laura Ingalls Wilder's eponymous series, Vivian Gornick traces the "ideology that visualize[s] freedom from government as an equivalent of freedom itself" to the triumphalist discourse of nineteenth-century westward expansion. Echoing Brown, Gornick asserts that "[t]he frontier mentality [that such contemporary Wilders as the Tea Party and President Donald J. Trump] still embody is less likely to shore up a potentially failing democracy than to wreck it altogether." In the same critical spirit, the nonprofit organization Action for Happiness, founded in 2010 with "no religious, political or commercial affiliations" other than patronage by the Dalai Lama, seeks to wrest credence from the notion that happiness comes from "material wealth" (Action). Yet apparently alive and well—no matter how objectionable—is the so-called prosperity gospel that material wealth comes to those who are inherently good, a credo, Anthea Butler argues, propounded by the likes of Trump—who, we must add, also fervently propounds the virtues of small government and the liberation of capital. While Brown dates neoliberal anti-institutionalism to the past thirty years (9), Gornick attributes the ideology of small government to nineteenth-century westward expansion. These are but two of the many recent attempts to periodize the origins of our current political moment. But is this abhorrence of vertical power in the service of horizontalized happiness and prosperity for all really something new?

Novel: A Forum on Fiction 51:2   DOI 10.1215/00295132-6846048   © 2018 by Novel, Inc.

I argue that an archaeology of our neoliberal narrative turns up a conceptual through-line that draws us back over two centuries to the origins of free-market economic philosophy, which proposed that organized government—albeit in monarchical form at the time—take its hands off capital and let the world of commerce turn on its own happy and institution-leery axis. The robust emergence of free-market economic philosophy actually dates back to the mid-eighteenth century in France and England, in the decades preceding the age of bourgeois revolution that would tear both countries out of royal mercantilism. In France, the etymological origins of the term *laissez-faire* lie in a crisscrossed set of textual references centering on a group organized around the signature concept of *physiocratie*, which Liana Vardi translates as the "reign of nature"; Vardi explains that its proponents, who would eventually be called the Physiocrats, were "initially known simply as the Economists" (7). What has outlived the idiosyncrasies of this group associated with the valorization of land and agriculture is the legacy of what Murray Newton Rothbard calls their "favour of complete freedom of trade"; Rothbard asserts that the Physiocrats were the "first economists to stress and develop the case for *laissez-faire*," a "concept that [had] developed among classic liberal oppositionists to the absolutism of late seventeenth century France" (368). Among countless others who recount this stuff of seventeenth-century legend, Michel Foucault signals the encounter between Physiocrats and French Crown as the moment when "the self-limitation of governmental reason" known as "liberalism" is discursively born (20). The legendary and exclusively anecdotal moment in question is a meeting circa 1680 in which Jean-Baptiste Colbert, Louis XIV's minister of finances, asks what the Crown can do for commerce, to which bourgeois merchant M. Le Gendre famously responds, "Laissez-nous faire." Beginning in 1751, the anecdote was reported and circulated in print among a group of Physiocrats that included Jacques Claude Marie Vincent de Gournay, Anne Robert Jacques Turgot, Baron de l'Aulne, René-Louis de Voyer de Paulmy, Marquis d'Argenson (see entry on "Laissez-faire, laissez-passer" in Palgrave 534; also Foucault 24–25n13–17). Of interest for our then-and-now perspective is the dedication of a 2013 *Economist* magazine blog on these Physiocrats that emphasizes their belief that a "natural evolution of the economy" had expanded a progressively developed imperative to "let do" (*laissez faire*), to "let do and let pass" (*laissez faire et laissez passer*), and then to "let do and let pass; the world turns on its own" (*laissez faire, laissez passer, le monde va de lui même*) (C. W.).

Adam Smith's conceptually analogous and contemporaneous "invisible hand" surfaces in both his *Theory of Moral Sentiments* (1759) and *The Wealth of Nations* (1776) to insist on the idea of a self-directing autonomic body politic whose own innate sense of equilibrium guides and optimizes the distribution of capital and wealth according to its own internal know-how. The "laws" of this body politic, if it may be said to have any in Smith's view, are natural tendencies toward morality without formalization in any authoritative or authoritarian code. The invisible hand is what I would call a decidedly disintellected symbol of self-governance that obeys somatic principles of order, an internalization of natural law that does not need the rational imposition of political law. Hands off! Off with the rationalizing head! In with moral sentiment as the natural, universalizing, and egalitarian administrator of capital flow. Again, I must ask, has the revolution of neoliberalism we are currently witnessing been stealthy, or has it been steady, perhaps some two to three hundred years in the coming?

In *Out of the Wreckage: A New Politics for an Age of Crisis* (2017), George Monbiot argues that neoliberalism was born—here, circa 1970 with the rise of iconic free-market economist Milton Friedman—on the strength of a narrative casting government as villain in both economic and moral terms (33–34). We will not shake neoliberalism so long as we keep telling this story. But it is not only the 1 percent that tells it, nor is it always told in strictly economic language. On the contrary, the epistemological narrative of laissez-faire capitalism is lifted from the language of the human condition itself: love, harmony, flow, self-regulation, organic know-how, balance, happiness. To understand how we are perpetuating this story, we have to examine its conceptual scaffolding. Those who do so soon discover that no matter which ideological side of the free market we believe ourselves to be on, we are nonetheless bound to reinforce its epistemology. In taking either side we fail to challenge the foundational precepts and epistemological contours they share. To put it another way, we cannot think our way out of a discourse that conflates the free-market narrative with that of the human condition itself. In devoting ourselves to identifying and dismantling imperialist discourse, we have overlooked not only the discursive—indeed, epistemological—means by which capitalism nevertheless keeps itself afloat but also the ways that we are complicit with its immanence. Who among us does not subscribe to the ontological merits of harmony, togetherness, organicity, love?

If this is indeed how we see ourselves, I ask, then how can we ever measure the extent to which free-market logic has played in the discursive cultural register to shape this self-understanding? How may we possibly separate physiological well-being from its discursive counterpart in the service of neoliberalism? We may decry the narrative of heroic neoliberalism on the grounds that such vastly asymmetrical wealth patently contradicts its claims to embodying and purveying horizontal happiness. If, however, we continue to lend acritical credence to its epistemological scaffolding, then this is, in effect, the story we continue to tell: the free-spirited and moral "everyman" liberates an economy in distress from the clutches of organized tyranny; extra-institutional morality and free capital live happily ever after. This, I contend, is our free-market epistemological model, not a rationality, as Brown argues, but an affectivity: a casting of knowledge, self, and world in the language of emotion and feeling, all bound up in the organizational principle of nonrational autonomic self-regulation.

Accounting for the Origins of Affect in the Age of Revolution

In addressing the question of bourgeois revolution and independence movements in the United States (1776), France (1789), and Latin America (1810–24), the cultural and intellectual historians who ask field-shaping questions about the prehistory of neoliberalism have inadvertently formed a substantial network of like-minded arguments on the power of emotion, sentimentality, morality, melodrama, or what I call epistemological affect. Nicole Eustace's *Passion Is the Gale: Emotion, Power, and the Coming of the American Revolution* (2008) argues that popular discourse vindicating the universal character of emotion conceptually underwrote the American Revolution. Peter Brooks's now classic *The Melodramatic Imagination: Balzac, Henry James, Melodrama, and the Mode of Excess* (1976) claimed that melodrama emerged as a function of the French Revolution, serving as a new venue for the formulation and articulation of social value and judgment in the vacuum left by the repudiated ancien régime. Matthew Bush's *Pragmatic Passions: Melodrama and Latin American Social Narrative* (2014) follows Brooks in valorizing melodrama as the predominant vehicle for articulating social critique in Latin American literature for the past two centuries, from the early nineteenth-century independence era forward. Dan Edelstein's "Enlightenment Rights Talk" (2014) posits that "[eighteenth-century] philosophes literally turned seventeenth-century rights talk upside down, replacing its rational foundation with a sentimental one" (532). In doing so they produced a conceptual break that informed the Déclaration des droits de l'homme et du citoyen (1789) and, in turn, the United Nations Universal Declaration of Human Rights (1948). The gaps in Edelstein's argument provide the basis for my own.

Edelstein's particular mission is to bring the silent century between Locke and the Declaration of the Rights of Man and the Citizen back into view, especially in the context of the French Enlightenment. Edelstein characterizes this century as an "epistemological dust-up" (532) between rationalist "jusnaturalists," who viewed natural law as centrally vested in nations, and their successors, the sentimentalist philosophes who viewed natural law as centrally vested in individuals. The key point of contention between the two groups, Edelstein argues, lay in the importance the philosophes granted to "conscience and *sensibilité*," which he does not find surprising in view of the fact that "a veritable cult of sensibility swept across French and British culture from the late seventeenth to the early nineteenth centuries" (542). It is both surprising and "remarkable" to Edelstein, however, that "this current also swept up traditional theories of natural right in its wake" (542). To explain this coextensive relationship, Edelstein echoes Lynn Hunt's argument in *Inventing Human Rights*: (1) eighteenth-century novels persuaded readers to perform "act[s] of empathy" for "other individuals, including those who may have been beneath their own social station," and (2) this "empathetic understanding of another's plight . . . was a necessary ingredient in the development of human rights" (543) linked to the "moral importance [that the philosophes granted to] conscience and *sensibilité*" (542).

Edelstein's ultimate stake in the influence of sentimental literature on the discourse of human rights, however, is to take issue with the characterization of its representation of empathy as a universalizing and universally applicable social force. He questions whether these sentimental novels "genuinely train us to empathize with everyone, or whether they train us to regard certain individuals as fundamentally evil, unworthy of our empathy, and, by extension, unworthy of rights" (546). "Rousseau even believed that it was beyond our capacity to empathize with those who were 'rich or noble,' who only awaken our envy," Edelstein adds (546). In this respect, he places qualifiers on Hunt's universalist empathy by showing that sentimentalist literary discourse drew a moral-affective line between the haves and the have-nots, which, in the final twist of his own argument, Edelstein then uses to explain how the revolutionaries could have believed themselves to be acting by a natural law of morality in supporting the have-nots while simultaneously committing the atrocities of the Terror against the haves (562–63). When it comes to explaining how rights discourse went "from being the prerogative of jurists and philosophers to a part of mainstream culture" over the course of the eighteenth century (543), I am suggesting, Edelstein falls back on the affective pedagogy of sentimental literature. In closing this gap in Enlightenment discourse, he, like Hunt, thus opens another, which I see as far broader in scope and implication. Could we not just as well regard the sentimentalist corpus as an evidentiary barometer of the level and stripe of affective sympathies of the times?

How else can we explain the cultural depth and diffusion of such affective sympathies? In seeming to explain the popularity of this kind of literature, the idea that sentimentalist novels instantiated and sustained a closed-cycle feedback loop with their readers forecloses the question of why they struck a chord for so long and with so many readers across Europe and in America. What made the public susceptible to be moved by this material? In this gap, I glimpse laissez-faire discourse rearing its head. I take my cue from Edelstein's observation that the revolutionary philosophes and authors of the Declaration of Rights understood the nation as a function of "the sentiments that nature engraved in the hearts of every individual" (560). For them, as he puts it, "the nation is not a community produced by an act of will, but rather a 'natural' community that predates—and ultimately makes redundant—the moment of joint consent" (561). What else is this assertion that social order arises organically from the ground up, instead of being imposed artificially from the top down, but the thesis of unregulated natural economic order—laissez-faire. No exogenous institutions, no artificial government, no tyrannical verticality of power. Moral self-governance replaces rational social contract. The same question of the relative presence or absence of the social contract in the revolutionary Declaration was uncannily reproduced in a debate over Adam Smith's *The Wealth of Nations* (1776) on the podcast *The Partially Examined Life*, hosted by a group of self-styled renegade philosophy PhDs (Linsenmayer). Throughout the hour-long episode, the first discussant refuses to relinquish the conviction that the Lockean social contract is an a priori building block of Smith's thought. A second discussant counters with even greater force of conviction backed by textual evidence to the effect that such an assumption is unfounded, nowhere in evidence in either *The Wealth of Nations* or *Theory of Moral Sentiments*. In writing the latter, this second and progressively impassioned discussant continues, Smith contemplates social structure in the tacit mode as an "organic" effect of the movements of the invisible hand, as it directs the flow of capital to ensure economic growth.

Circling back to the prospect of adopting a *longue durée* approach to the life of laissez-faire, then, could we say that the principles of natural law credited with the epistemological architecture of the French revolutionary credo "liberté, égalité, fraternité," as well as the democratic precepts of "life, liberty, and the pursuit of happiness," have their earliest and most foundational origins in free-market discourse? Could it be that any government that erects itself on a bedrock of free-market thinking is building on the idea of its own gratuitousness? In the context of the free market, have we been mistaken in thinking that the political precedes the economic rather than the other way around? When we start out to understand neoliberalism in terms of a retrospective dialectics—which we must do in order to understand the nuances of the blow-by-blow evolution of free-market capitalism over time—do we nevertheless miss the forest for the trees? Do we fail to entertain the possibility that current global neoliberalism has been the result of a slow and uneven but steady process of intensification since the inception of free-market discourse centuries ago?

The Discursive Life of Free-Market *Homo oeconomicus*

In their respective discussions of universal emotion, both Eustace and Edelstein call attention to the fact that the discourse on emotion suddenly spikes. For my purposes, this raises the question of where capital and happiness discursively begin and end, the economic and moral aspects of early capitalist philosophy being all but impossible to parse. Smith espouses an early trickle-down theory of capital and morality equitably traversing the whole of human society, from pauper to nobleman. Jeremy Bentham calls pleasure and pain the two masters of the human condition upon which all sociopolitical life is constructed as a secondary operation. In making this claim, he forges a link between David Hume's assertion that passion rather than reason determines human behavior and John Stuart Mill's belief in individual freedom as the condition for maximizing the happiness of all. A century later, American economist Henry George would say of his influential *Progress and Poverty* that the ultimate goal was to "show that *laissez-faire* (in its full true meaning) opens the way to a realisation of the noble dreams of socialism; to identify social law with moral law" (5). Universal emotion and natural rights discourses morally justify free-market economics: this is the natural state of every human being; this is freedom.

If monarchy once enjoyed a monopoly on rationality as well as gentility, relegating residual social elements—including the bourgeoisie—to the unruly passions, which classified them as unfit to govern, then the discursive turn toward universalizing common emotion would symbolically decapitate the monarch and relocate the bid for sovereignty "downward," so to speak. Championing a residual body politic, a self-styled bourgeois freed itself of empire and discursively legitimized self-rule on the basis of capital and innate moral virtue. Laissez-faire embeds itself within US democracy and European empire. Although it seemed to offer an alternative epistemological and political model to imperialism, liberal democracy nevertheless imperializes. Think not only of the longstanding failure to abolish slavery but also of Manifest Destiny, westward expansion, and US military incursions and political manipulations too numerous to count in Latin America during the nineteenth and twentieth centuries. US imperialism can be held responsible for establishing so-called banana republics and culminated in the Spanish-American War that in 1898 "liberated" Spain's last colonies to make them economically vulnerable to the United States.

At the same time, empire liberalizes as it adopts an economically driven, informal imperialism, which, as historians John Gallagher and Ronald Robinson explain it,

only formalizes its imperial apparatus when the economic interests of the imperial nation cannot be sufficiently stabilized by the cultivation of complicity with
the native elite. Hence, argue Gallagher and Robinson in their 1953 essay "The
Imperialism of Free Trade," Latin America was the ideal nineteenth-century neo-
colony and never had to be formally colonized, unlike its counterparts in India and
Africa. Even after mid-century decolonization and leftist revolutions, the vertical
rationality of empire persists through the Cold War era. It is only with the fall of the
Soviet Union that the affective epistemology of capitalism fully unfolds to achieve
cultural visibility and popular influence.

By linking affective epistemology with liberal democracy, I mean the sentimental
privileging of a feeling soma—a body politic that is headless in the sense of having dispensed with the verticalities of rational command but possessed of the
autonomic intelligence famously figured as Adam Smith's "invisible hand." This
"hand," as I have argued, moves both capital and moral sentiment through the
body politic as harmonious flow. The body politic as feeling soma self-governs
without any need for interference or intervention from above and so does away
with "tyranny." Rule of the people, by the people, for the people simply optimizes
the natural flow of capital and morality. Rather than the very form of order, verticalities consequently become anathema to this principle of order. The result is an
extreme horizontalization of relationships on an immanent plane; everything rests
within a body politic organized on the principles of organicity, harmony, happiness,
love, equality, trust.

By the linking of rational epistemology with imperialism, I mean the Cartesian
privileging of a thinking mind over a residual and even abject body—commanding,
regulating, decreeing, imposing, exploiting, colonizing, disciplining. The mode of
thinking thinks for and in place of the subject, who is always a third-person other,
always the object of discourse. The relationship between sovereign and subject is
consequently based on fear, suspicion, mistrust, strategy, repression, the unyield-
ing assertion of superiority—superiority of knowledge, decision making and
judgment, critical acumen. If morality finds its way into the justification for colonial
empire, it is during the epistemologically hybrid nineteenth-century period, still
staunchly cleaving nevertheless to the mold of verticality maximally expressed
in the discursive form of the British white man's burden or the French civilizing
mission, which claim the duty to bring orderly rational civilization as a gift to
lesser peoples who would otherwise languish in natural enslavement to their
own unruly and irrational passions. In this epistemology, a vertical dualism
organizes and segregates the ruling head from the subject body, reserving all
powers of governance for the head and imposing all duties of subservience on
the body as remainder.

If, since the advent of laissez-faire–inspired bourgeois rebellion, we see hybrid
affective-rational modalities between reason and affect in the resulting two-hundred-
year variations on an admixture between rationally vertical forms of rule of the
many by the few (i.e., imperialist governments) and rule of the people by the people
(i.e., liberal democratic governments), then we should be able to see the reflection
of this historiography of recombinant epistemological jousting in our cultural

production. We should be able to identify and decipher the epistemological discursive structures that shift over time to lend foundational legitimacy to the dominant social order and its archetypical model of politico-economic power.

To explain the aesthetic operations of affective free-market epistemology, I turn now to a comparison of two versions of the same artistic work, one made during the French Revolution, the other in our neoliberal present. This pair of cultural examples provides a means of reading the arc of intensifying cultural protagonism of epistemological horizontalized affectivity during the period 1793–2010. The work in question is *La Mort de Marat* (*The Death of Marat*), made by Jacques-Louis David in 1793 to honor the eponymous fallen Jacobin journalist and political figure. The 2010 remake is *Marat/Tião*, made by Vik Muniz in collaboration with a group of Brazilian landfill workers, one of them the subject of this updated work and the source of the new name in the title. I would like to look at these two works as a series in the discursive life of free-market *Homo oeconomicus*. In both cases, we see an aesthetically rendered rejection of verticality insofar as the representation of the subject works unrelentingly against its transcendence and exaltation; instead of any kind of rising above, there is a morally inflected insistence on immanence and dwelling within. In the case of David's *Marat*, this horizontality represents the revolutionary challenge to vertical ancien régime social order and the heroism of the common people; in the case of Muniz's *Marat/Tião*, it defies the same hierarchies of social class to an even greater extreme of locating heroism in garbage.

David, the French Revolution, and Plaster

There is arguably no aesthetic representation of the French Revolution more canonical or enduring than David's *La Mort de Marat*, which I read as being squarely situated in the epistemological break from imperialist rationality to free-market affectivity—not simply as a passive act of history but as an active conceptual representation that David sought to make to underscore the triumph from below of a revolutionary society composed of the dissident elements of the wealthy but titleless bourgeoisie plus the sansculotte lower class against the towering ancien régime of monarchy, nobility, and clergy.

In their early careers, both Jean-Paul Marat and his painter David mixed with elite society but nevertheless became supporters of the revolution. Marat, born into a poor but educated family, was able to become something of a bourgeois social chameleon by securing patients within aristocratic circles as a doctor despite lacking institutional credentials and by publishing his scientific experimentation on Newtonian theories of light and energy throughout the 1780s, though he was rejected from the Academy of Science (which, Stephen Jay Gould says, resulted in the 1794 execution by guillotine and mass-grave burial of chemist Antoine Lavoisier, who had blocked Marat's entry). Marat's 1789 political publication, *Offrande à la patrie, ou Discours au Tiers-état de France* (*Offering to the Nation, or Address to the Third Estate*), which initiated his revolutionary career, criticized the royal economic policies that had landed the country on the brink of bankruptcy and asserted the right of the Third Estate to be essentially cosovereign in perpetuity with the First (the clergy) and Second (the nobility). Shortly thereafter, he began publishing the fervently Jacobin newspaper *L'Ami du peuple* (*Friend of the People*). David, born into the affluent bourgeoisie, studied at the Royal Academy of Painting and Sculpture, won its Prix de Rome, and was admitted to the Royal Academy; yet he became the premier painter of the revolution and, like Marat, a member of the National Convention, the political body of the republic. Theirs was a moment in which, against the backdrop of Louis XVI's economic crisis, the Third Estate was being vindicated—in Emmanuel Joseph Sieyès's formulation, as "TOUT" (1). When Marat was murdered, David painted him as the embodiment of revolutionary political commitment.

Tracing the complicated life of the painting that involved both originals and reproductions is difficult and, for me, evokes Walter Benjamin's now classic definition, in "The Work of Art in the Age of Reproduction" ("Das Kunstwerk im Zeitalter seiner technischen Reproduzierbarkeit" [1935]), of "aura" art in reference to discrete art objects accessible to the elite consumer and affording their spectator the distance required for critical analysis. This, as opposed to "aura-less art": art objects that can be reproduced on a mass scale and thus democratized for the better yet that are—as maximally embodied in cinema—possessed of an immediacy and velocity that require acritical consumption. Benjamin's essay turned on the advent of a technological revolution in artistic reproduction, exemplified in cinema, as clearly demarcated before-and-after paradigms of access to art and the phenomenology of spectatorship. While it may appear that by lifting Benjamin's categories of "aura" and "aura-less" art from his historical and media-specific framework, I have stripped them of meaning along with their original context, that is not the case. In just this respect, I find that Benjamin's characterizations of aura art and cinema map well onto the epistemological categories of imperialist rationality and free-market affect that are still at work in contemporary culture. In this sense, I find them helpful in elucidating the epistemological stakes that *The Death of Marat* visualized and, in so doing, opening up another dimension of Benjamin's essay. The opposition between aura art and cinema shows him grappling with shifts in a deeper diachronic life than his historical moment and media would let him address directly.

David painted different versions of *The Death of Marat*, including one that hangs in the Louvre and another in the Royal Museums of Fine Arts in Brussels. In the sense that these paintings have become part of permanent museum collections, they appear to satisfy the definition of what Benjamin would consider aura art—original and one of a kind. Never mind that the revolutionary government that commissioned it ordered copies for other cities and made efforts to maximize its public visibility and spectatorship. It is not coincidental that a painting widely considered to be radically paradigm shifting—in Timothy J. Clark's view, the first work of "modernist" art (21)—should be accompanied by some measure of reproducibility and popular access. What Clark considers unprecedented was the "way it took the stuff of politics as its material and did not transmute it" (21).

I would underscore that these are not just any politics but rather the most cataclysmic European social upset in modern history: the toppling of the ancien régime by the economically powerful bourgeoisie in the name of the sansculotte commoners and the beginning of a new era—David dated the Brussels copy in year two of the revolutionary calendar that began civilized time anew in 1792. Both David and Marat had voted for the execution of King Louis XVI in what Amy Ione calls a "prevailing 'off with their heads' mentality" (203). The revolutionary regime wanted new heroes and tasked David with painting three portraits of their martyrs. *The Death of Marat* is the only one to be completed and to survive the era intact. Here we have a work of aura art that nevertheless rejects the elitism of that aura status, instead, in effect, seeking the attributes of cinema art as understood by Benjamin: *The Death of Marat* was meant to be reproduced for propagandistic dissemination and consumption under an intended democratization—or at least commonization, so to speak—of politics and culture at large. Perhaps universal dissemination of the image was impossible, but it seems to have been a goal to maximize access, cutting across lines of class hierarchy. The painting provocatively eschews symbols of elitism and religion, seeking instead to portray Marat as an everyday hero who claimed to hold the wellbeing of the people as his highest ideal.

Marat was assassinated by knife wound in his bathtub by Girondist-royalist sympathizer Charlotte Corday. In the painting, his body—some say lifeless, others on its last breath—slumps back, his head and right arm draping downward, plume in hand still poised to write, left arm resting on his makeshift desk, still grasping between thumb and forefinger the petition he believed Corday to have brought him. For the painting, David apparently revised the content of the original letter, which called for a list of executions by guillotine, so as to soften the moral content of what Marat was about to condone with his signature forever forestalled. David's editorializing was also in play in the unblemished representation of Marat's body, for in real life Marat suffered from a skin condition so severe as to oblige him to retreat from public life and to work from his medicinal bath. This motif of purity—not only in his physical aspect but in his moral character explicit in the epigraph of the Louvre Museum's version, "N'ayant pû me corrompre, ils m'ont assassiné" ("Not having been able to corrupt me, they assassinated me")—is punctuated by the single knife wound that some equate with Christ's stigmata. Critics frequently point to two sources of inspiration for David's neoclassical treatment of Marat's body. In pose and play of light, both sources feature Christ's body: Michelangelo Buonarroti's *Pietà* (1499) and Michelangelo Merisi da Caravaggio's *The Entombment of Christ* (*La Deposizione*) (1603–4). Both paintings position the body in a horizontal recline with similarly draped limbs and faces that capture the light source and, with it, the viewer's gaze.

If David's *La Mort de Marat* is a secularized representation of Christ's martyrdom, then it seems strange that the disposition of Marat's martyred body is framed so that it forecloses all the glory thereof. There is none of the classical symbolism of spiritual transcendence, no ecstatic Baroque meeting of his Maker, no wondrous ascendance into a grand beyond. The light source is agonizingly horizontal and unseen, with an easing of the darkness toward the upper right of the frame but no true relief from above or behind. There is neither horizon nor upward dynamism, thus no thereafter. The dingy and pitted wall of nondescript yellow-green-brown takes on its own protagonism, framing Marat's body and existence with an oppressive sense of no escape. If this is heroism, then it is painstakingly rendered in a visual language of everyday immanence with such banal details as the imperfections of the wall, the chaotic folds and stains in the linens surrounding the bathtub, and the grain of the rustic wood box that serves as both side table for the ink well and his de facto tombstone, inscribed with the epigraph to the Parisian version and the artist's dedication to the fallen hero followed by his signature in the Brussels counterpart. The play of light marks this as a death in mid-action, that of a devotee of his cause, perhaps a martyr—even one with the significance of Christ, though lacking signs of exaltation. There are only subtle suggestions of Marat's life and the moment he engineered. His arrested movement enshrines his intent, while the slight float of the paper in his hand indicates the political cause for which he died. In order to locate Marat's face far to the left, the eye has to travel the length of the wall, placing its dirty imperfections at the visual center of the painting. The only symbolic center of which to speak is the moral glow that bathes Marat's horizontally arranged body and illuminates his face in an expression somewhere between pain and peace. It is as though the very impossibility of his transcendence is being celebrated here—his ordinariness, his death mid-gesture in the carrying out of his revolutionary commitment, his eternal resting within Jacobin sansculottism as a principled rejection of the rising-above that characterized the ancien régime.

David's *The Death of Marat* has had an uneven afterlife. Richard Nilsen describes how it was immediately commissioned as part of a "propaganda machine" in which "a great public funeral was held—organized by David—streets were renamed for Marat, poems and songs were written. At least one new restaurant opened in the rue Saint-Honore called the Gran Marat," and David's painting, finished within three months of Marat's death, was "paraded around Paris like a Mexican *santo*," only to fall into oblivion for a half century until the class conflict of 1848 and the second short-lived French Republic brought it back into the public eye. This initiated an ideological oscillation of artistic interest investment between vindicating Marat and exonerating his assassin Corday. Edvard Munch and Pablo Picasso made early twentieth-century versions of the painting that in both cases foregrounded the role of the female aggressor. In Munch's case, the Corday figure was explicitly an autobiographical portraiture of the violence he purportedly suffered at the hand of his former lover. As in the time of the 1848 Second French Republic, so the early twenty-first century experienced a resurgence of interest in the painting and a sudden proliferation of versions by other artists from both the high art and online communities. The one to which I now turn puts a twenty-first-century garbage activist in the place of Marat.

Muniz, Neoliberalism, and Garbage

In 2010, Katherine Bindley of the *Wall Street Journal* hailed as "A Modern Marat" the "Pictures of Garbage" project by Brazilian-born and Brooklyn-based artist Muniz, as chronicled in Lucy Walker's *Waste Land* (2010), a documentary film that received dozens of international film festival awards from 2010 to 2012 as well as an Academy Award nomination for best documentary. Bindley notes that Muniz is "known for his use of oddball materials." Indeed, as Eva Respini, associate curator of photography for the Museum of Modern Art explains, Muniz has "fashioned the Mona Lisa from peanut butter and jelly, Elizabeth Taylor from diamonds, Caravaggio's *Narcissus* from junk, iconic news images from wet ink, and his self-portrait from dice." This list serves to contextualize the MoMA's acquisition of Muniz's *Action Photo, after Hans Namuth* (1997), in which dribbled chocolate—in a kind of visual onomatopoeia—reproduces the image in Namuth's photograph of Jackson Pollack at work famously making his action art. Respini's description of Muniz as "one of the smartest and funniest artists that [she has] had the pleasure of working with" supports Bindley's characterization of his materials as "oddball," those of a jokester.

But Muniz made his name with a 1996 series now owned by the Smithsonian American Art Museum that bears the following gallery label on each of the works (see any of the individual works listed below):

> *Vik Muniz drew portraits of the children of sugar cane workers he met on the Caribbean island of St. Kitts using sugar crystals on black paper, which he then photographed for the series he called "The Sugar Children." As he wipes the paper clean after creating each image and begins again, his actions and his subjects' lives take on symbolic value, suggesting that generations of cane workers have been consumed by the sugar industry.* (Smithsonian)

If the SAAM description interprets Muniz's procedural erasure as symbolic of the consumption of lives by the sugar industry, then the titles of these portraits seem to work precisely in the opposite direction by mitigating this invisible loss through the assertion of their idiosyncratic and irreproducible personhood: *Valentina, the Fastest*; *Big James Sweats Buckets*; *Valicia Bathes in Sunday Clothes*; *Jacynthe Loves Orange Juice*; *Little Calist Can't Swim*; and *Ten Ten's Weed Necklace*. The last portrait includes what seems to be a fibrous adornment around the subject's neck that could be construed as the "weed necklace" of the title. But the other titles bear no diegetic relationship to the traditional portrait pose of each subject; they seem more like terse poetic anecdotes, or short-story titles, that point to narratives of lived experience beyond each portrait's visible content. These faces are more than just anonymous human visages with meaningless first and last names, the titles insist; they belong to real living children who have run, sweated, bathed, drunk orange juice, tried unsuccessfully to swim. The storytelling titles are abbreviated invitations to endearment and empathic connection that make us chuckle and want to know more. They consequently make it impossible to maintain a relationship of affectless distance to the work we are beholding.

Muniz's portraits are a self-consciously complex combination of aura and aura-less art: the portraits themselves hang in one of the premiere high-art venues of the world, the modern epitome of aura art. Although one must travel and pay to gain access to view them in person, it is also true that one may take an online gallery tour without doing either, as I have. This digital open access nevertheless calls attention to difference in privilege between the institution holding the image and the subject represented therein. Surely it would not be impossible or inconceivable to trace a relationship between the national wealth derived from proprietary interests in the Caribbean sugar industry and the national wealth that constructed its venerable halls of culture. Even if there were no direct connection, any attempt to do so would be the effect of conscience evoked by the image itself. Monique Allewaert distinguishes colonial subjectivity from the liberatory personhood denied visible subjectivity by an economy that defines such subjects as what Kevin Bales calls "disposable people." At the same time, she suggests, this process affords them a means of escape from institutional capture, in the form of stories that remain cheerfully defiant in the face of any strategy of ownership or disposability. Whatever their social and historical circumstances of exploitation, these children are, without exception, represented as joyful and proud and, as such, possessed of radiant beauty. In the same way, with respect to the exhibition spaces and the spectators that frequent them, the dimension of aura art in these works gestures toward a critique of a social asymmetry that enables the sacrifice of others' lives for the production of consumables. At the same time, both institution and viewer, through the exculpatory route of affect, are spared a hard-line social critique in the form of an accusation or an admission that they are responsible for this sacrifice. Rather than force viewers to reflect rationally on their cultural culpability and complicity, these works afford an affective encounter with the inviolable personhood of these individuals on a horizontalized plane of equality forged of common emotional experience.

In Muniz's "Pictures of Garbage" project presented through the documentary vehicle of *Waste Land*, this same artistic procedure holds for creating an ephemeral portrait out of symbolic materials, photographing it, and then disassembling the original. The difference is that garbage becomes the raw material of portraiture, yielding an even more powerful and stark symbolism. The site of the project that Muniz chose, as chronicled by the documentary, is the now defunct landfill Jardim Gramacho, operative for thirty-four years (and closed in 2012) in Rio de Janeiro, in Muniz's home country of Brazil. CNN statistics help put into perspective what it means that Jardim Gramacho was, at the time, Latin America's biggest dump: "piled almost 300 feet high across 14 million square feet," it was the "equivalent of 244 American football fields" and "received close to 8,000 tons of trash daily" (Brochetto and Ansari). The landfill's closure had a happy ending for the several thousand *catadores*, or "pickers" of recyclables, who worked there, because they were able to negotiate more than $11 million in severance pay as well as a state government fund to pay for former *catadores'* education and training in recycling or another industry (Brochetto and Ansari). The man behind this negotiation is Associação dos Catadores do Aterro Metropolitano de Jardim Gramacho president Sebatião Carlos dos Santos, or Tião, as he is called, an energetic, optimistic, and incredibly articulate young Afro-Brazilian *catador* who became the face of *Waste Land* and the entire garbage art project: Muniz's Marat.

The protagonism of Tião becomes clear early on in the film. Muniz arrives at the dump thinking he will find and foreground trash; his surprise is that, instead, he finds people working there who give this trash a human face. These people, all *catadores*, become the focus of Muniz's journey and project, as the process of getting to know one another and sharing stories not only antecedes but eventually begins to constitute the artistic act. Here we watch Muniz develop the same reservoir of intimate personal narrative that we imagine must also exist in the case of his "Sugar Children" portraits. Within the film, Muniz defines himself autobiographically from the outset as coming from Brazilian poverty; he explains in a key conversation with Tião that he wants to use any clout and resources he has accrued as an international art phenomenon to help others. Eventually, all of Muniz's proceeds at auction from the Jardim Gramacho project would be donated back to the workers, along with all of the proceeds from the film's prize winnings (Bowen). *Huffington Post* blogger Lisa Kaas Boyle opines that this artistic intervention into the life of a landfill must surely have played a decisive role in the favorable outcome that Tião was able to negotiate for its workers when it closed.

In the course of *Waste Land*, we see Muniz develop the idea of working with the *catadores* to produce their own art. Muniz maintains his status as artistic director and is, ultimately, the artist credited with the works themselves, but he nevertheless ideates and executes a more participatory project than he had imagined. Selecting a group of interested and willing *catadores* based on preliminary meetings, conversations, and tours of the landfill, Muniz proposes to make a portrait of each one, some remakes of canonical works of art, others derived from personal photographs. For each piece, Muniz projects the image onto a warehouse-sized floor. The *catadores*-cum–artistic collaborators then gather and distribute trash onto the image projection, filling in the formal outlines with the raw material of their work life. Muniz oversees the artistic landfill from a balcony above the "coloring" floor. Only in these shots does he direct the image "fillers" from the balcony in a vertical relation to image production. Otherwise, the film puts Muniz on the same plane as the *catadores*, as a peer who has gained access to the cosmopolitan world of high culture through talent and hard work and without losing his humility or native sense of community.

In 2015, Muniz founded the nonprofit Escola Vidigal to offer free art programs to local children in the neighboring Rio de Janeiro *favela* (low-income neighborhood). The school's architectural and pedagogical design project, "Juntos," represented Brazil in the 2016 Venice Biennale. On the subject of its goals, Muniz again negates any vertical authority he and his collaborators might otherwise be seen to exercise—claiming, as reported by the *Wall Street Journal*, "We don't have all the answers yet"—and horizontalizes that authority by locating it in future grade-school students, claiming too that "[t]he main reason we're opening this school is to learn from the kids" (Kino, "Brazilian Artist Vik Muniz Builds a School"). In doing so, he is as much a contemporary David as Tião is a contemporary Marat. Both are invested in egalitarian alternatives to classic institutionality—of art, of education, of labor. Both perform their reshaping in the terms established by market culture and without the spilling of blood of their eighteenth-century counterparts, Tião waxing optimistic about the "promis[e]" of the recyclables market and its "nee[d] to be a humanized form of work" (Brochetto and Ansari).

Marat/Tião, as the *Death of Marat* homage garbage portrait is called, is, on the whole, pictorially faithful to the original: Tião is reclined in a bathtub pulled from the landfill, a cloth wrapped around his head, his right arm draped *Pietà*-style and grasping a writing plume, his left hand holding a bloodied paper. Interestingly, the knife, blood, and chest wound are all absent—as if that violence and struggle are not in fact part of whatever "revolutionary" cultural work they might be seen as doing. Also missing is the wood box that doubles in the original as a lapidarian moral of the story and/or dedication to the fallen martyr. This is possibly because a tombstone to this Marat who looks like he could be resting in a moment of inspiration would not make sense in a portrait that is not so much about death as it is about life.

The most obvious and significant change in this version, however, is the obtrusive and visually inescapable garbage. We might think of this as a visual equivalent of Jean-Paul Sartre's *Huis clos* (1945), in which the enclosure of eternal entrapment is made entirely of trash. The original *Marat*'s pitted ochre plaster wall has given way to a wall of garbage that has no beginning or ending; it represents a state of immersion by surrounding the bathtub on three sides. As in the original, the bathtub intersects the right edge of the frame. There is no light source. Outlined in trash, the silhouette of Tião as Marat stands out in beige by force of colorless contrast. The eye-catching prominence of two white toilet seats, extended to the full-and-open position and therefore immediately recognizable for what they are, also lends the trash a meta-identity as such. In the other portraits of the series, the trash background provides a colorful patchwork of undiscernible material identity, but in the photograph of Marat/Tião alone, garbage acquires life—simply, openly, and unapologetically—as garbage.

Waste Land shows us footage of all the steps required to produce the final Marat/Tião portrait. First, Muniz takes an initial photograph of Tião resting in a bathtub; second, that photograph is enlarged and projected onto some hundreds of square feet of work space, where Tião himself and the other *catadores* fill in the image with garbage; and third, Muniz then takes a second photograph of the enormous garbage-made image that constitutes the final work of art. I want to give special consideration to what happens to the background in the passage from the preliminary photograph to its reconfiguration in garbage. When he shoots his preliminary photograph of Tião, Muniz has an expansive baby-blue sky fill the frame above the trash heap in which the bathtub sits. But when the image is projected onto the studio work floor and "painted" with garbage, neither the sky nor a horizon of any kind can be seen. Instead, garbage completely saturates the area around the tub, turning it into an image of resting within rather than rising above the conditions of possibility for political subjectivity. As in David's original, so in Muniz's version, any visual position "above" is completely elided. The *Waste Land* version takes this sense of an all-inclusive material reality further, however, in using garbage to occlude the source of light that gives David's original Marat his moral glow. Marat's capacity for heroic transcendence appears to have bottomed out, leaving us with a perfect and thoroughly abject immanence—heroism constructed of and inextricable from society's waste—as the perfect hero for free-market affectivity. This is a revolutionary reversal of the original that lovingly affirms rather than violently counters. A monetary and moral alchemist of the neoliberal age, Tião turns trash into money, trash into altruistic advocacy, and, in the process, saves Western culture from its self-induced oblivion by rescuing books that include canonical literary texts to create a library for the *catadores*.

"I'm trying to step away from the realm of fine arts because I think it's a very exclusive, very restrictive place to be," Muniz says at the outset of *Waste Land* (also quoted in Kino, "Where Art Meets Trash"). "What I want to be able to do is to change the lives of people with the same materials they deal with every day." Indeed, with Muniz's help, Tião is able to make capital, culture, and social change from the same materials he deals with every day, namely, garbage. Muniz's *ars poetica* is one of moving away not only from high art to low art but also from the most powerful artistic centers that serve economic power and privilege and to the abject position of social excrement in order to humanize and valorize through art the people and objects that society has classified as waste.

The Happy Freedom of Horizontality

Muniz engages the discursive play of horizontalities over verticalities (immanence over transcendence, morality over rationality, equality over elitism) that we saw in David's original *Death of Marat*. Could we consider Muniz's garbage art to be the redemptive portrait of Brown's demos undone, inverse interpretations of a common epistemological eschewal of verticality and privileging of horizontality? Is this, in other words, the happy freedom of horizontality? The same preferential horizontality is notoriously at work in the rhetoric of the ultra-neoliberal Tea Party on the US political Right, which decries any perceived overreach of democracy into economic regulation as tyranny and its insufficiently free-market–friendly presidents as kings (Lepore). We also see in the philosophy of the likes of billionaire private political supporter Bob Mercer, a key Trump presidential campaign donor, the conviction that institutional government is the enemy of political autonomy, personal happiness, and, above all, economic freedom (Abramson and Shen; Mayer, *Dark Money*; Mayer, "Reclusive Hedge-Fund Tycoon"; "How Dangerous Is Dark Money?"). This present-day anti-institutionality strongly echoes laissez-faire revolutionary-era thought like that of the Physiocrats ("pour gouverner mieux, il faudroit gouverner moins" [to govern better, govern less]) and Adam Smith, whose invisible hand brings the social elements it traverses into harmony in order to perform much the same discursive decapitation of rational institutionality that his French contemporaries enacted shortly thereafter in the name of freedom (Argenson 362). Whether at work in the age of revolution on behalf of liberal democracy or during the present moment, when democracy itself seems on its way to the chopping block of tyranny, free-market logic tells the same story: (if they can't keep their) hands off (our money), (then) off with their heads!

"This Is the Good and This the Evil of Trade"

Lest we be tempted to think that neoliberalism comes across laissez-faire as a found object and molds it for the express purpose of undoing the demos, let me return to the period of US expansionism referenced above, in Gornick's critique of so many twenty-first-century "Wilders," with a second example that comes on the eve of the annexation of Texas and the Mexican-American War that increased US territory by more than 50 percent. To testify to its presence, I have excerpted a passage from "The Young American," an 1844 address by Ralph Waldo Emerson to the Mercantile Library Association of Boston. This independent organization was founded in 1820, featured a "Library and Reading Room for the use of young men engaged in mercantile pursuits," and was reputedly "the first association of the kind in the United States" (Mercantile Library Association 3). We should not be surprised, then, to find that "trade" is Emerson's word for "laissez-faire," which places him on our growing list of authors favoring nonverticality and evincing credence in an ordering principle at once moral and natural, all of which derives from the model of "trade." Here is how Emerson went about cultivating the spirit of trade in young Americans:

> We must have kings, and we must have nobles. Nature provides such in every society,—only let us have the real instead of the titular. Let us have our leading and our inspiration from the best. . . . Let the powers be well directed, directed by love, and they would everywhere be greeted with joy and honor. . . .
>
> [T]he historian will see that trade was the principle of Liberty; that trade planted America and destroyed Feudalism; that it makes peace and keeps peace, and it will abolish slavery. . . . Trade is an instrument in the hands of that friendly Power which works for us in our own despite. We design it thus and thus; it turns out otherwise and far better. This beneficent tendency, omnipotent without violence, exists and works. Every line of history inspires a confidence that we shall not go far wrong; that things mend. . . .
>
> Trade goes to make the governments insignificant, and to bring every kind of faculty of every individual that can in any manner serve any person, on sale. Instead of a huge Army and Navy, and Executive Departments, it converts Government into an Intelligence-Office, where every man may find what he wishes to buy, and expose what he has to sell, not only produce and manufactures, but art, skill, and intellectual and moral values. This is the good and this the evil of trade, that it would put everything into market, talent, beauty, virtue, and man himself. (Emerson)

In Emerson's vision, trade operates on a natural principle of cyclical birth and death that impedes the reification of verticalities, including government. The agents of trade are "real" rather than "titular" nobility who work against any hierarchy other than that born of "powers well directed . . . by love." Their enterprise is "in the hands of that friendly Power which works for us in our own despite," an affectively rendered divine agency reminiscent of Smith's invisible hand. Thus we return to my opening question.

From our vantage point, are we simply witnessing the latest falling waves of the sea, these movements in the hands of that friendly Power that works for us in our own despite, a beneficent tendency of self-correction and self-perfection— mending—that expresses the mind of mankind? What, exactly, is the balance of good and evil in trade's putting everything into market—"talent, beauty, virtue, and man himself"? Does our answer to this question mean that neoliberalism is evil—or is it good? How do we distinguish the arguments of so many Wendy Browns from those of so many Bob Mercers, who tell us, respectively, that we are in terminal ruin and salutary renewal?

This, I have suggested, is the ultimate consequence of the repudiation of verticalities, which we now seem to be witnessing for the first time unchecked by the countervailing constraint of imperialist reason. The fact is that free-market epistemology does not admit its hierarchical impulse in thought or in action. Free-market epistemology regards the rational head as the symbolic and epistemological terrain of the tyrant. In its purest form, free-market epistemology does not countenance the hierarchy implied by Cartesian dualism any more than it suffers the imposition of taxation without representation. The ultimate epistemological consequence of the universal triumph of laissez-faire is the cultural injunction against any form of superiority. As in Adam Smith, so in today's free-market discourse, money and morality move together, washing away any obstacles to their conjugal flow, including forms of moral judgment that do not organically emerge within the logic of that flow. Any assertion of contrary fact is met with a will toward symbolic decapitation. As the Dude says in the now iconic refrain from the cult film *The Big Lebowski* (1998), "That's, like, your opinion, man." Although the line is meant humorously to disarm the claims of his big-money alter ego, it also unwittingly reinforces the epistemological underpinnings of laissez-faire.

Indeed, what I have sought to show is that the same laissez-faire precepts of antiverticality that inform the neoliberal undermining of democratic structure—or any government perceived to stand in the way of the moral freedom of capital—are the same ones that also inform the aesthetic representation of horizontal heroism in works like the two Marats, both of which are treated as a form of common currency that circulates on the strength of morality through a body politic (better yet, a body economic). David's *Marat*, in its many late eighteenth-century copies and street parades, was an aesthetic of the everyman standard of equality; Muniz's *Marat/Tião*, endlessly disseminated as the face of *Waste Land*, with auction proceeds that undercut every form of profit (our new elitism) as donations to recycling labor activism, is an aesthetic of new extremes of horizontal relativism that strips the internal logic of hierarchy even from the notion of value itself by rendering worth equivalent to—and even subordinate to—its diametrical lack.

Do we think we may keep the heroism of the two Marats and reject democratic institutional implosion? What I want to argue is that this is not an epistemologically coherent proposition, for the two go hand in hand. Horizontality has its repercussions: our acceptance of a Marat or, eventually, a Tião—that is, respectively, a champion of the heroism of the everyman, or the embodiment of the heroism of the most abject nobody—is a vote against hierarchies of every kind: of power, of governance, of knowledge, of worth. The categories of fact and truth and the actions of rational critique and judgment cannot survive this epistemological shift because they assume the epistemological acceptance of relationships of superiority and inferiority; in a cultural climate dominated by laissez-faire logic, fact and truth and rational critique and judgment must cede, respectively, to opinion and affective preference. Rational vertical edifice yields to horizontal affective commerce. Affirmation and resistance—in short, politics—become rendered as so many variations of the Janus-like circulation of passion and capital in a world that sees itself as a freedom fighter for the natural right to turn on its own.

*   *   *

DIERDRA REBER is assistant professor of Latin American studies at the University of Kentucky and author of one book, *Coming to Our Senses: Affect and an Order of Things for Global Culture* (2016). She is now at work on a second book tentatively titled "Losing Our Minds: Free-Market Affect and the Disavowal of Reason."

Works Cited

Abramson, Alana, and Lucinda Shen. "Conservative Megadonor Robert Mercer Is Stepping Down as CEO of His Massive Hedge Fund. Read His Full Statement." *Fortune* 2 Nov. 2017 <www.fortune.com/2017/11/02/robert-mercer-renaissance-technologies-breitbart -news-steve-bannon/>.

Action for Happiness. "About Us" <www.actionforhappiness.org/about-us> (accessed 8 Dec. 2017).

Allewaert, Monique. *Ariel's Ecology: Personhood and Colonialism in the American Tropics*. Minneapolis: U of Minnesota P, 2013.

Argenson, René-Louis de Voyer. *Mémoires et journal inédit du marquis d'Argenson, Ministre des Affaires Étrangères sous Louis XV*. Ed. Charles Marc René de Voyer Argenson. Vol. 5. Paris: Jannet, 1858.

Bales, Kevin. *Disposable People: New Slavery in the Global Economy*. Berkeley: U of California P, 1999.

Benjamin, Walter. "The Work of Art in the Age of Reproduction." *Illuminations*. Ed. Hannah Arendt. Trans. Harry Zohn. New York: Schocken, 2007. 217–51.

Bentham, Jeremy. *An Introduction to the Principles of Morals and Legislation*. Oxford: Clarendon, 1907. Library of Economics and Liberty <www.econlib.org/library/Bentham/bnth PML1.html>.

The Big Lebowski. Dir. Joel Coen and Ethan Coen. Polygram, Working Title, 1998.

Bindley, Katherine. "A Modern Marat." *Wall Street Journal* 16 Oct. 2010 <www.wsj.com /articles/SB10001424052748703440004575548581385394008>.

Bowen, Stephanie. "One Man's Trash." *Daily Gumboot* 6 Oct 2010 <web.archive.org/web /20120313155922/http://dailygumboot.ca/2010/10/one-mans-trash/>.

Boyle, Lisa Kaas. "Finding Hope Down in the Dump: A Visit with Tiao Carlos dos Santos, Champion of Rio Garbage Pickers." *Huffington Post* 29 June 2012 <www.huffingtonpost .com/lisa-kaas-boyle/finding-hope-down-in-the-_b_1635927.html>.

Brochetto, Marilia, and Azadeh Ansari. "Landfill's Closure Changing Lives in Rio." CNN, 5 June 2017 <www.cnn.com/2012/06/05/world/americas/brazil-landfill-closure/index .html>.

Brooks, Peter. *The Melodramatic Imagination: Balzac, Henry James, Melodrama, and the Mode of Excess*. New Haven: Yale UP, 1976.

Brown, Wendy. *Undoing the Demos: Neoliberalism's Stealth Revolution*. New York: Zone, 2015.

Buonarroti, Michelangelo. *Pietà*. 1499. Marble. St. Peter's Basilica, Vatican City.

Bush, Matthew. *Pragmatic Passions: Melodrama and Latin American Social Narrative*. Madrid: Iberoamericana Editorial Vervuert, 2014.

Butler, Anthea. "The Cheap Prosperity Gospel of Trump and Osteen." *New York Times* 30 Aug. 2017 <www.nytimes.com/2017/08/30/opinion/trump-osteen-harvey-church.html>.

Caravaggio, Michelangelo Merisi da. *The Entombment of Christ*. 1603–4. Oil on canvas. Pinacoteca Vaticana, Vatican City.

Clark, Timothy J. *Farewell to an Idea: Episodes from a History of Modernism*. New Haven: Yale UP, 1999.

C. W. "Who Were the Physiocrats?" *Economist* 11 Oct. 2013 <www.economist.com/blogs /freeexchange/2013/10/economic-history-0>.

David, Jacques-Louis. *La Mort de Marat*. 1793. Oil on canvas. Louvre Museum, Paris.

——. *La Mort de Marat*. 1793. Oil on canvas. Royal Museums of Fine Arts of Belgium, Brussels.

Edelstein, Dan. "Enlightenment Rights Talk." *Journal of Modern History* 86.3 (2014): 530–65.

Emerson, Ralph Waldo. "The Young American: A Lecture Read before the Mercantile Library Association, Boston, February 7, 1844." American Transcendentalism Web <tran scendentalism-legacy.tamu.edu/authors/emerson/essays/youngam.html> (accessed 26 Nov. 2017).

Eustace, Nicole. *Passion Is the Gale: Emotion, Power, and the Coming of the American Revolution*. Chapel Hill: U of North Carolina P, 2008.

Foucault, Michel. *The Birth of Biopolitics: Lectures at the Collège de France, 1978–1979*. Ed. Michel Senellart. Trans. Graham Burchell. New York: Picador, 2004.

Gallagher, John, and Ronald Robinson. "The Imperialism of Free Trade." *Economic History Review* 6.1 (1953): 1–15.

George, Henry. *Progress and Poverty: An Inquiry into the Cause of Industrial Depressions and the Increase of Want with Increase of Wealth*. New York: Cosimo, 2006.

Gornick, Vivian. "Little House, Small Government." *New Republic* 16 Nov. 2017 <www.new republic.com/article/145410/little-house-small-government-laura-ingalls-wilder-frontier -vision-freedom-survival-lives-trump-america>.

Gould, Stephen Jay. "The Passion of Antoine Lavoisier." *Natural History* 98.6 (1989): 16–25.

"How Dangerous Is Dark Money?" Crooked Conversation, *Crooked* 15 Nov. 2017.

Hunt, Lynn. *Inventing Human Rights: A History.* New York: Norton, 2007.

Ione, Amy. *Art and the Brain: Plasticity, Embodiment, and the Unclosed Circle.* Leiden: Brill
Rodopi, 2016.

Kino, Carol. "Brazilian Artist Vik Muniz Builds a School in Rio." *Wall Street Journal* 18
May 2016 <www.wsj.com/articles/brazilian-artist-vik-muniz-builds-a-school-in-rio
-1463581385>.

———. "Where Art Meets Trash and Transforms Life." *New York Times* 21 Oct. 2010
<www.nytimes.com/2010/10/24/arts/design/24muniz.html>.

Lepore, Jill. "Tea and Sympathy: Who Owns the American Revolution?" *New Yorker* 3 May
2010 <www.newyorker.com/magazine/2010/05/03/tea-and-sympathy-2>.

Linsenmayer, Mark. "Episode 174: Adam Smith's 'Wealth of Nations' (Part One)." *The
Partially Examined Life* (blog) 16 Oct. 2017 <www.partiallyexaminedlife.com/2017/10
/16/ep174-1-adam-smith/>.

Marat, Jean-Paul. *Offrande à la patrie, ou Discours au Tiers-état de France.* Paris: Temple de la
Liberté, 1789.

Mayer, Jane. *Dark Money: The Hidden History of the Billionaires behind the Rise of the Radical
Right.* New York: Doubleday, 2016.

———. "The Reclusive Hedge-Fund Tycoon behind the Trump Presidency." *New Yorker* 27
Mar. 2017 <www.newyorker.com/magazine/2017/03/27/the-reclusive-hedge-fund
-tycoon-behind-the-trump-presidency>.

Mercantile Library Association. *A Catalogue of Books of the Mercantile Library Association of
Boston: Together with the Act of Incorporation, and the By-Laws and Regulations Adopted January,
1848.* Boston: Mercantile Library Association, 1848. Google Books <books.google.com
/books?id=DVlBAQAAMAAJ&dq>.

Muniz, Vik. *Action Photo, after Hans Namuth.* 1997. Chromogenic color print. Museum of
Modern Art, New York.

———. *Big James Sweats Buckets.* The Sugar Children Series. 1996. Gelatin silver print.
Smithsonian American Art Museum, Washington, DC <www.americanart.si.edu/artwork
/big-james-sweats-buckets-36328> (accessed 26 Nov. 2017).

———. *Jacynthe Loves Orange Juice.* The Sugar Children Series. 1996. Gelatin silver print.
Smithsonian American Art Museum, Washington, DC <www.americanart.si.edu/artwork
/jacynthe-loves-orange-juice-36329> (accessed 26 Nov. 2017).

———. *Little Calist Can't Swim.* The Sugar Children Series. 1996. Gelatin silver print. Smithsonian American Art Museum, Washington, DC <www.americanart.si.edu/artwork
/little-calist-cant-swim-36330> (accessed 26 Nov. 2017).

———. *Marat/Tião*. 2010. *Waste Land*, dir. Lucy Walker, Almega Projects and O2 Filmes, 2010.

———. *Ten Ten's Weed Necklace*. The Sugar Children Series. 1996. Gelatin silver print. Smithsonian American Art Museum, Washington, DC <www.americanart.si.edu/artwork/ten-tens-weed-necklace-36331> (accessed 26 Nov. 2017).

———. *Valentina, the Fastest*. The Sugar Children Series. 1996. Gelatin silver print. Smithsonian American Art Museum, Washington, DC <www.americanart.si.edu/artwork/valentina -fastest-36332> (accessed 26 Nov. 2017).

———. *Valicia Bathes in Sunday Clothes*. The Sugar Children Series. 1996. Gelatin silver print. Smithsonian American Art Museum, Washington, DC <www.americanart.si.edu/artwork/valicia-bathes-sunday-clothes-36333> (accessed 26 Nov. 2017).

Monbiot, George. *Out of the Wreckage: A New Politics for an Age of Crisis*. New York: Verso, 2017.

Nilsen, Richard. "Death and 'Marat.'" *Richard Nilsen* (blog) 20 Jan. 2014 <www.richard nilsen.com/2014/01/20/death-and-marat/>.

Palgrave, Robert Harry Inglis. *Dictionary of Political Economy*. Vol. 2. New York: Macmillan, 1912.

Respini, Eva. "Vik Muniz: Painting with Chocolate." MoMA, *Inside/Out* (blog) 12 Nov. 2009 <www.moma.org/explore/inside_out/2009/11/12/vik-muniz-painting-with -chocolate/>.

Rothbard, Murray Newton. *Economic Thought before Adam Smith: An Austrian Perspective on the History of Economic Thought*. Vol. 1. Cheltenham: Elgar, 1995.

Sartre, Jean-Paul. *Huis clos*. Paris: Gallimard, 1945.

Sieyès, Emmanuel Joseph. *Qu'est-ce que le Tiers état?* Paris: Boucher, 2002 <www.lebou cher.com/pdf/sieyes/tiers.pdf>.

Smith, Adam. *An Inquiry into the Nature and Causes of the Wealth of Nations*. Ed. Edwin Cannan. 5th ed. London: Methuen, 1904. Library of Economics and Liberty <www .econlib.org/library/Smith/smWN.html>.

———. *Theory of Moral Sentiments*. Ed. Ryan Patrick Hanley. Intro. Amartya Sen. New York: Penguin, 2010.

Smithsonian American Art Museum. Vik Muniz. "Description." SAAM catalog data <collections.si.edu/search/detail/edanmdm:saam_1998.31.6> (accessed 21 Feb. 2018).

"Undoing the Demos: Neoliberalism's Stealth Revolution." Overview of *Undoing the Demos: Neoliberalism's Stealth Revolution*, by Wendy Brown. MIT P <www.mitpress.mit.edu /books/undoing-demos> (accessed 26 Nov. 2017).

Vardi, Liana. *The Physiocrats and the World of Enlightenment*. Cambridge: Cambridge UP, 2012.

Waste Land. Dir. Lucy Walker. Almega Projects and O2 Filmes, 2010.

The Microeconomic Mode:
Survival Games, Life-Interest,
and the Reimagination of Sovereignty

JANE ELLIOTT

Since the late 1990s in North America and Britain, the field of contemporary aesthetics has been marked by the appearance and growing prevalence of what I call *the microeconomic mode*. This mode has proliferated across media and genres as well as across the demarcations between high and low culture; it gives form to some of the most celebrated recent literary novels as well as some of the most reviled products of popular culture. Texts in this mode are characterized by a combination of abstraction and extremity, a fusion that we can witness everywhere from the *Saw* horror-film series (2004–10) to Cormac McCarthy's *The Road* (2006), from the reality TV franchise *Survivor* (1997–) to Steve McQueen's art-house film *Hunger* (2008). Abstraction results from a focus on delimited or capsule worlds in which option and decision, action and effect, have been extracted from everyday contexts and thus made unusually legible—for example, the life raft, the desert island, the medical experiment, the prison cell. Extremity registers in forms of painful, grotesque, or endangered embodiment, including deprivation, torture, mutilation, self-mutilation, and various threats to life itself. The combination of the two results in situations in which individuals make agonized choices among unwelcome options, options that present intense physical or life-threatening consequences for them or their loved ones. In its fullest manifestations, the aesthetic effect of this mode is brutal, in every sense of the word: crude, harsh, ruthless, unrelenting, and unpleasantly precise.

In order to suggest what this mode looks like in operation, I want to begin with a particularly stark and telling example: the film *127 Hours* (2010), based on the memoir titled *Between a Rock and a Hard Place* (2004) by rock climber Aron Ralston. Aron, played by James Franco, becomes trapped in a slot canyon when his arm is wedged between a falling boulder and the canyon wall; eventually, after nearly dying from exposure and deprivation, he cuts off his arm in order to escape the canyon and find help. Some of Aron's personal history appears in flashbacks, but it isn't presented as qualifying or shaping the life-or-death choice that confronts him. The few elements with causal significance in the canyon—the trapped arm, the lack of food and water, the number of hours—concern Aron's sheer existence as a conscious mind that inhabits a body with certain essential needs and capacities. It is difficult to imagine any human being with this sort of body experiencing Aron's situation very differently, whatever the specifics of his or her personal psychology or place in the social order. Not only does Aron's decision to cut off his arm appear detached from any external processes that would render it something more than an expression of sheer individual choice, but the horrible nature of the act simultaneously throws into relief the fierce determination with

Novel: A Forum on Fiction 51:2   DOI 10.1215/00295132-6846066   © 2018 by Novel, Inc.

which his choice is enacted. I refer to this experience of highly consequential, utterly willed, and fearsomely undesired action as *suffering agency*.

In animating interest in this way, I argue, works such as *127 Hours* offer a searing incarnation of the microeconomic model of human behavior. Often described via Lionel Robbins's now canonical description of economics as "the science which studies human behavior as a relationship between ends and scarce means which have alternative uses," this model combines methodological individualism and the foreclosure of interpersonal utility comparison with the presumption that the choosing individual operates according to the parameters of allocative choice, weak rationality, and utility maximization (Robbins 15).[1] There are significant disputes regarding the meaning and parameters of each of these terms even among contemporary orthodox economists, but these differences have not invalidated this approach so much as given shape to various schools and approaches within mainstream economics as a discipline.[2] In practice, microeconomics relies on this axiomatic foundation to produce elaborate mathematical descriptions for the aggregate phenomena guided by consumer behavior—for example, demand curves or price points. My focus instead is on the principles governing individual choice in this underlying model—what I call *the microeconomic imagination*—which emerges most visibly via the granularity of microeconomics as a subdiscipline even as it guarantees the discipline as a whole.

We can get a sense of the conceptual power of this model by turning to the work of Chicago School economist Gary S. Becker.[3] Because of its movement into areas

[1]   On the gradual canonization of Robbins's definition as a measure of shifts in the topics and methods of postwar economics, see Roger Backhouse and Steven G. Medema. Although often seen as crystallized in Robbins's phrase, the perception of economics as a science of individual choice has a much longer history linked to the emergence of the so-called marginalist revolution of the 1870s. For a critical account of marginalism that explicitly ties it to the ills of contemporary free-market capitalism, see Regenia Gagnier. The methods and topics now specifically linked to microeconomics began to coalesce substantially before its recognition as a named subfield. For an overview of the twentieth-century history of the topics now associated with microeconomics before the subfield was designated as such, see Backhouse 284–94.

[2]   In general, the various components I have described here combine in different ways in different areas of choice theory as follows: (1) game theory: strong rationality, specific definition of utility (narrow self-interest), individual focus; (2) macroeconomics: weak rationality (transitive preferences), specific definition of utility (e.g., maximization of consumer satisfaction or material welfare), aggregate focus (view of the massed phenomena created by individual decisions); (3) microeconomics: weak rationality, specific definition of utility, individual focus (specific economic units including consumers, workers, firms, and markets). The other significant branch of choice theory, rational choice theory, combines many of these elements but eschews the focus on allocative choice that defines macro- and microeconomic approaches. Its model involves weak rationality, a nonspecific definition of utility, and an aggregate focus in the context of nonallocative choices. Because it is nonallocative, rational choice theory does not belong to the analytic rubric described by Robbins's definition. On the evolution of rational choice theory, see S. M. Amadae's excellent *Rationalizing Capitalist Democracy*. For an example of the range of approaches possible with regard to utility in particular, see Daniel M. Hausman and Michael S. McPherson, esp. 238–39.

[3]   The foundational status of this view of individual choice can be glimpsed in its treatment in microeconomic textbooks, which customarily situate the discipline in relation to these features

normally associated with sociology, his work represents a methodologically radical edge of microeconomics, but it is for this reason that it is especially revealing. When he applies the microeconomic view of choice "relentlessly and unflinchingly" to areas formerly consigned to other disciplines, Becker distills what he calls "the economic approach to human behavior" from its usual content and makes its self-reinforcing nature apparent (5, 3). For Becker, what makes the microeconomic understanding of human behavior unique is precisely its universality: not only is there no act of human choice to which the model cannot be said to apply, but also the model renders every choice by definition equally rational and allocative.[4] Becker's overarching methodology depends on aggregate presumptions of market efficiency and equilibrium, but his description of the individual as a "decision unit" functions without reference to such aggregate factors (167). Instead, it emerges from the tautologies that make up the model alone.[5] Because allocative choice necessarily takes place in conditions of scarcity, resources distributed in one area are necessarily not available for distribution in another. In effect, that is, every benefit comes with a cost, and vice versa. Add to that closed system the definition of choice as the

in their opening pages before descending into disciplinary complexities. For example, *Principles of Microeconomics* asserts that "economics is the study of how individuals and societies choose to use the scarce resources that nature and previous generations have provided. The key word in this definition is *choose*. Economics is a behavioral, or social, science. In large measure, it is the study of how people make choices. The choices that people make, when added up, translate into social choices" (Case, Fair, and Oster 35). *Microeconomics and Behavior* declares that "[e]very choice involves important elements of scarcity. Sometimes the most relevant scarcity will involve money, but not always. Coping with scarcity is the essence of the human condition" (Frank 3). And *Microeconomics* offers this account: "Is economics about money: How people make it and spend it? Is it about business, government and jobs? Is it about why some people and some nations are rich and others poor? Economics is about all these things. But its core is the study of *choices* and their *consequences*" (Parkin 1). The remarkably ubiquitous recourse to italics in such passages indicates something of the axiomatic nature of these features; the centrality of choice, consequence, and scarcity is declared via emphasis rather than justified through logical explanation.

[4]   In similar if more sweeping terms, Michel Foucault argues that for Becker, "economic analysis can perfectly well find its points of anchorage and effectiveness if an individual's conduct answers to the single clause that the conduct in question reacts to reality in a non-random way" (Foucault, *Birth of Biopolitics* 269). I am of course indebted here to Foucault's analysis of Becker, but it proceeds from a level of generality that leaves aside the way in which Becker's approach evolves from specific microeconomic concepts such as utility maximization. Whereas Foucault stresses the extent to which Becker goes further than the economic mainstream, I am more concerned with the ways in which Becker's work proceeds from and illuminates foundational axioms of the discipline. For a similar reason, I do not emphasize the link Foucault makes between the subject of interest and neoliberalism. Suffering agency can be understood as part of the extension of economic rationality that has been seen as a defining feature of neoliberalism—and I have explored this connection in previous work—but texts in the microeconomic mode fixate on one very specific aspect of this shift: the experience of allocative choice in one's own best interest as a frame for every possible human action (Elliott). My terminology is thus intended both to signal this focus and to enable consideration of what it is this focus reveals—which may not be visible via more large-scale optics of neoliberal governmentality as a concept.

[5]   Becker describes his method as tautological but defends it on the grounds of its predictive power (7).

expression of individual preference, and any choice that at first glance appears irrationally costly can be understood to meet preferences that are not immediately apparent. If an individual choice does not yet appear to us to maximize utility, then that is only because we have not yet identified the evaluation of cost and benefit, means and end, that guided the choice in question.

When combined with methodological individualism, this tautological account transforms every human action into an expression of individual agency. Not only does methodological individualism strip out contextual factors that might determine or mitigate individual choice, but also the factors that do remain in play become transposed into the closed system of costs and benefits. In this way, the very existence of constraints becomes the vehicle through which we manifest our capacity to act in our own best interests. For example, in his analysis of life expectancy, Becker posits that every death must be considered in some sense a suicide, since it "could have been postponed if more resources had been invested [by the subject] in prolonging life" (10). Even seemingly self-destructive behavior becomes the logical result of the pursuit of some goal other than that of prolonging life. And once the existence of that goal is taken as proved by the presumption that it was chosen, the choice can retroactively be determined to be an expression of interest since it led to this end. By foreclosing the importance of any contextual factor that does not function as either a resource to be distributed or an end to be met, this model turns even the negotiation of profound constraints—for instance, the finitude of life itself—into the rational enactment of sheer individual will. In this model, taking action in one's own best interest is not a measure of true liberty or full personhood but rather an inescapable feature of human life itself.

In *127 Hours*, we witness a relentless, nearly unbearable literalization of this conviction that, for human beings, to be alive is to be interested. From the geographic reproduction of methodological individualism in the stark emptiness of the canyon to the binary nature of the decision Aron confronts, the film incarnates the microeconomic imagination of choice in near algorithmic form. Through his serial and evolving enactment of the choice between life and limb, Aron endures a nightmare version of the comparison process that underlies the presumption of rational allocative choice: 127 hours of weighing the benefit of his life against the cost of cutting off his arm. Moreover, as his example demonstrates so viciously, the intrinsic quality of interest in life does not take away the subject's capacity for choice; instead, to borrow Becker's terminology, Aron postpones his death by choosing to put his every resource, including the determination required to amputate his own arm, toward life. Aron's experience manifests at the forcible intersection of profoundly agential choice and his existence within a container of living flesh. Yet, as the film's title also suggests, Aron's fierce attachment to life registers not only in his final decision but also in his sheer endurance of his circumstances. With each hour that passes, the effects of exposure and deprivation on Aron increase, so that the progression of time itself becomes a measure of both his torment and his commitment to survival. As he nears death, Aron's every breath signals that he is still clinging to life, with all the grasping desperation that the phrase suggests. When being alive transforms from a largely background, involuntary function to a profoundly important feat of individual will, the unfolding of life becomes both the object of interest and the moment-by-moment demonstration of that interest. Aron's interest is in life, and his life expresses his interest.

Across the microeconomic mode, we witness this conversion of interest from an analytic constant into a palpable, propulsive element of our status as corporeal human organisms—into what I call *life-interest*. Or, put from the opposite direction, we might say that the combined abstraction and extremity of the microeconomic mode emerges as an aesthetic technology through which the pressures and powers of life-interest can be imagined. By taking versions of the so-called survival instinct as their central example of individual interest in circumstances variously stripped of ordinary vectors of social determination, works in the microeconomic mode depict the contemporary individual as primarily a subject of life-interest. As a manifestation of a shift in the imagination of political subjectivity that has thus far escaped cognition even if it has not escaped perception, this mode both registers and fills a gap in our understanding of the present, and that is why I need recourse to an unfortunate number of neologisms to describe its central concerns. If apt terms were already in existence—if the transformation in question were either less radical or more established—then this mode would likely not exist in its same ubiquitous form. That my central terms here—suffering agency, life-interest, the microeconomic mode—seem to embody or unfold across seeming contradictions indicates something of the stress this shift places on our usual ways of comprehending political experience. By reading the microeconomic mode as a form of compressed knowledge about this ongoing transformation, I aim to uncover what it is that this mode seems to know about our situation that has otherwise remained unthought.

In this essay, I offer one segment of this analysis by interrogating the form that is most prevalent in the microeconomic mode: the survival game. Survival game texts participate in the microeconomic mode almost by definition; not only is the survival game created from the intersection of the necessarily abstracted game form and extreme life-and-death consequences, but it also requires, propagates, and harnesses each contestant's seemingly ineradicable interest in life. I focus first here on Gillian Flynn's novel *Gone Girl* (2012) and unpack the arguments it makes about the situations in which survival games come to be constituted. Unlike the majority of survival-game texts, *Gone Girl* interrogates the utility of the survival game as a response to the circumstances that make up its created world; the novel attempts to identify not only how the survival game functions but what its function is. One of these functions, I will argue, is to model and test a set of transformed relationships among interest, sovereignty, and the biological status of human being. Although this model resonates in certain ways with contemporary theorizations of affective labor and the biopolitical, it cannot be mapped against our existing assumptions about these categories, which may explain why the microeconomic mode has unfolded in a critical blind spot. In what follows, I document the way in which the microeconomic mode requires us to think very differently about what is meant by the political capture of life itself in the present. In order to track this thinking, I approach the survival game not as an object of existing theoretical discourse but rather as the theory that it is.

*   *   *

The plot of *Gone Girl* centers on a young wife, Amy, who has gone missing, and her husband, Nick, who is suspected of having murdered her. Although the opening clearly designates the novel as a thriller, the account of what has led Nick and Amy to this pass is closer to social realism in tone, with a specific emphasis on the social effects of contemporary capital. We learn that Amy's character has been shaped by the fact that, since her early childhood, her parents have been cowriting and publishing books for children based on her life, called the *Amazing Amy* series. Rather than cherishing her for her own sake, they seem to have taken Becker's infamous microeconomic analysis of parental motivations as their instruction manual: they treat Amy's existence as an investment and reap the financial rewards accordingly (Becker, Murphy, and Spenkuch). When Amy uses her trust fund to bail out her parents after the 2008 stock market crash, she can no longer support Nick, who has lost his job as a writer due to the casualization of journalism in the Internet age, and they move from Manhattan to Nick's hometown, North Carthage, Missouri. The town's status as postindustrial backwater is neatly signaled by the fate of the local mall: having gone bust, it now houses an encampment of men who became homeless after they lost their jobs when the local plant shut down. In sum, Amy and Nick's arrival in North Carthage is determined by a confluence of monetization, flexible employment, financialization, and Web 2.0—in other words, by the real subsumption by capital of the most ephemeral, minute, and personal aspects of human behavior.[6]

What makes *Gone Girl* revealing is that it turns this canny if familiar account of immaterial labor in America into fuel for a mystery-thriller potboiler, complete with bizarre twists, misplaced trust, and a killer on the loose. And that generic shift gives the novel an imaginative reach quite different from what we find in contemporary Marxist theory. Tellingly, the hinge between *Gone Girl*'s social-realist and thriller registers is another feature of the social landscape associated with the regime of immaterial labor: the gamification of dating.[7] By only slightly exaggerating the approach recommended by dating manuals such as *The Rules: Time-Tested Secrets for Capturing the Heart of Mr. Right* (Fein and Schneider), *Gone Girl* skewers the expectation that women can find love provided they understand what men

---

[6] For key accounts of this shift, see Gilles Deleuze; Michael Hardt and Antonio Negri; Maurizio Lazzarato; Paolo Virno; Neferti X. M. Tadiar, "Life-Times in Fate-Playing"; and Tadiar, "Life-Times of Disposability." Although there are significant disagreements among these theorists in terms of the way they describe the form, reach, and global dispersion of this shift in contemporary capital, I focus on their general areas of overlap in order to illuminate the particular, overarching distinction that concerns me here: that between the subject of immaterial labor and the subject of life-interest. Although I use the term *immaterial labor* instead of *affective labor* in this essay, both terms circulate as a means to describe this transformation and both have been subject to arguments regarding their limitations.

[7] In general, gamification refers to the creation or amplification of gamelike features within a system that exists for reasons other than the experience of playing a game. For a popular argument in favor of gamification, see, for example, Jane McGonigal. For a critique of such arguments focused on the relationship between neoliberalism and gamification, see, for example, McKenzie Wark.

really want and have the discipline to play the game accordingly. After meeting Nick at a party, Amy intuits that he is looking for what she calls "the Cool Girl." Self-confident but undemanding, a gorgeous size 2 yet addicted to hot dogs and burgers, the Cool Girl can be easily identified by her professed love of football, poker, cheap beer, threesomes, and anal sex (222). Winning Nick requires that Amy convince him that she is the Cool Girl of his dreams, who of course would never be so uncool as to modify her behavior to catch a man. Once Amy successfully embodies the Cool Girl and captures Nick's affections, however, she comes to the outraged realization that playing love like a game is an inherently self-canceling project. Transforming herself into someone to whom Nick will commit turns out to mean that Amy has foreclosed the possibility that she will be loved for herself, since it is not Amy that Nick has chosen but the Cool Girl she has been impersonating. Not only is winning in this scenario indistinguishable from losing, but it is also specifically Amy's capacity to game the system that has caused her to wind up with the booby prize. Precisely because it creates such a clear and instrumental path to the goal of love, the power of Amy's will turns into a source of self-injury. When capturing Mr. Right is just another form of rational action in one's own best interest, *Gone Girl* suggests, it becomes a form of suffering agency for the woman involved.

This realization sparks the novel's thriller plot because, as readers discover in the novel's central twist, Amy is actually a psychopath who cannot bear to have her will thwarted or her amazingness denied. In part 1 of the novel, we read a series of diary entries by Amy cataloguing her relationship with Nick from their first meeting in Manhattan to his gradual shift to selfish indifference and finally violent outbursts. At the start of part 2 of the novel, however, narrator-Amy gleefully informs the reader that "diary-Amy" is a fake, created to cast suspicion on Nick. Instead of being a victim of forces beyond her control, Amy turns out to be a monster whose villainy is directly tied to her creepy but not at all supernatural capacity for goal-directed action, from secretly crafting her faux-diary over months to slicing into her own arm to leave her blood at a staged crime scene. As she advises readers, "You just have to decide to do it and then do it. . . . Discipline. Follow through. Like anything" (388). What infuriates her about the results of her Cool Girl initiative is not that she has missed out on real love but rather that her feat of discipline and follow-through somehow failed to garner the results it should have. Amy's ultimate interest is in coming out on top, in having her will always and everywhere recognized as superior to everyone else's, and the prizes that accrue along the way are welcome but largely superfluous. As a villain, Amy embodies interest taken to a ludicrous yet logical extreme, and that is why her capacity for evil emerges full-blown when she encounters the problem of suffering agency. Suffering agency belies the principle that successful action in one's own best interest is always beneficial, and Amy rightly understands herself as that principle incarnate. She figures the outraged, spiteful energy of a person betrayed by a system whose dictates she has followed with unimpeachable fidelity.

In order to reverse this defeat, Amy does something only a villain could do: she forces Nick to play a survival game that she designs. She fakes her own death in a fashion that will cast suspicion on Nick, and then leaves a series of clues for Nick to solve seemingly based on details of their relationship, which he can solve provided he has been paying attention to their interactions. Not only does Nick have no choice but to "play the Missing Wife game," as he describes it, but he also reminds readers that, given that Missouri is a death penalty state, this game is life-or-death for him (42). In order to humble Nick on the same ground where her victory turned to defeat, Amy designs her survival game to resemble the gamification of love as viewed from a heterosexual male perspective. Familiar from countless sitcoms and rom-coms, this is the narrative in which women baffle men by turning communication into guesswork and minor interactions into symbolic relationship landmarks that men fail to note at their peril. Amy's sly twist is that, in this case, the clues actually refer to Nick's affair with a much younger woman, and with each riddle he solves he digs himself in deeper with the police. When she gets Nick to play the survival game she has created, Amy successfully traps him in an all-consuming structure that threatens to be fatal for him but is a voluntary and delightful fabrication for her. She uses the survival game to materialize a division between those with the power to legislate a self-contained realm governed by rules of their own design and those who cannot help but treat these manufactured, artificially delimited worlds with all the seriousness reserved for matters of life and death.

This division is what makes the survival-game designation more than simply a category error. In the survival game, the game-form's characteristic distance from necessity persists for the game's designers even as it is eradicated for the game players, who must inhabit the game whether they like it or not. As Amy's example suggests, survival-game designers demonstrate their power by ensuring that others must pursue tremendously important ends through inexpedient means—that contestants will play out their real lives in a fabricated world, like lab rats running a maze. Yet because these contestants are playing for their lives, this form of power over others specifically requires that subordinated subjects also take agential action of the most consequential kind. Amy proves herself the ultimate subject of interest not only because of her supreme capacity to act in her own best interest but also because her revenge depends on Nick's lesser capacity to do the same. She does not take away Nick's ability to choose; she *captures* his capacity for choice, and that is how she performs her dominance over him. She relocates his will inside a set of life-and-death parameters whose very existence expresses her will, and in so doing, she proves that hers is the meta-will. Or, to put it in more familiar terms, she proves that her will is sovereign. But what the survival-game designer decrees is not who lives or dies but rather the terms by which players may either win or lose their lives. Sovereign is he—or she—who decides on the rules of the game.

Because it locates the survival game within a mystery-thriller plotline that centers on the real-world game of love, *Gone Girl* creates a through-line from the ubiquity of gamification to the imposition of the survival game. As the title of *Gone Girl* suggests, Amy's successful disappearance from the field of play is what indicates her triumph—not only over Nick but over gamification at large; it is by decisively exiting the fray in favor of the game designer's spectator seat that she aims to prove her superiority. Of course, we might doubt Amy's assertion that being thwarted in the game of love is what drove her to create the Missing Wife game, especially given that her critique of heterosexual romance appears in the second part of the novel, voiced by Amy as unmasked psychopath. Yet even if it is clearly insufficient motivation for the specific action she takes, Amy's sneering dissection of contemporary dating mores in this section is too well observed and resonant for it to read as merely her insanity talking. Women readers may not go as far as Amy in attempting to capture the heart of Mr. Right, but there is a reason that "the Cool Girl" became a media obsession after the novel's publication. In skewering a recognizable dating dynamic, Amy's assessment of the gamification of love still participates in the novel's social realism even as her insane response to her defeat becomes the primary engine of the novel's genre-fiction status, both authorized and pathologized by its mystery-thriller conventions. Amy's takedown of the Cool Girl provides the conceptual switching-point between the novel's two generic and epistemological registers—the one that purports to represent the world as it is and the one that features the shocking acts of individuals who interrupt everyday life with their evil machinations.

One result of this nexus is to undercut the reader's identification with the feminist ire in the novel's satire of heterosexual dating habits by making it the motivation for an over-the-top form of revenge that readers cannot be expected to endorse. More importantly for my specific purposes here, however, this structure suggests that the survival game in *Gone Girl* is not a meditation on or metaphor for the process by which each human life becomes a locus of capital but rather an example of the profound, outsized measures required to set oneself outside—above—that process. The survival game is Amy's answer to the question: what does it take to achieve sovereignty over the countless games in which everyone acts in their own best interests? It can provide this answer because, as Nick learns to his peril, the survival game captures life in a very different way than gamification does. The assumption that underwrites gamification—the perception that everyday life activities operate as and are best approached as games—emerges from a regime of immaterial labor that codifies and monetizes the sum total of human behaviors as constantly shifting flows of affect and action. The survival game works in the opposite direction. By activating each player's interest in life, it forcibly locates each individual agent inside the container of its single, irreplaceable human organism. Amy knows Nick will play her game because, short of science-fiction measures, even a man who subsists on his protean charm cannot charm his way to inhabiting a second living human body should his first be taken by lethal injection. The human organism is where the buck of exchangeability stops—not for capital but for the individual who necessarily has one and only one body and who can usually be expected to act to preserve it. If the survival game stages a form of sovereignty particular to the present, then this is a power that guarantees that the same aggregation of human being expressed as countless shifting streams of interfused data will also be spooled up into individual life forms, piloted by conscious agents who have no choice but to keep making choices.

From one type of Deleuzian perspective, this insistence on the individual agent as a unit of domination may seem out of keeping with contemporary forms of control, but *Gone Girl* also brings to mind Gilles Deleuze and Félix Guattari's insistence that the molecular and the molar operate simultaneously (Deleuze; Deleuze and Guattari 157). Precisely through its crude distortions, the novel crystallizes a world in which the same subject who dissolves into various monetized flows of information can also be an individual whose one and only life is irreversibly blighted by a felony conviction or a bad credit score or the closing of the local plant—that is, by permanent consequences that attach to a single, identified human life. This, I want to suggest, is what life-interest is for: it constitutes the reterritorialization that accompanies the deterritorialization of the subject in contemporary capital. Although biopolitics and immaterial labor have been frequently understood as elements of the same process, the microeconomic mode thus represents their interaction quite differently. Instead of the mass populations we find in Michel Foucault's account of biopower, life-interest concerns the singularity of each living human body; instead of legislating a boundary between full persons and mere life as in the arguments of Giorgio Agamben, sovereignty over life-interest fuses the capacity for agential action with human being itself, whether that human life has been recognized as possessing political personhood or not. Life-interest is a biopolitical category, but it is one that scrambles our usual ways of thinking about the term.

*   *   *

Before gesturing toward some of the implications of this shift, I want to step back for a moment and consider this conceptual gap between life-interest and contemporary theorizations of life itself. Although there are also important distinctions to be made between life-interest and the approach to the politics of life associated with biophilosophy, I will concentrate here on a theoretical trajectory that is more revealing in terms of locating life-interest: that emerging from Michel Foucault's argument regarding the relationship among biopolitics, the subject of right, and the subject of interest. As is by now well known, Foucault posits in *"Society Must Be Defended": Lectures at the Collège de France, 1975–76* that biopower fosters or abandons human life in the aggregate in order to augment and strengthen national populations. That is, this form of power is focused on masses of human lives in terms of its operation and its goal. In contrast, the liberal subject of right famously possesses a self-evident right to life, but this right refers not to individuals' ability to sustain their own lives but rather to a guarantee that these lives will not be cut short by undue interference from others. In both the liberal and the biopolitical approaches to life, the active, ongoing necessity of individual self-preservation—the defining feature of life-interest as I have traced the category here—is set outside the sphere of governmental power, albeit for opposing reasons. The framework of biopolitics does not envision the individual's engagement with self-preservation as significant, while the framework of liberalism treats life's continuance as a baseline and given unless it is unjustly interrupted.

When Foucault turns to interest, however, he does so in order to describe a third explanatory framework, which serves as a necessary supplement to both the biopolitical and the liberal regimes. In *The Birth of Biopolitics: Lectures at the Collège de France, 1978–79*, he argues that, for John Locke and the other English empiricists, interest operates as the "principle of . . . [a] non-transferable atomistic individual choice which is unconditionally referred to the subject himself," and as such it "constitutes something irreducible in relation to the juridical will" (274, 272). For this reason, "the subject of interest constantly overflows the subject of right. . . . He overflows him, surrounds him, and is the permanent condition of his functioning"

(274). According to Foucault, this subject of interest occupies an economic arena increasingly understood as an opaque realm whose autonomy must be respected. Whereas political economy, with its investment in the national welfare as a whole, can easily be envisioned to align itself with the sovereign exercise of biopower over mass populations, economics after the marginalist revolution specifically concerns the choices made by the individual in situations of inherent scarcity. This analytic framework rests on the inescapable quality of human bodily needs: it is because we exist as living organisms with finite lifespans that we can be expected both to consume and to choose what to consume. Even had we every satisfaction possible on offer, our finite time on earth would ensure that we would be forced to opt for some pleasures over others. Obviously, the economic realm also contains forms of production and consumption that are far removed from the base demands of human existence, but as Foucault's genealogy indicates, the converse is not true: neither the liberal regime of rights nor the sovereign exercise of biopower addresses the subject's own relationship to continued existence as a living organism. It is only in the economic realm that we find the essential, active experience of self-preservation conceptualized as an ongoing area of individual concern.

This schema resembles the public/private divide that characterizes industrial capital, but Foucault's account is distinctive in insisting on a fundamental asymmetry between the subject of interest and the subject of right. The private realm should not be breached by juridical will, and its boundaries form part of the negotiated border between subjective rights and sovereign powers that characterizes the liberal regime. In contrast, interest is a feature of individual interiority that by definition cannot be broached by sovereign will. Interest can be engaged only by acting on the environment in which the subject assesses his or her options rather than on the individual assessment of interest itself. Whereas subjects of right can be forged into a mass by the "totalizing unity of the juridical sovereign," economic subjects of interest thus exist in "non-totalizable multiplicity" (*Birth of Biopolitics* 282). In contrast to the utilitarians' conflation of utility with happiness or pleasure, interest is defined by the subject alone and thus cannot be aggregated. Even should every subject of interest declare an interest in happiness, the impossibility of interpersonal utility comparison makes it impossible to measure or assess that quality across persons.[8] Rather than offering a new tool of political rule, interest in this phase belongs to the economic sphere and defines its boundaries as free from sovereign interference.

Crucially, Foucault identifies Becker's version of *Homo oeconomicus* with a postwar shift in this relationship between the political and economic spheres. In this phase, government increasingly operates not only in the service of but also via the methods that characterize late capital. Competition, enterprise, and exchange come to "play a regulatory role at every moment and every point in society," with the result that the objective of government becomes "a general regulation of society

---

[8]   Many of the most famous interventions of rational choice theory concern the revelation of logical fallacies that haunt the attempt to define collective forms of utility and the approach to public policy that should be adopted in the wake of these insights. See for example Kenneth J. Arrow.

by the market" (*Birth of Biopolitics* 145). In the large body of work that has been influenced by these lectures in particular, Foucault's argument has been taken to describe the expansion of economic logic to what was formerly the purview of distinct types of political rationality and action. Thus while this expansion means that governmental structures must shift to accommodate the subject of interest, the result is an approach to politics that itself appears an instantiation of economic reason. From a Marxist perspective, this transformation appears as one aspect of capital's increasing subsumption of life itself, understood here as the totality of human behavior. As basic units of human sociality come to be quantified and circulated within the flows of capital, it is no longer possible to identify some actions as belonging to or signifying solely within the political arena. In general, what we appear to be witnessing is not so much the convergence of the political and the economic as the replacement of the former by the latter.

Yet Foucault's genealogy also suggests that there is another key component of this process, one that extends rather than eradicates political subjectivity. If we attend to life understood not as the sum total of human behaviors but rather as the status of humans as living beings with inherent needs, then it appears that the economic sphere includes life itself *before* the post-Fordist expansion of capital. As I have suggested, it is the economic subject of interest rather than the juridical subject of rights who exists as a self-preserving living being with inherent physical needs. From this perspective, then, the dissolution of the boundary between economic and political rationality also destroys a long-standing, constitutive barrier between the subject's own relationship to his or her continued existence and the purview of sovereign power. That is, not only do new facets of human sociality become available to incorporation by capital; features of human being once confined to the economic realm alone—including the individual relationship to physical requirements for existence—also become available for political incorporation. The same process that conjoins capital and life itself also opens a new aperture between our status as subjects of juridical will and our existence as self-preserving living beings with inescapable bodily needs. What results is a political category keyed to the expansion of capital it accompanies: the subject of life-interest.

*   *   *

I want to conclude by turning very briefly to a survival game that has an express connection to American geopolitics in order to suggest something of the permeation of life-interest as a biopolitical category. Usually referred to as the ticking-time-bomb scenario, this survival game has been the subject of political debate as well as being famously and frequently incarnated in the television series *24*. Its central features are a hidden bomb that will soon go off, a tortured terrorist who knows where the bomb is, and an American who must decide if torture is justified in these extraordinary circumstances.[9] In its archetypal form, torture in general

---

[9] On the ubiquity of and political and ethical problems with the ticking-time-bomb scenario, see, for example, David Luban. I am grateful to audience members at the ASAP/5 conference in October 2013 for questions regarding the relationship between the ticking-time-bomb trope and

offers what might be the ultimate version of the abstraction and extremity that characterize the microeconomic mode: through the stripped-down confrontation between the torturer and the tortured, it aims to produce interests in the torture-victim so profound that they blot out and render irrelevant everything else in the world.[10] In the ticking-time-bomb scenarios through which American torture has been most frequently fictionalized and debated, however, more attention has if anything been paid to painful interests of not the tortured but the torturer, who must steel himself to withstand the moral agony of undertaking horrific actions in order to serve the greater good.[11] Whereas in Elaine Scarry's famous account, the eradication of agency via torture serves to turn the victim's pain into the torturer's power, torture in the ticking-time-bomb scenario instead transforms the victim's pain into the torturer's pain. That is, in facing an unbearable choice that requires subordinating one profound interest to another, the torturer manifests his or her own version of suffering agency.

Although there is an obvious political utility in imagining the torturer as an even greater victim than his victim, I think this depiction suggests that the ticking-time-bomb scenario also has a more specific function, which may explain some of its more puzzling features. Numerous commentators have noted a mismatch between the ticking-time-bomb scenario and the historical context in which it emerges. Not only does this scenario appear as a feature of public debate almost immediately after the destruction of the World Trade Center, well before there is any official acknowledgment of the United States' engagement or need to engage in "enhanced interrogation techniques," but also the torture that was eventually revealed to have been perpetrated by the United States in the War on Terror bears very little resemblance to the dynamic that drives the ticking-time-bomb scenario.[12] However, the early, repeated, and erroneous recourse to the ticking-time-bomb scenario makes a different kind of sense if we understand its purpose otherwise: not as means of mediating the actual use of torture in the War on Terror but, instead, as a way to negotiate the uncanny, powerful, and disturbing resemblance between the "suicide bomber" as a figure and the form of individuality guaranteed by life-interest.

The dangers of this resemblance become evident if we consider this figure's decision in light of the model of choice I have been examining here. Not only is life-interest by definition nonfalsifiable and incontestable—it is unquestionably in my interest to blow myself up if I decide that it is—but the suicide bomber also pays for his or her choice in the very currency that underwrites agential action in the present: the embodiment of life-interest. Considered from this perspective, it is

the microeconomic mode. At the time, I was unconvinced of the connection, but the discussion encouraged me to consider the issue further.

10   For the classic account of this type, see Elaine Scarry.

11   For the same dynamic imagined in another morally charged context, see *The Tortured* (2010), a film about parents who torture a man to find out the location of a kidnapped child. In raising the question of who precisely is being tortured, the title of the film insists viewers consider the perpetrators to be sufferers also, if not equally, in this scenario.

12   On the chasm between the scenarios through which we theorize torture and its current manifestations in the War on Terror, see, respectively, Stephanie Athey and Michael P. Vicaro.

difficult to refute the logic that leads one individual to judge the benefit of making a fatal strike against one's enemies to be worth the cost of his or her life. In fact, once self-preservation operates as the clearest sign of interest, acting against self-preservation in order to achieve another objective becomes the most profound expression of suffering agency, of the commitment to attain one interest at the expense of another held almost equally dear. And unlike the self-sacrifice of the soldier who flings himself into the breach to save his comrades, the premeditated nature of suicidal bombing puts the focus on the calculated trade-off that brings a person to see something else as more valuable than continuing to live. When the confluence of life and choice operates as the medium of individual will, deliberately and consciously turning suicide into a weapon may come to seem one of the most cogent and agential acts a subject can take.

To be clear: my point is not that this logic has any bearing on the actual motivations of American proponents of "enhanced interrogation" or of those labeled as terrorists within the context of twenty-first-century geopolitics. Rather, I am suggesting that the ticking-time-bomb trope is in part an attempt to engage and revalue a perceived resemblance between the deployment of life-interest by the figure of "the terrorist" and the experience of life-interest that guarantees political subjectivity within post-Fordist capital. If the suicidal terrorist appears to triumph through an ingenious renegotiation of this fusion of life and will, then it becomes imperative to imagine an American victory over this particular form of power. In order to both activate and overcome the life-interest of the terrorist, it is not sufficient in this version for the torturer to force the victim to subordinate one profound interest for another, since it is the terrorist's profound capacity to do exactly this that constitutes the threat to be eliminated. Rather, in order to prove his power, the torturer must demonstrate that he can best the victim on the same ground on which the terrorist has gained the advantage: the enactment of suffering agency. That is why the reluctant torturer is not outside the game, a sovereign designing its rules, but inside it: a player fighting to win; that is why he must be both torturer and self-torturer. In order to stage the defeat of an enemy who has found a way to weaponize life-interest, the ticking-time-bomb scenario demonstrates that its American hero can withstand more suffering for his agency than the terrorist can.

Taken together, the texts and tropes I have examined begin to suggest the potent elasticity of life-interest as a biopolitical category. On one hand, *Gone Girl* demonstrates that life-interest can function as a reterritorialization of the subject because of its presumed status as a feature of each sentient human being. On the other hand, the ticking-time-bomb scenario clearly indicates an anxiety regarding this very universality, which means that there can be no necessary, categorical distinction between humans who do and do not master life-interest. Even in survival-game texts that insist on life-interest as a stable site of sovereign power, the very frenzy of representation that has given us so many texts in the microeconomic mode points to the unfinished and inconclusive nature of these imaginative experiments. What a regime based on life-interest can enable, contain, or set loose is a question currently subject to near-constant hypothetical extrapolation, in the innumerable forking paths of the narratives that make up the microeconomic mode. In its melding of the state of nature with sovereignty, living being with choosing subject, suffering with agency, the microeconomic mode registers a rethinking of contemporary political subjectivity whose reach and consequences are still being worked out around us.

*   *   *

JANE ELLIOTT is senior lecturer in the Department of English at King's College London and author of *Popular Feminist Fiction as American Allegory: Representing National Time* (2008), coeditor of *Theory after "Theory,"* and coeditor of a special issue of *Social Text* titled *Genres of Neoliberalism*. A second monograph, *The Microeconomic Mode: Political Subjectivity in Contemporary Popular Aesthetics*, was published in 2018.

Works Cited

Agamben, Giorgio. *Homo Sacer: Sovereign Power and Bare Life*. Stanford: Stanford UP, 1998. Meridian Series.

Amadae, S. M. *Rationalizing Capitalist Democracy: The Cold War Origins of Rational Choice Liberalism*. Chicago: U of Chicago P, 2003.

Arrow, Kenneth J. *Social Choice and Individual Values*. 1951. New Haven: Yale UP, 1963.

Athey, Stephanie. "The Torture Device: Debate and Archetype." *Torture: Power, Democracy, and the Human Body*. Ed. Zalloua Zahi and Shampa Biswas. Seattle: U of Washington P, 2011. 129–57.

Backhouse, Roger. *A History of Modern Economic Analysis*. Oxford: Blackwell, 1985.

Backhouse, Roger E., and Steven G. Medema. "Retrospectives: On the Definition of Economics." *Journal of Economic Perspectives* 23.1 (2009): 221–33.

Becker, Gary S. *The Economic Approach to Human Behavior*. Chicago: U of Chicago P, 1976.

Becker, Gary S., Kevin M. Murphy, and Jörg L. Spenkuch. "The Manipulation of Children's Preferences, Old-Age Support, and Investment in Children's Human Capital." *Journal of Labor Economics* 34.S2 (2016): S3–30.

Case, Karl E., Ray C. Fair, and Sharon M. Oster. *Principles of Microeconomics*. 12th ed. Hoboken, NJ: Pearson Higher Education, 2017.

Deleuze, Gilles. "Postscript on the Societies of Control." *October* 59 (1992): 3–7.

Deleuze, Gilles, and Félix Guattari. *A Thousand Plateaus: Capitalism and Schizophrenia*. Trans. Brian Massumi. London: Bloomsbury, 2013.

Elliott, Jane. "Suffering Agency: Imagining Neoliberal Personhood in North America and Britain." *Social Text* 31.2 [no. 115] (2013): 83–101.

Fein, Ellen, and Sherrie Schneider. *The Rules: Time-Tested Secrets for Capturing the Heart of Mr. Right*. New York: Warner, 1995.

Flynn, Gillian. *Gone Girl.* London: Weidenfeld and Nicolson, 2012. Kindle edition.

Foucault, Michel. *"Society Must Be Defended": Lectures at the Collège De France, 1975–76.* Trans. David Macey. New York: Picador, 2003.

———. *The Birth of Biopolitics: Lectures at the Collège de France, 1978–1979.* Trans. Graham Burchell. London: Palgrave Macmillan, 2008.

Frank, Robert H. *Microeconomics and Behavior.* 9th ed. New York: McGraw-Hill Education, 2015.

Gagnier, Regenia. *The Insatiability of Human Wants: Economics and Aesthetics in Market Society.* Chicago: U of Chicago P, 2000.

Hardt, Michael, and Antonio Negri. *Empire.* Cambridge, MA: Harvard UP, 2000.

Hausman, Daniel M., and Michael S. McPherson. "The Philosophical Foundations of Mainstream Normative Economics." *The Philosophy of Economics: An Anthology.* Ed. Daniel M. Hausman. 3rd ed. Cambridge: Cambridge UP, 2008. 226–50.

Lazzarato, Maurizio. "Immaterial Labor." Trans. Paul Colilli and Ed Emory. *Radical Thought in Italy: A Potential Politics.* Ed. Michael Hardt and Paolo Virno. Minneapolis: U of Minnesota P, 2006. 132–37.

Luban, David. "Liberalism, Torture, and the Ticking Bomb." *Virginia Law Review* 91.6 (2005): 1425–61.

McGonigal, Jane. *Reality Is Broken: Why Games Make Us Better and How They Can Change the World.* London: Penguin, 2011.

Parkin, Michael. *Microeconomics.* Global ed. Harlow, UK: Pearson, 2016.

Ralston, Aron. *Between a Rock and a Hard Place.* New York: Simon and Schuster, 2004.

Robbins, Lionel. *An Essay on the Nature and Significance of Economic Science.* London: Macmillan, 1932.

Scarry, Elaine. *The Body in Pain: The Making and Unmaking of the World.* Oxford: Oxford UP, 1985.

Tadiar, Neferti X. M. "Life-Times in Fate Playing." *South Atlantic Quarterly* 111.4 (2012): 783–802.

———. "Life-Times of Disposability within Global Neoliberalism." *Social Text* 31.2 [no. 115] (2013): 19–48.

Vicaro, Michael P. "A Liberal Use of 'Torture': Pain, Personhood, and Precedent in the U.S. Federal Definition of Torture." *Rhetoric and Public Affairs* 14.3 (2011): 401–26.

Virno, Paolo. *A Grammar of the Multitude: For an Analysis of Contemporary Forms of Life.* Trans. Isabella Bertoletti, James Cascaito, and Andrea Casson. Cambridge, MA: MIT P, 2004.

Wark, McKenzie. *Gamer Theory.* Cambridge, MA: Harvard UP, 2007.

Drone Form:
Mediation at the End of Empire

NATHAN K. HENSLEY

I traced a triangle in my mind up from our restaurant table to the satellite in space that would receive the signal, then back down to Time Control's office where the satellite would bounce it. I remember being buffeted by wind, the last full memory I have before the accident.

—McCarthy, *Remainder*

When [the missile] hit, we couldn't tell the difference between night and day. . . . It was day before and it immediately became dark, and I couldn't see my grandma anymore.

—Zubair ur Rehman, age thirteen

Enemies' Dead Strewed the Town

At the British Library, dispatches from the front lines of England's merciless counterinsurgency campaign in India, 1857–58, are collected into folders marked "Miscellaneous Indian Mutiny Papers" and "India Office Records and Private Papers." Copied on thin paper, the documents read as a perverse and staccato kind of poetry. They shape tidings of insurrection and its brutal suppression into the idiom of war-state bureaucracy. Antiseptic and technical, dehumanizing by design, this administrative jargon is further formalized during its compression into the argot of electronic telegraphy. And if compression names "the process that renders a mode of representation adequate to its infrastructures" (Sterne 35), then telegraphy of the so-called Indian Mutiny is perhaps best understood as conveying not simply the content that any given message contained, encoded, and transmitted—the movement of troops, the reports of losses, the accounts of battle—but a cipher of the war-making infrastructure of nineteenth-century imperialism.[1]

In earlier form, portions of this essay appeared in *e-flux journal* 72 (2016). I thank Stephen Squibb for his editorial help and for permission to reprint here. I have learned much about drones and representation from Katherine Chandler, Jennifer Rhee, Paul K. Saint-Amour, and J. D. Schnepf; I thank them here.

[1] C. A. Bayly explains that the British chains of information exchange were crucially vulnerable in ways the 1857 uprising exposed: "Their chain of surveillance was at its most vulnerable where the body of elite, literate officers stretching down from the district town linked up with the hereditary servants and information collectors of the village" (8). Thus did vernacular and indigenous networks of information exchange—gossip, word of mouth, "social

One of these communiqués, marked "Copy of message received by Electric Telegram" and dated August 17, 1857 (Havelock), originated with General Havelock in Cawnpore (Kanpur) and was sent to his superiors in Calcutta. It reports a qualified victory over the massed peasants then arrayed against British paramountcy. Insurgents captured some cannon, Havelock reports, "But enemies' dead strewed the town—I estimate their loss of three hundred killed & wounded." It is an everyday update during this yearlong campaign, an event hardly worthy of notice and occasioning nothing beyond straight accounting of enemy casualties: part of the paperwork of empire. On the form itself, the message is copied in barely legible handwriting. At the bottom of the page, the account is dated "Calcutta, Elec. Tel. Office, 17 Aug't 1857," verified again ("A true copy"), and finally signed in pencil by a receiving clerk. These marks verify the contents' correct transcription from the telegraphic original. They show us that this act of state killing has been reported by dictation, transcribed into writing, configured into telegraphic code, transmitted over vast distances of copper wire, received, decrypted, transcribed again by hand (now in pencil) onto a paper form, and then copied longhand and finally double-verified by a functionary who signs his own name: J. S. Seale, LT. Elaborately mediated yet insisting via seal and signature on its perfectly lossless transmission, the document, like many others during the Victorian era's long war—no single year of the queen's reign was without armed conflict—is a document of asymmetrical warfare that announces most of all its status as an act of mediation.

This essay is about the mediation of war in material form. After establishing the crucial role of mediation in wartime activities across periods of imperial rule, my first aim in what follows is to underscore the material nature of these aesthetic mediations—their intercombination with physical channels, technological apparatuses, and built infrastructures—and to suggest how these acts of mediation themselves become visible or apprehensible, as form becomes content and vice versa. "We see things shroudedly, as through a veil, an over-pixellated screen," says the reflexively named hero (U) of Tom McCarthy's network novel *Satin Island* (2015). "People need foundation myths," he continues, "a bolt that secures the scaffolding that in turn holds fast the entire architecture of reality" (3). The point U is making is the Derridean one; the same one sealed in Lieutenant Seale's seal, above: human beings yearn for immediacy, for presence and grounding, but mediation—the true subject of McCarthy's novel—is all there is. Writing, translation, compression, transmission, recoding: "a perpetual state of passage, not arrival," U calls it. "[N]ot *at*, but *between*" (87): "transfer points, rather than destinations in and of themselves" (5). I will return at the end of this essay to McCarthy's technofetishistic experiments in metamediation: those sexless, theoretical fictions about the circuitry and wiring of our late-imperial sensorium. A second aim in what follows, though, is to identify, in the instances of what I will call drone form arranged here, an abiding problem of nonreciprocal action: a constitutive dissymmetry between viewer and viewed, subject and object, that becomes, I argue, an obsessive preoccupation of fiction in the drone era and that is the special focus of nearly all of

communication"—threaten importantly the techno-rationalist network of infrastructural communications maintained by the empire.

McCarthy's novels. Focusing on drones, then, what I aim to describe here is the relationship between the means of distributing death in our late imperial moment and the regime of mediation in which that sovereign power is transmitted, recoded, and ultimately visited on human bodies.

The mutiny telegram cited above already showed that all imperial power is crucially a matter of mediation: the physical channels and formal languages by which information is transmitted and, in that act of transmission, inevitably changed. But today's infrastructures of wartime communication, like our technologies for delivering violence, are no longer those of the nineteenth century: bayonet, telegram, and cannon have been replaced by data mining, satellite reconnaissance, and long-distance strikes by weaponized drones. This is the technic sensorium suffused by "[e]lectric birdsong," as McCarthy has it in C (52), "a set of signals . . . repeating, pulsing, modulating in the airspace" (McCarthy, *Transmission and the Individual Remix*, i). All aesthetic forms presuppose and in turn ratify an episteme or regime of perception by means of which subjects apprehend their world.[2] My suggestion is that to chart the shifting relations between mediation and death in our contemporary moment—to identify the way of seeing proper to the drone era— might in turn help us to comprehend our place in the cycle of American empire that observers like Giovanni Arrighi (*Long Twentieth Century*) already in 1994 saw shifting toward decline.

The isomorphisms between imperial cycles at which I have only hinted suggest that attending to the twilight of the British world system might provide analytical purchase on, and resources for understanding, the waning days of the American phase of hegemony and vice versa.[3] But for observers of art, it bears noting that the forms of mediation that were central to the normatively demarcated "culture" of the nineteenth century, and that are central to my own training in that period— poetry and the literary novel, say—are no longer dominant but residual or even niche categories, boutique commodities for a narrow subset of sometimes self-consciously nostalgic consumers. McCarthy's own novels exhibit a snobbish disdain for the "dumb" and facile "mainstream" (McCarthy, "Interview" 675) but play wittily with their own residual status as media objects. Moments of such self-consciousness aside, the academic fields of contemporary literature and contemporary novel studies arguably exist uneasily in tension with the novel form's ever-failing position in our grid of cultural production: criticism continues to massively overrepresent cultural forms (like the art novel) of minimal import to the sensory and affective lives of media consumers today.[4]

---

[2]   "The fundamental codes of a culture—those governing its language, its schemas of perception, its exchanges, its techniques, its values, the hierarchy of its practices—establish for every man, from the very first, the empirical orders with which he will be dealing and within which he will be at home" (Foucault xx).

[3]   I have approached these questions at more length in "Allegories of the Contemporary."

[4]   Thus did a special issue of *Novel*, titled *The Contemporary Novel: Imagining the Twenty-First Century* (Bewes), justify its existence by noting that the current moment "marks a point of crisis and transition in the history of the novel" (Duke University Press n. pag.). But the issue (including an essay by the present author) addressed only prestige fiction and art novels, by such consecrated

This is hardly news, however, and I want to flag, without resolving, this issue of how disciplinary object choice fits often uneasily with contemporary regimes of cultural and social practice. My topic here is drones, or unmanned aerial vehicles (UAVs), and particularly military ones. These machines for remote seeing and killing should be understood, I argue, to signify an end of empire in two senses. First, an end as in *conclusion*, or terminus. Hannah Arendt, among others, has noted that proliferating death is a sign not of hegemony but of its waning: "[r]ule by sheer violence," she notes, as though gazing toward contemporary Afghanistan, "comes into play where power is being lost" (53). This means that the still-proliferating assassinations undertaken in the name of an American phase of accumulation are the sign not of its strength but of its weakness; drone war is, to twist Fernand Braudel's evocative phrase, a "sign of autumn" (246).[5] Second, an end in the Aristotelian sense of *telos*, or purpose. If we take seriously the fact that empire is best understood not as culture or discourse but as a monopoly on putatively legitimate violence—the stretching of the state's power to kill even beyond its "own" citizenry—then the power of sovereign decision crystalized in remote assassination machines is the very essence of empire: its *telos*, or end. President Obama's now infamous "kill list meetings" only sharpened to an obscene purity the state's power of decision over life and death and thus allegorize as event the very crystal of imperium as such.

Drones, I am arguing, are at once a symptom and a realization of the empire's end. But they are also a regime of figuration, a way of seeing and, therefore, a modality of thought. In the words of Roger Stahl, drones have "capacity as a medium" (659). Even a small survey of the artifacts that have drawn on the drone's odd coincidence between media form and instrument of sovereignty would stretch across the field of cultural production. Such a survey might start in the corporate world of mass-market films and massively capitalized video game franchises by major game studios like Sony Interactive, Activision, or Bethesda Softworks, today's version of golden-age Hollywood's studio system. But it would move toward vernacular forms like Twitter bots and dissident public art installations, reaching all the way to the anxious dreams recorded in the drawings of victims.[6]

But any survey of drone form would need to move all the way up the hierarchy of cultural value, too, reaching to the self-consciously rarefied idioms of prestige fiction and gallery art: works that, like McCarthy's self-consciously avant-garde fictions and

figures as Michael Chabon, Vikram Chandra, Don DeLillo, Jonathan Safran Foer, Jonathan Franzen, David Lodge, Ian McEwan, Michael Ondaatje, and Orhan Pamuk. McCarthy's C, which makes media nostalgia its subject, toys self-reflexively with the residual status of its own form, the novel; but it also, in its promotional front matter, refers to McCarthy as "the standard-bearer of the avant-garde novel" (n. pag.), wearing its place on the restricted end of the Bourdieusian grid on its sleeve. That is OK, since as McCarthy never tires of explaining in interviews, the vulgar and problematically realist "entertainment industry" is "dumb" compared to the modernist art-objects he presumes we too will fetishize (McCarthy, "Interview" 677, 675).

5   Arrighi's final book, *Adam Smith in Beijing*, points to the future his analysis imagined beyond American hegemony.

6   See, for example, the wobbly and haunting sketches of Predator drones by nine-year-old Nabeela ur Rehman of Pakistan, whose mother was blown apart in a 2012 drone strike by US forces (Knefel).

the monumental contemporary-art photographs I examine below, attempt to represent critically the ontological and political, and therefore also aesthetic, novelties generated by our drone era. There is even—and this will be a focus in what follows—a clutch of mass-market novels about drones produced for a global anglophone audience, generated from the very epicenter of the "entertainment industry" to which McCarthy condescends ("Interview" 677). Seen together, what the cheaply printed best sellers and high-art productions mutually help sketch is a comparative analysis of the aesthetic technologies that have emerged to structure the sensory regime of our endless late-imperial war.

Consolidated Vision

The visual rhetoric of drone optics, with targeting sight, framing flight data, and conspicuous pixelation, has become a cliché. Figure 1 shows a still from a Predator drone feed, part of a five-minute wordless video that was intercepted by a hacker in 2009 while being transmitted over unencrypted DOD satellite circuits.[7] A year later, and by the magic of changed context, this pirated feed became an installation artwork titled "Drone Vision," which appeared under the name of Trevor Paglen, the conceptual artist and contemporary art cause célèbre I will discuss shortly.

The point is that UAV optics are now part of our everyday image-world, defining how we apprehend the present: they structure million-hit YouTube videos of actual drone kills (Stahl 663) but also massively profitable video game franchises, big-budget films, and television dramas up and down the scale of so-called quality. The fourth season of *Homeland* (2014), near the top of this mass-cultural prestige hierarchy, kicked off with Claire Danes's character overseeing an assassination of a suspected terrorist by video feed seconds before enjoying cake at an office birthday party ("Drone Queen") (figure 2).[8] An over-the-shoulder shot positions us as spectators: watching sovereign bureaucrats as they watch something else, a drone feed, which in turn watches the Afghan farmhouse where a fictional terrorist has been incinerated along with forty civilians.

Reminiscent of the Velázquez painting that opens Foucault's famous account of the modern episteme in *The Order of Things*, this scene's baroque perspectival scenario—frames within frames—begins to suggest that drone vision is not only about crosshairs and black-and-white targets. But where the complex sightlines of *Las Meninas* meant, for Foucault, that the object watched back, creating a "pure reciprocity" of gaze—a "slender line of reciprocal visibility" (4)—in drone form, sight runs only one way. As I will suggest, the regime of perception inaugurated by the drone is marked instead by its precise negation of the reciprocity Foucault ascribes to the classical episteme; this is the same reciprocity that, not

---

[7]   They were not encrypted because in 2009, doing so introduced too much latency in the feed, extending to a tactically disadvantageous length the delay between events on the ground and the drone pilot's apprehension of the information. That delay is now, with encryption, down to about two seconds.

[8]   I thank Scott Selisker for alerting me to this episode and for his expert feedback on aspects of this argument.

coincidentally, commentators from Hegel and Emmanuel Levinas to Judith Butler have identified as the prerequisite for ethical life. But drone vision cancels reciprocity while extending the classical order's will to knowledge in ways Foucault could scarcely have imagined.

Figure 1. *Drone Vision*, 2010. Archival pigment print, 16×20 in. Copyright Trevor Paglen. Courtesy of the Artist, Metro Pictures New York, Altman Siegel San Francisco

As Grégoire Chamayou explains in *A Theory of the Drone*, the order of vision proper to drones rests on at least three principles: (1) persistent surveillance or permanent vigilance in the present; (2) a totalization of perspectives or synoptic viewing, covering all space; and (3) total archival retention, aggregating surveillance diachronically in storage (38–39). All of this adds up to what Chamayou calls a "revolution in sighting" (38). The US Air Force's incredibly named Gorgon Stare program, for example, offers what its advocates call an "unrelenting gaze": mounted on a "hunter-killer" MQ-Reaper, which can hold two tons of weaponry and remain airborne fully loaded for fourteen hours, the Gorgon Stare setup uses 192 different cameras and can store the data it collects for thirty days, enabling "after-action forensic analyses," a diachronic capacity that makes this technology "the number-one reconnaissance asset that warfighters crave" (Thompson). That is not least because with it, the state can "discern patterns in the behavior of insurgents—where they hid, how they operated, who they interacted with—that would have been unknowable using other surveillance systems" (Thompson). Transforming long-durational observation into databases massive enough that individual behaviors might algorithmically be predicted from that general set, drone surveillance thus reverses at the level of warmaking technology the relationship between instance and category that Catherine Gallagher identifies in the realist novel, say, where "a general referent was . . . indicated through a particular, but explicitly nonrefrerential, fictional individual" (61–62). Here, concrete and indeed living individuals are indicated by general pattern, with lethal but unevenly accurate results.[9]

Diachronic, totalizing, and aspiring to omniscience, drone form is also, as a result of all this, predicated on massive asymmetries of perspective—a point *Homeland*

[9]   In a November 2017 exposé called "The Uncounted," *New York Times Magazine* reported that "one in five of the coalition strikes we identified resulted in civilian death, a rate more than 31 times that acknowledged by the coalition" (Khan and Gopal).

Figure 2.   Screen shot, "The Drone Queen," *Homeland* ep. 37
(season 4, ep. 1), Showtime, 2014

hammers home by melodramatically juxtaposing birthday cake and state murder. As Chamayou notes, the weapons-loaded drone eliminates reciprocity from the scene of killing and turns seeing, and with it the risk of death, into a one-sided operation: I see you but you don't see me, and a drone operator at Creech Air Force Base in Nevada or at a situation-room birthday party on *Homeland* can kill but is not herself at risk of being killed. This constitutive dissymmetry of drone vision has tactical and legal ramifications but is also a political-aesthetic problem. It means that the dilemma of unevenly distributed narrative space that Edward W. Said detailed in *Culture and Imperialism*, for example—where the core speaks and has the power to act, while the margins figure only as silence—now describes the tactical raison d'être of a new war-making technology, its operational advantage. Recall that the relevant chapter in *Culture and Imperialism* is titled "Consolidated Vision." Said's argument about uneven representation within the novel-space has long been critiqued for construing imperial power as a representational or cultural and not properly political problem. In this vein we might note, for example, how that text slips in its description from optics to power, silently analogizing "vision" with political sovereignty by referring, in a chapter titled "Consolidated *Vision*," to "what I have been calling . . . consolidation of *authority*" (77; emphasis added). Representational capacity is not identical to political authority, but drone technology helps us see that in fact, "consolidated vision" was always naming a problem of sovereignty, albeit one that in 1993 still awaited the wartime infrastructure that would make it so. Drone form makes this coincidence between vision and power explicit, since it twins representational capacity—the power to see and to observe or, as Said has it, to narrate—with the capacity to kill.

Twitter bots like Dronestream seek to interrupt drone form's unidirectional or vectored omniscience, since they push information about drone strikes happening in "peripheral" zones like Waziristan, Yemen, or Afghanistan back to the core, using that social networking platform to make the darkness of drone war visible. "Early Tuesday," as one post read, "in a village south of Thal, a US drone fired missiles at a house. Two people were killed (Pakistan)" (@dronestream). Iraqi-born artist Wafaa Bilal exposed the perversity of these seemingly unthinkable spatial dissymmetries in *Domestic Tension* (2007). This thirty-day performance piece saw Bilal sitting in a Chicago art gallery while Internet users across the world, anonymously and at any time, could click a button to shoot him with a paintball gun. As Bilal's website explains, this interface "transform[ed] the virtual experience into a very physical one." Other artists, working yet more explicitly in the idiom of drone war, have attempted to redistribute the unequal representational and political space on which remote killing depends. Khesrau Behroz's "Everybody knows where they were when they heard that Kennedy died" is an app that uses Twitter, Tumblr, and Instagram to send push notifications to followers as soon as a drone strike is reported. Often remediating notices from sites like Dronestream or *Agence France Presse*, these notifications include details of the numbers killed and wounded, the location of the attack, and, occasionally, a brief description of the scene. What Behroz adds, juxtaposed against these notifications of drone execution, are, in his words, "picture[s] of where I was when I heard about the news." The resulting collages set a space of precarity against one of safety, putting periphery against core and underscoring, in the process, the obscene anonymity of these killings. Unlike after the Kennedy assassination for which the series is named, no one remembers where he or she was when these unnamed individuals die. What Behroz's project generates is the characteristically contemporary affect—flat, numbed, endlessly sad—that critics (as we will see) without quite knowing why consistently ascribe to McCarthy's fiction.

In January 2013, Teju Cole likewise turned to the media platform of Twitter to test how drone war might tweak, invert, or satirically revise famous examples of a once-dominant media form. His "Seven Short Stories about Drones" jarringly bolt onto the plots of classic novels conclusions provided by drone killing: "Someone must have slandered Josef K.," reads number 5 in the series, "for one morning, without having done anything truly wrong, he was killed by a Predator drone" (@tejuecole). Compressing vast, complex, and almost exclusively modernist novels into 140-character clips, Cole's unevenly successful experiment aimed to expose a disjunction between drone killing and novel form itself. Here the capaciousness of what it performatively suggests is modernity's signal form (Cole's examples include *Ulysses*, *Mrs. Dalloway*, and *Invisible Man*) is jammed with ironizing compression into tweet-sized bites, sealed with death: "human" stories reshaped into inhuman form. This process of self-consciously sloppy reduction may subscribe to a humanist ideology of the novel form and fetishize mainline modernism; it certainly exposes what it suggests is the violence of compression, performing (contra Sterne) the message's inadequacy to its media infrastructure. It goes further, I think, to associate the brevity of the tweet form (against the implicitly more substantial novels it ironizes) with the anti-deliberative and all-but-instantaneous violence of weaponized UAVs.[10]

Cole's tweets hint at a formal observation about mediation, simultaneity, and drone war that they nevertheless do not fully theorize. By contrast, the digital chromogenic prints of multimedia artist Paglen—vast in format, variously opaque and hyperreal in their macro-scaled high resolution—seek avowedly to reverse or reorient the protocol of seeing that is constitutive of the drone state. (The function of the MQ-9 Reaper, according to an Air Force fact sheet, is to "find, fix, and finish targets" ["MQ-9 Reaper"].) Inverting this vector of predication, Paglen's artworks deploy sophisticated surveillance technology to find and fix the state, if not to "finish" it: they use long-range

---

[10]   One resident of Datta Khel, North Waziristan, interviewed by Stanford researchers in 2012, "remembered hearing the hissing sound the missiles made *just seconds* before they slammed into the center of his group" (Cavallaro 59; emphasis added).

Figure 3.   Trevor Paglen, *Untitled (Reaper Drone)*, 2010. C-Print, 48 × 60 in. Edition of 5 plus 2 AP. Copyright Trevor Paglen. Courtesy of the Artist, Metro Pictures New York, Altman Siegel San Francisco.

lenses and military-grade optics to turn the object of the state's gaze into its subject and vice versa. They depict secret interrogation sites, half-visible drones, and private tarmacs used to transport detainees to overseas gray zones for torture. Paglen uses long exposures to reveal the orbits of secret government surveillance satellites in transit, for example, inverting the state's powers of vision to disclose the regimes of watching that are, for citizens, normally occluded. I wrote "depict," "reveal," and "disclose," but the point is that these images aim to redirect the desire for immediacy and presence that is inherent to drone vision (find, fix, finish) and that structures war-state informatics logic more broadly—or so the mutiny telegram with which I began would suggest.

Rather than the frictionless transfer of information or "documentary" accuracy, Paglen's work aims, in his words, to be "useless as evidence": "I want photography that doesn't just point to something" he continues; "it actually *is* that something" (Stallabrass and Paglen 11, 4). The point of these works, then, is to bring into focus not the thing observed but the technologies of seeing themselves, and an image like *Untitled (Reaper Drone)* (2010), for example (figure 3), from his series of quasi-abstract drone photographs from 2009–10, announces itself as a grandly beautiful depiction of color itself, its wash of graduating blue-red referencing mid-century color-field painting by people like Barnett Newman and Mark Rothko no less than J. M. W. Turner's smeared depictions of suicidal modernity from the Victorian phase of accumulation. With concentration, Paglen's haunted vacancy becomes legible as an evening sky. The Reaper drone flecking the corner of the frame, once noticed, becomes the photograph's maddening focal point, impossible to unsee. That is the point: for instead of *objects* or *content* these images show walls of distance, highlighting the forms of mediation, recoding, and transmission—aesthetic, technological, spatial—separating it from us.

Of course, even as they comment, obliquely but critically, on the militarized ways of seeing proper to our fading hegemony, Paglen's self-consciously high-cultural artifacts occupy a specific (elevated) place in the contemporary culture industry, hanging in galleries, headlining exhibits, and acquiring the fetish character that remains the sine qua non of the marketplace for cultural capital that is the world of contemporary art. (Paglen was awarded a MacArthur "genius" award in 2017.) Yet Paglen is rare among fixtures of this milieu in his commitment not just to noting the paradoxes of critiquing of the contemporary art world's fetish character from inside it (this is common enough among the *October* set of avant-garde artists) but also to weaponizing this very art-world success in hands-on projects and noncommodified happenings funded by sales of the gallery work. This strategy is evident, for example, in Paglen's dissident public works, like *Code Names of the Surveillance State*, in which he projected NSA code names onto the British Parliament (2015); his monumental tube stop installations, like *An English Landscape* (*American Surveillance Base near Harrogate, Yorkshire*) (June 15, 2014–July 13, 2016); or his work (as producer and provider of still images) for Laura Poitras's documentary about Edward Snowden, *Citizenfour* (2014).

The Sting of the Drone

To shift from the "restricted" to the unrestricted end of our contemporary field of cultural production, I move now from the gallery spaces of "art-as-pure-signification" (Bourdieu 114) to the "field of large-scale cultural production" (115; emphasis removed), where art is money and the point is to sell in volume. The "drone thriller" is a relatively recent subgenre of fiction that has begun to occupy a niche, albeit a small one, in the contemporary mass market for literature.[11] These emergent forms are pitched as stories for a new era, but they triangulate themselves within well-established conventions in the literary middlebrow. Yet these conventions themselves point up many of the same cognitive and political tangles that artworks like Paglen's address in the key of enlightened critique. The cover of Dan Fesperman's *Unmanned* (2014) announces the book as "part mystery and part thriller," while *Sting of the Drone* (2014), a clunky exercise by former US counterterrorism czar Richard A. Clarke, is unmistakably a "thriller"—unmistakable because the word is repeated five times on its back cover. ("This first rate thriller," one apparently anxious blurber says, is "a cross between a techno-thriller and a docu-thriller.") Among the most delightful of these openly derivative offspring of Clancy is Mike Maden's "Troy Pearce" series of "intense, page-turning novel[s]" (*Drone*, cover copy), whose phallically named, eponymous hero is "still lean and cut like a cage fighter despite the strands of silver in his jet-black hair" (15). Pushed out in quick sequence, the series kicks off with *Drone* (2013) and moves through *Blue Warrior* (2014), *Drone Command* (2015), and *Drone Threat* (2016).[12] (Maden's latest project

---

[11]   Nielsen Bookscan reports that sales in this new subgenre have yet to storm the culture industry, though their numbers as of February 2016 would be the envy of many academics. Mike Maden's series had sold about 23,600 copies (*Drone*: 6,493 cloth, 9,838 paper; *Blue Warrior*: 1,285 cloth, 5,469 paper; and *Drone Command*: 609 cloth); Richard A. Clarke's *Sting of the Drone* about 7,600 (4,849 cloth, 2,760 paper); and the literarily aspirational Dan Fesperman clocked in last—at around 1,250 copies for *Unmanned* (985 cloth, 268 paper). By comparison, Tom Clancy's latest book, *Commander-in-Chief* (Greaney), has sold 145,000-plus copies. I thank Sam Douglas and Becky Cole for tracking down these figures.

[12]   Maden is sophisticated in his awareness of how the conventions of his chosen genre both enable and constrain his capacity to dream up new scenarios and characters. He has noted the

closes the generic loop, since it finds him writing *as* Tom Clancy in *Tom Clancy: Point of Contact—A Jack Ryan Novel* [2017].)

I call them "delightful" because as all their names and titles—*Warrior, Command, Pearce*—suggest, Maden's interventions into this new subgenre operate unapologetically as masculine fantasia. In defiance of the rules of narrative point of view, they include full specifications for every gun and piece of war-making technology to grace their pages and feature a no-nonsense female president, her frame "strong and lean" from "years of swimming and Pilates" (*Drone* 17), who drinks bourbon and shows no patience for fussy questions of human rights. What President Margaret Myers unknowingly discloses is the ghost of matriarchal authority tangled into the DNA of the drone's technological history: as J. D. Schnepf has noted, the term *drone* was originally chosen by American officers in homage to the early British radio-controlled craft called the *Queen Bee*, because these mindless vehicles were, from the Navy's perspective, "male subordinates, constitutionally subservient to a female queen" (Schnepf 275). Says one military historian: "The term fit, as a drone could only function when controlled by an operator on the ground or in a 'mother' plane" (quoted in Schnepf 275).

But the gender complications that have marked drone technology from its advent become sublated—enhanced, cancelled, and heightened to something like art—in Maden's novels. President Myers "wore a black Nike long-sleeve polo shirt and a matching golf skort and shoes, very subdued. She still had the toned arms and shapely runner's legs to carry off the ensemble smartly. She was more than fifty but looked a decade younger. Heads turned when she entered a room—men and women both" (*Drone Command* 18). In Maden's plots, the lean and gym-toned female president leagues with the cage fighter Pearce to scrub the world of Mexican gangsters and Iranian terrorists. The fantasy president from Texas nonetheless balances her badassery with fetchingly conventional maternal instincts, nearly starting a pointless and politically disastrous war with Mexico—but only to avenge the death of her son (17). "[S]he had a bigger nut sack than any man he knew in politics," Pearce reflects (*Drone* 353); "[s]he hit from the same tee box as the men" (*Drone Command* 20). The novels' adolescent gaze, seemingly standard-issue for a subgenre aimed at (in Maden's words) "bring[ing] current technology into stories in a powerful and entertaining way" ("A Conversation"), leaves no equipment or human body unadmired, and its taste, as suggested by the president's skort, runs to the conventional. But the lady president's nut sack announces gender as a site of contestation and helps us see that, in this novel and all drone fictions, the stabilization of gender identities along familiar axes of power is less an ideological solution than a fraying, constant problem. In Maden, "Madame President" "pour[s] herself another bourbon" (*Drone* 17), but a female scientist has "long legs, soft curves, and cloying eyes . . . more like a Bollywood movie star than a Ph.D. in robotics engineering" (*Drone* 32); the enemy

requirements of creating familiar characters and scenarios that nonetheless (and paradoxically) feel new and identified a father figure for all the drone books I have just named. "In my opinion," Maden told me, "everyone who writes in the action-thriller genre today is essentially writing a variant of a Tom Clancy novel" (personal interview). I am grateful to Maden for taking the time to speak with me about his novels and his process for writing them.

(and male) Castillo twins, meanwhile, are "[n]aked and tan, their muscled bodies glisten[ing] with sweat" (*Drone* 37). As a character, Pearce himself might have been ripped from the rhetorical vocabulary of ads for impotence drugs ("[I]t was his blue eyes that grabbed most women" [*Command* 116]) and, as we will see, this potency is always at risk. He drinks beer and splits logs shirtlessly between fishing trips, chainsaw maintenance, and sexual conquests, all while organizing assassinations by robot (*Drone* 158). "Men want to be him," as Maden summarized to me in an e-mail exchange, risking a familiar phrase; "women want to $^&% him" (personal interview).

However mottled by the shadow of matriarchy, the *Drone* books' internally divided aspiration toward infantile masculinity is important, because this gender trouble only enciphers at the level of sex a larger concern about the category of agency itself. As Chamayou helps us to see, the constitutive absence of reciprocity in drone technology—what one air force pamphlet calls the "FREEDOM FROM ATTACK" combined with the "FREEDOM TO ATTACK" (*Global Vigilance* 4)—demands a dramatic restructuring of the category of masculine military agency. This restructuring becomes legible as a lingering, obsessive concern about potency—a worry about action as such—stretching across these aspirationally masculine texts, a castration anxiety that shouts from nearly all of the books' titles: *The Sting of the Drone*, *Drone Command*, *Point of Contact*. Where Dan Fesperman's 2014 novel raises drone war's crisis of male authority to the level of explicit problem in his *Unmanned*—get it?—marking his book as the most safely middlebrow of the novels (it sold by far the fewest of these titles; see note 11), the others labor unevenly to solve it. Heroic action must now be recast to include sitting at a desk and pushing buttons. *Tom Clancy: Point of Contact* finds Maden reviving the Jack Ryan franchise for the era (as a press release puts it) of "quantum-powered AI-generals and AI-admirals waging land, sea and air drone campaigns" ("Conversation"). But if this new world of artificial intelligence and mediated action feels antiheroic, at removes from the direct action of real combat, it is the media form of the thriller itself—with its male heroes, identifiable antagonists, love interests, and resolutions—that emerges to graft onto this brave new informatic world a structure of direct agency we have seen before. As Maden writes in a promotional interview, "a two-fisted, red-blooded Jack Ryan, Jr. . . . will be right in the middle of all that digital mayhem, if I have any say in the matter" ("Conversation"). As though to hammer home the point, the book's cover depicts only an enormous, grayscale knife, charming in its phallic simplicity.

In an interview, Maden explained what his novels more artfully show, which is that the structure of action mandated by the bourgeois novel, in which *characters* perform *actions* against backgrounds of *setting*, fits only unevenly with the hyperdistributed and ultramediated nature of drone warfare. This distention of the field of action presents a challenge, he explained, for the thriller form itself. The "factual reality" of drone war, Maden said, "is often mind-bogglingly complex"; "[f]or example, a military deployment of a long-range drone like Reaper typical entails 80 + people in the loop—from maintenance personnel on the ground to JAG lawyers in D.C. in oversight positions. Fully describing each of those functions would completely bog the story down" (personal interview). But a "readable" and "interesting" story, he continued, cannot afford to distribute its action across this too-vast chain of actants; the result would be boring. Instead, translating drone form into the media technology of the thriller requires devising scenarios in which red-blooded and two-fisted men can do red-blooded and two-fisted things. Did Maden find it difficult to create a hero who performs daring acts in the context of drone war?

> The short answer is "Yes" for many of the reasons you've already stated, e.g., long distance, "push button" warfare. I work around that challenge thusly: (a) using pre-drone historical storylines and action events in Troy's life (e.g., Iraq); (b) focusing on bad actors who don't have drone resources (though this category is becoming scarcer by the day) who are battling with Troy; (c) featuring non-military drone activity (e.g., rhino conservation) where there are no expectations of combat; (d) finally, by emphasizing tactical drone warfare where operators are necessarily present on the battlefield (and also deploying conventional weapons) rather than on the larger, long range systems like Reapers that are operated from stateside. (personal interview)

All of this shows admirable insight into the difficulties of matching a chosen subset of novel form with the technical novelties of its subject. It also highlights for us the misfit between a residual media regime and the emergent one it seeks gropingly to describe.

Yet the tangle that arises when the bourgeois novel meets bureaucratic and multiply mediated warfare is conceptual too and, like all conceptual tangles, plays out perhaps most vividly at the level of syntax. This mismatch between forms—which, as I have suggested, plays out around the gendered problem of action—generates, in Clarke's book, a hero called Dougherty and another with "still firm pecs" (10)[13] but also syntax like this, where the sentence itself must strain to find a human agent for its act of killing: "The mechanical extension of Major Bruce Dougherty, the thing that moved in the air when Bruce's hand made adjustments with the joystick in his cubicle, was pressing ahead . . . against the cold wind two miles above the canyon" (Clarke 6). Dougherty's virtual piloting leads in the end to an execution, and after the novel gives us the scene of explosion, it switches erratically to Creech Air Force Base. Here, a world away from human bodies dismembered by explosives, and on the other side of the novel's vigorous formal crosscutting, fake pilots are high-fiving and cheering, giving "hoots and applause" (8). "Righteous shoot. Big Kill," says the secure digital message summarizing the bombing, a detail that aims to cleanse these pseudo-pilots'—and readers'—consciences about this act of digitized killing (8). But the compensatory, conscience-assuaging work of Clarke's novel is not done, for the chapter follows Dougherty's copilot, Erik Parsons, as he drives home from Creech in "his black Camaro" (8) to a

---

[13]   If infantry warfare had heroes, in the drone era it is cubicle-bound bureaucrats who exercise the state's putatively legitimate monopoly on violence. Dougherty's name fairly advertises this supposed degeneration, while Erik Parsons, Dougherty's CO, is described in the mode of mock heroic: "If pilots were supposed to look like the cartoon hero Steve Canyon, tall and blond, Erik Parsons looked more like a wrestling coach" (4).

clichéd hot wife the novel does not bother to describe, and the chapter that began with the detonation of an encampment of "human life-forms" (6) ends with the drone operator and his "night owl" spouse (9) having very straight sex in a hot tub after downing Heinekens: "Jennifer Parsons ran her fingers through the thinning black hair on his head and then through the graying hair on his still firm pecs" (10). If this is the sting of the drone, it is a sting that does not fully convince, and when Parsons, just before coitus, tells his wife, "We're finding them, Jen. We're winning," we might be forgiven for entertaining doubts (10). And when Ray and Sandra, later in the novel, find themselves in their DC love nest, postcoitally talking drone bombing, the prose must again labor to convince itself of its hero's manful decisiveness:

> She slipped her fingers slowly through the hair on his chest . . .
> "Some people think we are murderers," Ray [said].
> "Does that bother you still?" she sighed.
> "No, never did," he said. "I know who the murderers are. The guys we go after." He took both of her breasts in his hands and buried his head in between them.
> She felt behind her with her right hand until she found it. "Seems like you're ready for me to show you something this time. In this one, I play the cowgirl and you play the horsey." He let out a loud neighing noise. (142)

Interrupted by a Blackberry chirping with news of a drone operation in Pakistan, this aspirationally erotic scene, intercut with a pseudo-debate about the morality of drone murder, leaves its central, obsessive topic unresolved. Who is the rider and who the horsey in this cartoonish, and elaborately failed, attempt to renarrate our drone hero as a confident and unbothered leading man? The point is that these aspirationally macho texts are everywhere marked by gender inversion, confused vectors of agency, and highly choreographed scenarios of (lapsed) mastery—a combination that suggests their own slantwise insight into the difficulties novel form has in bearing out the network-logic and multiply mediated chain effects of drone war causality.

Where Clarke turns this problem into a sexual scenario in which gendered mastery is literally reversed ("[h]e let out a loud neighing noise"), Maden's books work at the level of plot structure and sentence to recover, and paint in bright colors, the heroic male agency that drone war erodes in its very structure. Pearce himself, named "'Troy' as in 'Trojan, warrior' and 'Pearce' as in 'pierce' with a spear point" (personal interview), cannot avoid admitting that killing by remote "almost didn't seem fair" (*Drone* 177). He concedes, too, that the bomb blast that ends the book "wasn't as satisfying as killing the bastard Ali with his own hands" (406). But a short epilogue, literally an addition to the novel, exorcises any worry that this new form of killing is not quite manly enough. "I kill you with my bare hands," Pearce explains to his enemy and to us, after bursting in to settle his final score (412). In this tacked-on, masculinity-saving scene—an actual and not just Derridean supplement—the remote killings, proxy agency, and murders by push button resolve at last into mano a mano, the cage fighter standing against his rival (now Russian) to banish the specter of mediated war in favor of The Real Thing. The sequence works hard, I mean, to recapture as compensatory fantasy exactly the direct agency that drone war makes impossible. The scene is a blaze of active verbs and phallic knife work: "Pearce jabbed a laser-pulsed drug injector against Britnev's neck before he could scream, paralyzing him. He pushed the Russian back inside the apartment, kicked the door shut, and guided the whimpering, gurgling man onto a modular white leather sofa" (413). All this manful action, this jabbing and "inject[ion]" arriving just at the end of the book, puts away forever any doubts about whether remote warfare can be heroic. Or does it?

Some Relation between Me and the Machine

I have so far tracked drone content, not drone form, and it is important to note that the particularities of this new delivery system for sovereign violence are legible not just as compensatory masculinity or tangled erotic tableaux but as dilemmas of narrative point of view, themselves aesthetic ciphers or codes for what I am suggesting is the episteme of our drone era. Despite conventional associations of drone technology with "god's eye" surveillance, none of these novels unfolds in a third-person omniscient voice: think of Dickens's Shadow from *Household Words*, "the omnipresent, intangible creature . . . which may get into any place" (*Letters* 622) or the "far-reaching visions" of Eliot's consciousness-penetrating narrator in *Adam Bede* (5). The hero of *Unmanned* does wonder "what it would be like to lead a life in which every action was observed from on high for hours at a time" (Fesperman 8), but the novel does not pursue such perspectival effects as formal strategy. Rather than structurally mirror drone sighting with omniscient structures, I mean, and instead of turning this perspectival dilemma into a problem—as *Bleak House* does, say, when it formally shifts between Esther's on-the-ground narration and high-flying omniscient chapters—the drone thrillers just surveyed uniformly deploy third-person limited point of view. They follow thriller convention in heading sections with dates and named locales—Langley, Creech, Kandahar—a "meanwhile" effect that works acrobatically to negotiate the constitutive spatial caesura, the impermeable separation between there and here, on which drone war is predicated.

Only Fesperman's novel gives this crosscutting a rest, but its comparative stillness follows from its primary interest in domestic surveillance: so Nevada, Maryland, and New Hampshire rather than (as in Maden) Yemen, "Gulf of Mexico" (*Drone* 365), and "On board the Pearce Systems HondaJet" (221). Yet the effort to police social space and point of view in this way, separating perspectives by chapters headed with datelines and exotic locales, also breaks down, and Clarke's narrative, for example, proves unable to maintain its distinction among gazes, shifting as it does so haphazardly from limited points of view in the killing scenes—operator, commander, victim, witness—that it becomes simply impossible determine who is seeing what, as in the following.

A few people *heard a bang, when the triangle hit Mach 1, but it was so soon followed by the crash of the glass façade when the triangle hit it, and then by the muffled thump when the triangle exploded in the Cigar Bar.* Wilhelm actually saw *the triangle as it came through the outer glass façade, less than a second before it went through the Cigar Bar door where he was headed.* His eyes registered the flash *of light when the triangle exploded in the bar,* but his brain did not have enough time to process what his eyes had seen *before the steel shards sliced his eyes and his brain and all the rest of him into a bloodied pulp on the burning carpet.*

The visual feed *from the Myotis triangle, Bird Two,* had looked *blurred, incomprehensible shapes on the screen as the aircraft had hurtled toward the narrow laser beam projected from Bird One. Then* the camera feed from Bird Two, *the black triangle, had stopped.*

"Target hit. Warhead ignited. No secondary. Fire seems contained," Bruce reported *into his mouthpiece after* he turned his attention back to the image *from Bird One.*

"Fire alarm has gone off in the building, automatically signaling to Feuer Brigade around the corner," said a voice from Maryland.

"Zoom Bird One's camera in on the room, please," someone in Virginia said, and Bruce *[in Creech AFB, Nevada]* adjusted the view. *"Thanks, not much left there."*

Bruce switched the camera back to wide angle *and the image on the screen showed the hotel guests filing out of the front door in orderly fashion, guided by hotel staff, as two fire trucks rolled to a stop at the curb.* (Clarke, *Sting* 31–32; emphasis added)

The point in quoting at length this hopelessly muddled perspectival scenario is to show how far the narrative technology of these novels must stretch to give shape to the nonreciprocity of gaze on which drone technology is predicated. The conceptual novelty of the subject, I mean, generates difficulties for the perspectival regime of narrative fiction, a mismatch between message and medium that is legible in these drone thrillers at the level of the sentence itself. Here is Maden, describing from the point of view of its victim what Clarke's cheering flyboys called a "righteous kill": "His brain barely perceived the blinding flash [of the explosion], and that for only an instant. He was dead before the slower-moving sound waves could strike his eardrum and stimulate the aural nerve. In fact, his entire brain case, including the aural nerve, had been splattered like an overripe melon against the bathroom wall tiles, which were also a lustrous pink terrazzo" (*Drone* 170). This can be called third-person limited only with the caveat that the perspective is not a perspective at all, since it explains what Castillo "didn't hear," "didn't notice," and "barely perceived." (The same formula appears in Clarke's experiment, above, when the victim's "brain did not have enough time to process what his eyes had seen before the steel shards sliced his eyes and his brain and all the rest of him into a bloodied pulp.") Depictions of occluded perspective and snuffed-out sentience like these, despite their inadvertently complex formulations, betray origins in infantile sexuality and pornographic militarism; they also perversely literalize Said's argument about the silence of the colonial periphery, doing so by crystalizing this nonreciprocity at the level of form.

At the other, more elevated end of the literary field, these dilemmas of sex, mediation, and point of view play out in an apparently more self-conscious register, and quite apart from the dirty business of actual warfare. As consecrating reviewers have breathlessly noted, McCarthy's anerotic, theoretical novels are concerned with taking the measure of our hypermediated contemporary. But despite their uniformly fetishistic interest in death,[14] these novels eschew direct confrontation with the contemporary war state in favor of obliquely narrated, first-person accounts by white men in imperial capitals; they are antihumanist experiments aimed at (in one reviewer's words) "expos[ing] as an empty delusion the bourgeois reader's pitiable need for alluring characters, emotional heights and narrative closure" (Hogan). Concerned not with human bodies but with the processes of mediation, compression, replication, and repetition connecting them, these professedly anticommercial works play out, in U's words, in "the hiatus created by the passage of command down a chain, the sequence of its parts; the interim between an action and its motion, like those paralytic lags that come in hideous dreams" (McCarthy, *Satin Island* 60). The point is that where the drone thriller seeks variously to suture or overwrite the gaps separating subject and object in this highly technologized modernity, McCarthy dwells in them and, like Paglen, turns the "paralytic lag" or "hiatus" of mediation into his works' very subject. *Satin Island* begins in an Italian airport, like other hubs that are "predominantly transfer points, rather than destinations" (4–5).

My purpose is not to celebrate these media-fetishistic texts as heroic exposures of a technical modernity that the drone novels only blunderingly evoke. Instead, I want to suggest that McCarthy's ostentatiously rarified novels examine the same hypermediated and violent modernity that Maden and Clarke do, and to similarly anti-erotic and genre-stretching effects. And McCarthy's technical fetishism, so structurally similar to Maden's, described above, limits the capacity of his affectively flat texts to comprehend the human damage of our drone world. As in the horsey and Heineken-swilling thrillers described earlier, these novels' attempts to account for the spatial and infrastructural sinews connecting the drone world manifest at the level of erotics—or their absence. Where the drone fantasias attack this problem of mediation with a hypercharged but auto-demolishing masculine virility, McCarthy's barren works are all but expunged of sexuality. In *Remainder*, this affectively neutralized failure of sexual contact is raised to plot point and theme, as the book's aphasic narrator numbly fails to connect with Catherine, just in from Africa, in what should have been a boozy, night-ending hookup. But it turns out that for McCarthy's narrator, the mediated form of this female person is preferable to the real thing:

---

[14] McCarthy's "International Necronautical Society"—an avant-garde collective project he runs with philosopher Simon Critchley and others—lists in its manifesto a belief that "there is no beauty without death, its immanence. We shall sing death's beauty—that is, beauty" ("Manifesto"). "Our ultimate aim," says the manifesto, "shall be the construction of a craft that will convey us into death in such a way that we may, if not live, then at least persist." This tonally ambiguous document concludes with a Bataillean flourish: "[M]ankind's sole chance of survival lies in its ability, as yet unsynthesised, to die in new, imaginative ways. Let us deliver ourselves over utterly to death, not in desperation but rigorously, creatively, eyes and mouths wide open so that they may be filled from the deep wells of the Unknown." Such rhetoric would be impossible, probably, from the point of view of actual victims of the "famine, war, [and] disease" the authors cite as characteristic of their present; they close this list with "asteroid impact," making a mockery of disasters that, from the perspective of victims, are likely not as funny as they are made to seem here.

"Catherine had already begun to annoy me. I preferred her absence, her spectre" (39). Such elaborately constructed preferences for disembodiment, voiced by male narrators whose own investments track toward the cerebral, marks these professedly avant-garde works as theory-boy discourse translated to aesthetic form.[15]

As before, sex is where the dissymmetry of novel form and media regime plays out. In *Satin Island*, after spectacularly denarrating his relationship with an undescribed woman called Madison ("When I arrived at Madison's, we had sex. Afterwards . . . " [20]), U reoutfits "vanguard theory" in the shape of Badiou and Deleuze for marketing campaigns (33). McCarthy plays this hyper-theoretical, antiseptic tendency for laughs when, in *Remainder*, blue liquid spurts onto the lap of the unnamed title character, whose numbed-out mind is too focused on remediating old experiences ("translating them into manoeuvres to be executed" [87]) to take action in collaboration with any other human body. "The idea that his flesh could melt and fuse with the machine parts pleases him," we're told of Serge Carrefax, hero of *C*. "When they sing their song about taking cylinders out of kidneys, [Serge] imagines the whole process playing itself out backwards: brain and connecting rod merging to form one, ultra-intelligent organ, his back quivering in pleasure as pumps and pistons plunge into it, heart and liver being spliced with valve and filter to create a whole new, streamlined mechanism" (164).

This relentlessly mechanical, cyborg world is characterized by transmission, relay, and death, and here the only pleasure comes, perhaps paradoxically, from the supercession of body by machine, its becoming-drone in the performance of "manoeuvres." Even Madison herself, in *Satin Island*, finds a slanted eroticism—some pleasure "beyond sexual," she says—in feeling (as she poses for a stranger's camera) "some kind of relation between me, the angles of my limbs and torso, and the machine, the rhythms of its crackles, beeps and oscillations" (166–67). At this

---

[15]   Toril Moi has offered the following taxonomy of the theory boy:

> *Every year some female graduate students tell me that they feel overlooked, marginalized, silenced in some seminars. They paint a picture of classrooms where the alpha males—so-called "theory boys"—are encouraged to hold forth in impossibly obscure language, but where their own interventions elicit no response. These women, in short, say that they are not listened to, that they are not taken seriously, and that they get the impression that their perceptions of the matter at hand are of no interest to anyone else. Such experiences tend to reproduce a particularly clichéd ideology in which theory and abstract thought are thought to belong to men and masculinity, and women are imagined to be the bearers of emotional, personal, practical concerns. In a system that grants far more symbolic capital, far more intellectual power, to abstract theorizing than to, say, concrete investigations of particular cases, these women lose out in the battle for symbolic capital. This is bad for their relationship to the field they love, and it is bad for their careers in and out of graduate school. This is sexism, and all this goes to show that sexist effects often arise from the interactions of people who have no sexist intentions at all.* (4)

Moi continues with an important addendum, relevant to McCarthy's novels: "But there is another side to this. Sometimes I have a conversation with someone who has been described to me as a theory boy. Then I invariably discover that the theory boy doesn't at all sound like an intellectual terrorist. He is, simply, profoundly, and passionately interested in ideas. He loves theory and precisely because he loves it, he has strong theoretical views" (4). An eighteen-page 2013 interview generated the names of no fewer than fifty-six writers, artists, philosophers, and critical theorists, of whom (by my tally) four were women (McCarthy, "Interview"; my analysis).

point, technology becomes a literal fetish, as McCarthy's novels play out with self-conscious relish the fact that humanized forms like the novel cannot be adequate to our brutal new networked sensorium, thick with "hordes of bits and bytes," "uber-server[s]," "stacks of memory banks, satellite dishes sprouting all around them, pumping out information non-stop, more of it than any single person would need in their lifetime, pumping it all the way in an endless, unconditional, and grace-conferring act of generosity" (*Satin Island* 73).

Remainder concludes its own antihumanist experiment in transforming bodies to machines with the endless, suicidal looping of an aircraft, the culmination of the narrator's efforts to "ma[k]e all our actions passive. We weren't doing them: they were being done. The guns were being fired, I was being hit, being returned to the ground" (216). All of this boils down, I mean, to a concern with agency and with the strange between-space where action and passivity intertwine, a tangled scene of capacity and helplessness in the face of determining systems that plays out, as it does with drones, as a problem of observation, knowledge, and data. Like the Reaper drone that aspired to omniscience, U's "Great Report," in *Satin Island*, seeks the total knowledge or perfect social anthropology that drone surveillance too holds out as its aspirational conclusion or *telos*. "It's about identifying and probing granular, mechanical behaviours," U tells us, "extrapolating from a sample batch of these a set of blueprints, tailored according to each [client's] brief—blueprints which, taken as a whole and crossmapped onto the findings of more 'objective' or empirical studies (quantitative analysis, econometric modeling and the like), lay bare some kind of inner social logic, which can be harnessed, put to use" (23). My point is that here as in the drone-focused texts above, a concern with weaponizing aggregated data gained by "'objective'" study transforms into a problem, at once formal and thematic, of agency and its lack. It is true that McCarthy's novels, despite their interest in surveillance, replication, communications technologies, and human-machine relations—and despite the fact that planes, airports, and remote technologies feature in all of them—are unconcerned with UAVs at the level of plot. Still, I am suggesting they can be usefully redescribed as drone novels.

U's dream in *Satin Island* is that he is flying, drone-like, "over a great, imperial city, the world's greatest—all of them, from all periods: Carthage, London, Alexandria, Vienna, Byzantium and New York, all superimposed on one another the way things are in dreams" (141). In this palimpsest of Arrighi's imperial cycles—empire upon empire, with more superadded—what U sees is a hybrid image of imperium itself. At the core of this power is a burning pile of trash, glowing: "Yes, *regal*—that was the strange thing: if the city was the capital, the seat of empire, then this island was the exact opposite, the inverse—the other place, the feeder, filterer, overflow-manager, the dirty, secreted-away appendix without which the body-proper couldn't function" (142). Concerned here to chart a connection between the empire's regal core and its abject outside, McCarthy's novel now bears witness to the caesura in contemporary social space that Maden and Clarke's drone thrillers attempt more disorientingly to coordinate. The realization that occasions this dream of modernity's cataclysm is the narrator's recollection of Claude Lévi-Strauss, in which he (the narrator) imagines the human beings on the receiving end of the anthropologist's gaze. "[F]or them," the novel's narrator reports, "civilization represents no less than a cataclysm. This cataclysm . . . is the true face of our culture—the one that's turned away, from *us* at least" (141). McCarthy's novels fetishize the technical regime of their hypermodernity and revel in the "structures of untold complexity" available to rich male narrators in Western capitals. In this they are test cases in the consolidated vision Said long ago described. But if these experiments in narrating the "order and harmony of the West"—as *Satin Island's* narrator puts it (140–41)—do not have the capacity to imagine the experiences of those human beings on the West's receiving end, they at least labor to mark those experiences as unknowable from within the form of the metropolitan "literary" novel as such. Like Maden's equally experimental thrillers, McCarthy's upmarket fictions work to translate the relationship of violence and mediation of our contemporary into a residual form, the novel, and in so doing show how this misfit itself becomes apprehensible most fully as a problem of action.

My Heart Was on Fire

The hyperviolent twilight of the American century has been bracketed under various periodizing rubrics, including neoliberalism, late capitalism, or, with Elizabeth Povinelli and others, "late liberalism," the "lates" and the "neos" suggesting at once continuity and rupture with the orders that came before it (see Povinelli). However named, our extending present is characterized not just by new forms of warmaking or an expanded capacity for profit extraction and the capture of nature, but by dizzying proliferation of material technologies and digital genres. These new forms have emerged to mediate and monetize lived experience in late capitalism. One of these forms remains the novel itself, which I have suggested has stretched and, in some instances, all but fallen apart in an effort to comprehend the coincidence of mediation and death in our contemporary moment. To the jarringly sexual, late-imperial drone fables by Maden and Clarke we might oppose aspirationally critical artworks about mediation, violence, and modernity's trash-heap deathworlds by Behroz, Bilal, Paglen, McCarthy, and others, even as we note how the seemingly obvious distinction between critical and affirmative culture breaks down. Which group is symptomatic, and which critical, of our brave new antihuman sensorium? It may be that these familiar categories of ideology critique also stretch to breaking in the face of these media objects. However we answer, it is clear to me that against all such forms—high and low, critical and affirmative, and including our own criticism—we should array the testimony of people like Faheem Quershi, a fourteen-year-old boy whose skull was fractured and eye destroyed by shrapnel in a 2009 strike in Pakistan, one of President Obama's first "signature strikes." Faheem's first-person account comes at the end of one section of Stanford's long 2012 report, *Living under Drones* (Cavallaro). The section is titled "Voices from Below." "[I] could not think," reports Faheem. "I felt my brain stopped working and my heart was on fire" (70). In the words of another voice from below: "I started weeping. Lots of people there were weeping . . . weeping fiercely" (65).

*   *   *

NATHAN HENSLEY is associate professor of English at Georgetown University and author of *Forms of Empire: The Poetics of Victorian Sovereignty* (2016). He is also coeditor, with Philip Steer, of *Ecological Form: System and Aesthetics in the Age of Empire* (2019).

Works Cited

Arendt, Hannah. *On Violence*. New York: Harcourt, Brace, and World, 1969.

Arrighi, Giovanni. *Adam Smith in Beijing: Lineages of the Twenty-First Century*. New York: Verso, 2007.

———. *The Long Twentieth Century: Money, Power, and the Origins of Our Times*. New York: Verso, 1994.

Bayly, C. A. *Empire and Information: Intelligence Gathering and Social Communication in India, 1780–1870*. Cambridge: Cambridge UP, 1996.

Behroz, Khesrau. *Everybody Knows Where They Were When They Heard That Kennedy Died*. Twitter (no longer available), Instagram <www.instagram.com/p/8MFyQft-CN/>, Tumblr <whenkennedydied.tumblr.com> (accessed 28 Dec. 2017).

Bewes, Timothy, ed. *The Contemporary Novel: Imagining the Twenty-First Century*. Spec. issue of *Novel* 45.2 (2012).

Bilal, Wafaa. *Domestic Tension*. Chicago: Performance, 2007 <wafaabilal.com/domestic -tension/>.

Bourdieu, Pierre. "The Market of Symbolic Goods." 1971. *The Field of Cultural Production: Essays on Art and Literature*. Ed. Randal Johnson. New York: Columbia UP, 1993.

Braudel, Fernand. *The Perspective of the World: Civilization and Capitalism, Fifteenth-Eighteenth Century*. Vol. 3. Trans. Siân Reynolds. Berkeley: U of California P, 1992.

Cavallaro, James, Stephan Sonnenberg, and Sarah Knuckey. *Living under Drones: Death, Injury, and Trauma to Civilians from US Drone Practices in Pakistan*. International Human Rights and Conflict Resolution Clinic (Stanford Law School) and Global Justice Clinic (NYU School of Law), 2012 <law.stanford.edu/publications/living-under-drones -death-injury-and-trauma-to-civilians-from-us-drone-practices-in-pakistan>.

Chamayou, Grégoire. *A Theory of the Drone*. 2013. Trans. Janet Lloyd. New York: New Press, 2015.

Chandler, Katherine. *Drone Flight and Failure: The United States' Secret Trials, Experiments, and Operations in Unmanning, 1936–1991*. Unpublished MS.

Clarke, Richard A. *Sting of the Drone*. New York: St. Martin's, 2014.

Cole, Teju. "Seven Short Stories about Drones." Twitter, 14 Jan. 2013 <storify.com/josh begley/teju-cole-seven-short-stories-about-drones>.

———. *The Letters of Charles Dickens.* Vol. 5. Ed. Graham Storey and K. J. Fielding. Oxford: Clarendon P, 1981. 1847–49.

"The Drone Queen." *Homeland.* Ep. 37 (season 4, ep. 1). Showtime, 2014. Hulu.

@dronestream. Twitter, 19 June 2017, 11:18 a.m. <twitter.com/dronestream/status/876866 813673472002>.

Duke UP website. "Description." *The Contemporary Novel: Imagining the Twenty-First Century,* spec. issue of *Novel* 45.2 (2012) <www.dukepress.edu/the-contemporary-novel-imagining -the-twenty-first-century>.

Eliot, George. *Adam Bede.* 1859. Ed. Carol A. Martin. Oxford: Oxford UP, 2008.

Fesperman, Dan. *Unmanned.* New York: Knopf, 2014.

Foucault, Michel. *The Order of Things: An Archaeology of the Human Sciences.* 1970. New York: Vintage, 1994.

Gallagher, Catherine. "George Eliot: Immanent Victorian." *Representations (Berkeley, Calif.)* 90.1 (2005): 61–74.

Global Vigilance, Global Reach, Global Power for America. US Air Force, 2014 <www.af.mil /Portals/1/images/airpower/GV_GR_GP_300DPI.pdf>.

Greaney, Mark. *Tom Clancy: Commander-in-Chief; A Jack Ryan Novel.* New York: Putnam, 2015.

Havelock, Henry. "Telegram from Havelock to Calcutta," 17 Aug. 1857. Unpublished MS, British Library, London, India Office Select Materials, MSS Eur 124/19.

Hensley, Nathan K. "Allegories of the Contemporary." *Novel* 45.2 (2012): 276–300. <doi:10 .1215/00295132-1573976>.

Hogan, Phil. "*Satin Island* by Tom McCarthy: Review—A Brief Theory of Everything." *Guardian* 22 Mar. 2015 <www.theguardian.com/books/2015/mar/22/satin-island-tom -mccarthy-review>.

Khan, Azmat, and Anand Gopal. "The Uncounted." *New York Times Magazine* 16 Nov. 2017 <www.nytimes.com/interactive/2017/11/16/magazine/uncounted-civilian-casualties -iraq-airstrikes.html>.

Knefel, John. "Individuals, Worlds Apart, United by the Trauma of Drone Strikes." *Rolling Stone* 29 Oct. 2013 <www.rollingstone.com/politics/news/individuals-worlds-apart -united-by-the-trauma-of-drone-strikes-20131029>.

Maden, Mike. *Blue Warrior.* New York: Putnam, 2014.

———. "A Conversation with Mike Maden, Author of *Tom Clancy: Point of Contact*." Interview. *Signature* 13 June 2017 <www.signature-reads.com/2017/06/a-conversation -with-mike-maden-author-of-tom-clancy-point-of-contact/>.

———. *Drone*. New York: Putnam, 2013.

———. *Drone Command*. New York: Putnam, 2015.

———. *Drone Threat*. New York: Putnam, 2016.

———. Personal interview. 15 Aug. 2017.

———. *Tom Clancy: Point of Contact*. New York: Putnam, 2017.

"Manifesto of the Necronautical Society." International Necronautical Society, 1999 <www .necronauts.org/manifesto1.htm>.

McCarthy, Tom. *C*. New York: Knopf, 2010.

———. "An Interview with Tom McCarthy." Matthew Hart and Aaron Jaffe, with Jonathan Eburne. *Contemporary Literature* 54.4 (2013): 656–82 <muse.jhu.edu/article/537956>.

———. *Remainder*. 2005. New York: Vintage, 2007.

———. *Satin Island*. New York: Vintage, 2015.

———. *Transmission and the Individual Remix: How Literature Works*. New York: Vintage, 2012. Also available on Google Books <books.google.com/books?isbn=0345803272> (ac- cessed 26 Dec. 2017).

Moi, Toril. "Discussion or Aggression? Arrogance and Despair in Graduate School." *The Grind: Duke Graduate Student Newsletter* 4.1 (2003): 4. Also available at <www.torilmoi .com/wp-content/uploads/2009/09/Moi_Arrogance-and-despair_2003.pdf> (accessed 31 Dec. 2017).

"MQ-9 Reaper: Fact Sheet." US Air Force. 23 Sept. 2015 <www.af.mil/About-Us/Fact -Sheets/Display/Article/104470/mq-9-reaper/>.

Paglen, Trevor, producer. *Citizenfour*. Dir. Laura Poitras. Praxis Films, 2014.

———. *Code Names of the Surveillance State*. 2015. Projection on building. British Parliament, London. <www.paglen.com/?l=work&s=code_names_of_the_&i=1>.

———. *Drone Vision*. 2010. Archival pigment prints, 16 × 20 inches. Metro Pictures, New York; Altman Siegel, San Francisco. <www.paglen.com/?l=work&s=drones&i=10>.

———. *An English Landscape (American Surveillance Base near Harrogate, Yorkshire)*. 15 June 2014–13 July 2016. Tube stop installation, London.

———. *Untitled (Reaper Drone)*. 2010. C-Print, 48 × 60 in., edition of 5 plus 2 AP. <www .paglen.com/?l=work&s=drones>.

Povinelli, Elizabeth. *Economies of Abandonment: Social Belonging and Endurance in Late Lib- eralism*. Durham: Duke UP, 2011.

Said, Edward W. *Culture and Imperialism*. 1993. New York: Vintage, 1994.

Schnepf, J. D. "Domestic Aerial Photography in the Era of Drone Warfare." *MFS* 63.2 (2017): 270–87. <doi:10.1353/mfs.2017.0022>.

Stahl, Roger. "What the Drone Saw: The Cultural Optics of Unmanned War." *Australian Journal of International Affairs* 67.5 (2013): 659–74. <doi:10.1080/10357718.2013.817526>.

Stallabrass, Julian, and Trevor Paglen. "Negative Dialectics in the Google Era: A Conversation with Trevor Paglen." *October* 138 (2011): 3–14 <www.jstor.org/stable/41417903>.

Sterne, Jonathan. "Compression: A Loose History." *Signal Traffic: Critical Studies of Media Infrastructures*. Ed. Lisa Parks and Nicole Starosielski. Urbana: U of Illinois P, 2015. 31–52.

Thompson, Loren. "Air Force's Secret 'Gorgon Stare' Program Leaves Terrorists Nowhere to Hide." *Forbes* 10 Apr. 2015 <www.forbes.com/sites/lorenthompson/2015/04/10/air-forces-secret-gorgon-stare-program-leaves-terrorists-nowhere-to-hide/#1d4ede8f7be4>.

The Abstract, the Concrete, and the Labor of the Novel

EMILIO SAURI

Comprising, almost exclusively, photographs taken from a bridge overlooking Mexico's Federal Highway 85, Alejandro Cartagena's widely celebrated series of photographs, *Carpoolers* (2011), captures construction workers and landscapers who commute daily from the blue-collar suburbs of Monterrey to San Pedro Garza García in the backs of pickup trucks (see figures 1–4). Each picture is composed of the same elements: truck, road surface, and the contents found in the truck's flatbed, including workers on their way to San Pedro who remain oblivious (for the most part) to the camera above. As one art critic puts it, each truck is "transformed from a vehicle into a frame, the rectangular bed of the truck becoming a kind of bounded canvas on which [Cartagena's] narratives and compositions are arranged" (Knoblauch). When the dozens of photographs that make up the series are viewed together, the uniformity of composition becomes all the more conspicuous, making clear that the point is not to highlight the differences between individual pictures. While the beholder might take note of the dissimilarities among the arrangements of elements, among the models and makes of the trucks, among their cargoes, and among the persons they carry, the differences among those persons are softened not just by the repetition of these elements but also by the camera's distance from the scene, by the materials with which workers share the flatbeds, by the clothing and hats they wear, and more often than not by their postures. The unchanging background of gray pavement with white and yellow road markings, moreover, has the effect of decontextualizing the images, abstracting the figures from the setting in which they are found. Cartagena's series raises the question of whether these are in fact simply pictures of laborers who commute to and from the lower-income suburbs of Monterrey or whether the beholder is being prompted to see something else altogether.

Cartagena prompts the question when he describes his photography as a "search for an understanding of the space where we live" and of "why things look and operate the way they do" ("Beauty"). Of course, the *why* is crucial, for in making *Carpoolers* something more than a document, it urges the beholder to look beyond the surface of the photographic image. But the *why* is also a problem insofar as it requires Cartagena's series to compel the conviction that these are not just pictures of individuals laboring under unfavorable conditions, but rather

Portions of this essay were presented at the Arts and Sciences Workshop at Harvard University's David Rockefeller Center for Latin American Studies, at the University of Pennsylvania's Department of Hispanic and Portuguese Studies, and at the symposium The Novel and the Concrete, hosted by *Novel* at Brown University. I am grateful to those who organized and participated in these events and particularly to the editors of *Novel* for their feedback and comments. Special thanks as well to Alejandro Cartagena for the use of his images.

Novel: A Forum on Fiction 51:2   DOI 10.1215/00295132-6846102   © 2018 by Novel, Inc.

they are photographs of the unseen social forces that demand such conditions in the first place. In the course of the last three decades, development schemes and growth strategies associated with neoliberalism have created those conditions throughout Latin America by way of market reforms, privatization, and the abrogation of collective agreements, resulting in fewer protections for workers in countries like Mexico. Thus in asking "why things look and operate the way they do," Cartagena poses the problem of how photography visualizes the abstract forces that shape society in such decisively concrete ways. And in attempting to resolve that problem, *Carpoolers* insists that recording the experience of individuals alone does not offer a more complete picture of their situation.[1]

Or, as Roberto Schwarz, recalling Bertolt Brecht, reminds us, "Once reality has migrated into abstract economic functions, it can no longer be read in human faces" (35). Importantly, Schwarz offers this insight in relation not to photography but to the novel, and while it is specifically nineteenth-century Brazilian realism he has in mind, the question of how individual works picture abstract functions is no less relevant to the novel in Latin America today. As we will see, it is just as crucial to contemporary Mexican fiction, and particularly to Yuri Herrera's trilogy of novels, *Trabajos del reino* (2004), *Señales que precederán al fin del mundo* (2009), and *La transmigración de los cuerpos* (2013) (translated into English, respectively, as *Kingdom Cons*, *Signs Preceding the End of the World*, and *The Transmigration of Bodies*). At the same time, *Mexican* is a problematic term here, for despite being concerned with issues that have come to define the experience of millions in Mexico today, including violence, migration, and exploitation, Herrera's style involves abstracting such issues from the real-world contexts to which his trilogy alludes but that it rarely mentions. The result is a narrative counterpart to *Carpoolers'* images. If Cartagena conceives of abstraction as a means to visualize "why things look and operate the way they do" in photography, Herrera points to something similar in the novel when he observes that "literature's virtues and possibilities lie not in its ability to reflect reality, but in its ability to shed light on certain issues that do not appear in other forms of writing or that do not appear within the everyday public sphere" ("Las palabras").[2] The novel, Herrera suggests, affords the means to visualize abstract functions, lending them the status of the concrete.

---

[1] This is not to say that the difference between abstract and concrete can be reduced to the distinction between the visible and the unseen; the fact that such principles cannot be seen does not make them any less concrete. This is precisely the insight offered by the Hegelian-Marxist concept of "real abstraction," which, as David Cunningham puts it in a related context, refers to "those forms of abstraction that, precisely in the specific set of circumstances of capitalist modernity, come to have an actual (and thus paradoxically concrete) objective social existence, most specifically in the real abstraction of the value form" (313–14). Yet this also means that we cannot assume that merely documenting the concrete will provide a more complete understanding of those circumstances. For Cunningham, then, "the 'objective' reality that the novel confronts in capitalist modernity must be . . . one in which the social totality can itself *only* be understood in abstract terms" (314).

[2] Translations of Spanish- and Portuguese-language texts are my own unless otherwise noted.

Figure 1. Alejandro Cartagena, *Carpoolers, no. 12*, 2011. Permission of the artist.

Figure 2. Alejandro Cartagena, *Carpoolers, no. 48*, 2011. Permission of the artist.

To begin to understand how, it is worth remembering Karl Marx's claim that the "concrete is concrete because it is the concentration of many determinations, hence unity of the diverse," and therefore must appear "in the process of thinking . . . as a result, not as a point of departure, even though it is the point of departure for observation [*Anschauung*] and conception" (*Grundrisse* 101). For Marx, then, "the method of rising from the abstract to the concrete is only the way in which thought appropriates the concrete" (101). From this perspective, the challenge for any novel—or work of art for that matter—is to alter our conception of the concrete itself; that is, to grasp society as the concentration of abstract determinations that ordinary perception fails to see. But this also means that an attention to experience alone will not yield a clearer understanding of the concrete, and as Cartagena and Herrera make clear, this is just as true for the beholder's or reader's experience. For both photographer and novelist, abstraction in the work of art functions not only to visualize a structure but also to mark the irrelevance of the subject's experience to that structure. To put the point this way, of course, is to presume that society exists and that works of art are still possible in a situation in which neither of these claims is self-evident. And yet it is precisely this situation that both Herrera's trilogy and Cartagena's photography aim to address.

 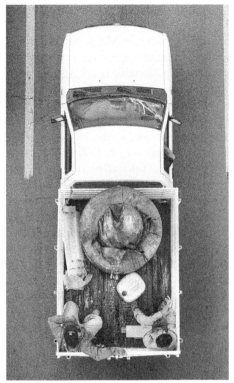

Figure 3.   Alejandro Cartagena, *Carpoolers, no.*   Figure 4.   Alejandro Cartagena, *Carpoolers, no.*
61, 2011. Permission of the artist.   *70*, 2011. Permission of the artist.

Border

Herrera's second novel (and the first to be translated), *Signs Preceding the End of the World*, provides a sense of what apprehending the concrete involves in the only instance where it makes direct reference to Mexico. Shortly after crossing the border into the Big Chilango, Herrera's protagonist finds herself in an unnamed city described as "an edgy arrangement of cement particles and yellow paint" (56). "Out on the concrete and steel-girder plain," however, Makina senses "another presence straight off, scattered about like bolts fallen from a window: on street corners, on scaffolding, on sidewalks: fleeting looks of recognition quickly concealed and then evasive" (57). She quickly realizes, "These were her compatriots, her homegrown, armed with work: builders, florists, loaders, drivers," and after wandering into several restaurants, she further realizes "they were here, too, more armed than anyplace else, cooks and helpers and dishwashers" (57–58). "All cooking is Mexican cooking," she jokes to herself, making it clear to the readers what has merely been implied until now: that the setting of Makina's story is the United States–Mexico border and that the figures she comes across on the street are Mexican just like her (58).

Even so, as the story of a young woman who travels from the Village to the Little Town and across the border into the Big Chilango in search of her estranged brother, *Signs* never refers to Mexico by name again. Considering Herrera borrows the structure of Makina's narrative from pre-Columbian Mexica visions of the afterlife—particularly Mictlán, the kingdom of the dead, whose nine distinct levels correspond to the novel's nine chapters—his decision to avoid any mention of Mexico is significant. And this decision is complicated further by the novel's language. In addition to his extensive use of neologisms, one of Herrera's more remarkable achievements as a writer is a style of prose rendered in a vernacular, "peppered," as his translator Lisa Dillman puts it, "with language—colloquialisms, slang, expressions, culturally-embedded references—that could only take place in Mexico (or on the Mexico-USA border)" (111). Thus if the appearance of the word *Mexican* connects the novel's settings and characters to the forms of sociality that "Mexico," "the United States," or even "the border" name, it also has the effect of making the absence of any such markers throughout the rest of the novel even more conspicuous. Not unlike the builders, florists, loaders, drivers, cooks, helpers, and dishwashers who emerge from the "concrete and steel-girder plain" to become Makina's "compatriots," Mexico comes into view briefly as the setting only to recede back into landscapes like the Earth, the Place Where the Hills Meet, the Place Where the Wind Cuts Like a Knife, the Place Where Flags Wave, and the Place Where People's Hearts Are Eaten.[3] Like Cartagena's *Carpoolers*, Herrera's *Signs* can be said to dramatize a process that aims to abstract figures and settings from the concrete particularity of real-world milieus.

Herrera's *Signs*, and his trilogy on the whole, might therefore be read as soliciting a kind of critical attention to setting that David Alworth has usefully called "site reading." Against longstanding views, Alworth argues that settings are not just the "static background for narrative action" but rather a means to grasp how literary fiction "theorizes sociality." As his account makes clear, this mode of reading also entails a departure from more "conventional" approaches to literary studies (2). Citing the growing skepticism toward the "project of locating the deep roots and meanings of literary form in the social forces that underlie it"—which critics such as James English, Franco Moretti, Rita Felski, Stephen Best, and Sharon Marcus have identified with the enterprise of critique—Alworth imagines site reading as contributing to a growing catalog of alternatives to "symptomatic reading" and the "hermeneutics of suspicion" (2). This attention to setting consequently reveals how the "figuration of sites, vibrant assemblages of persons and things, might occasion a new inquiry into the nature of sociality." But it does so with an eye to meeting the demand for a new way of doing literary interpretation stemming from the conviction, following Bruno Latour, that "there is no such thing as society or the social"—that is, "no such thing as a special domain of reality (distinct from, say, the material or the natural) governed by abstract laws, structures, and functions" (Alworth 3–4). Challenging approaches that have long understood literary form as a mediation of those abstract laws, structures, and functions, site reading insists that attending to such figurations will occasion a new sociology of literature.

---

3   These are among the titles that Herrera gives to several of the novel's nine chapters.

Herrera appears more or less attuned to this view when he claims in an interview, "Literature serves not so much to denounce as it does to think about and look at reality from another place," implying what seems to be a similar skepticism toward critique ("Las palabras"). And yet, as we have already seen, he also maintains that literature provides unique insight into matters that fail to appear in other forms of writing and speech. In contrast to recent tendencies within literary studies in general and within Latin American studies in particular, Herrera holds that the novel's potential—whether social, political, or artistic—stems from its capacity to make visible that which common perception cannot. But this means that rather than begin with the question, "what if there is no such thing as society?" his attentiveness to setting not only presupposes the existence of a society governed by abstract laws, structures, and functions but also signals the degree to which the novel is unthinkable without it.

To begin to understand why, we might note that *Signs Preceding the End of the World* is a work of fiction about migration that is not about migrating to or from any place in particular. Responding to an interviewer's remark that the "word immigration does not appear even once" in the novel, Herrera explains, "There are also no concrete references to the places in which the story is set" because "I didn't want the novel to be read solely as a novel about Mexican migration" ("Herrera, viajes" 42). Even as *Signs* draws on Mexica visions of the underworld, Herrera insists that "[j]ust as the descent to Mictlán was a journey full of tests that everyone had to face with their own means, migrants are forced to overcome the innumerable contingencies that separate them from their final destination, be this Paris, Houston, London, Madrid, or New York" ("Herrera, viajes" 42). The Mexica parallel determines Makina's narrative, but not in a way that would make her migration appear Mexican in any putatively cultural sense. Instead, the question of setting emerges forcefully in *Signs* as the problem of representing a phenomenon that is inexorably site specific, but it does so by means that undermine such specification. In Herrera's fiction, the possibility of overcoming specification emerges as one of seeing beyond the concrete immediacy of *lo fronterizo*, or "border condition," a condition that refers less to a geographic situation than to "any situation where you have different individuals and different communities exchanging values, exchanging goods, always in conflict but also in different levels of dialogue" (Herrera, "Border"). According to Herrera, the protagonists in *Signs*, *Kingdom Cons*, and *The Transmigration of Bodies* all share this condition, even where the actual border does not figure prominently. Each work consequently draws on the same set of techniques, formally abstracting settings, characters, and plotlines from real sites like the United States–Mexico border, with an eye to representing *lo fronterizo*.

For this reason, *Signs* is as much a border novel as a theory of how the border works as a structure.[4] This becomes all the more apparent in a scene in which a cop detains Makina and several others. Having snatched a book from one of the presumably undocumented detainees, the cop says, "Poetry. Lookie here at the educated worker,

---

4   For an excellent account of the "novel as theory," see Anna Kornbluh, for whom "[t]he novel is a kind of thinking concerned with a problem, both of which exceed the parameters of experience" (403).

comes with no money, no papers, but hey, poems" (98). The cop orders the man to start writing, but Makina soon after snatches the pencil and book from the "worker" and begins to write her own poem, which the cop reads aloud:

We are to blame for this destruction, we who don't speak your tongue and don't know how to keep quiet either. We who didn't come by boat, who dirty up your doorsteps with our dust, who break your barbed wire. We who came to take your jobs, who dream of wiping your shit, who long to work all hours. We who fill your shiny clean streets with the smell of food, who brought you violence you'd never known, who deliver your dope, who deserve to be chained by neck and feet. We who are happy to die for you, what else could we do? We, the ones who are waiting for who knows what. We, the dark, the short, the greasy, the shifty, the fat, the anemic. We the barbarians. (99–100)

At first glance, Makina's poem might be read as an attempt to solicit a kind of empathy from both the "patriotic officer" and the reader alike (98). This interpretation is more or less confirmed by the reaction of the cop, who "had started off in a mock-portentous voice but gradually abandoned the histrionics as he neared the last line, which he read almost in a whisper" (100). From the perspective of the reader, however, the pronoun *we* is an obstacle to any empathetic identification: with whom is the reader being asked to empathize? What Makina's poem presses the reader to see is a formal structure, the mutually determining relationship between "we" and "you," between, that is, two logical positions within that structure belonging to no group in particular.

Further, it is precisely this formal abstraction that marks Herrera's distance from recent theorizations of the border. Consider, for example, what Sandro Mezzadra and Brett Neilson call "the multiplication of labor," a concept from which capitalist development can be "analyzed in terms of [its] consequences for the subjective composition of living labor" (22). Drawing on Marx's notion of living labor, Mezzadra and Neilson's method would seem to provide a gloss on Makina's poem when they explain, "To affirm that the border plays a decisive role in the production of labor power as a commodity is also to contend that the ways migratory movements are controlled, filtered, and blocked by border regimes have more general effects on the political and juridical constitution of labor markets, and thus on the experiences of living labor in general" (20–21). Even so, it would be a mistake to understand Herrera's characters as figurations of such "living labor," and this becomes even clearer when they observe that "there is a need to stress the qualities of the container of labor power—that is, the body in its sexualized and racialized materiality" (110). Where Mezzadra and Neilson look to the "specificity of the positions and subjective experiences of these figures" (96), *Signs* looks to a structure that gives rise to such positions and experiences overall.

Which is to say that Herrera intends to make that structure visible by taking up the problem of how to depict the border as a condition that exceeds not just place but also culture and identity. Recalling Cartagena's *Carpoolers, Signs* powerfully dramatizes what the solution to this problem looks like in its closing pages, where Makina is guided to "The Obsidian Place with No Windows or Holes for the Smoke," a place that was "specific, yet inexact" (105). Here, Herrera's protagonist realizes her journey has come to an end when, in a somewhat fantastic scene, she is a given a file and sees, "There she was, with another name, another birthplace. Her photo, new numbers, new trade, new home. I've been skinned, she whispered" (106). Nevertheless, Makina, we are told, almost immediately

> *stopped feeling the weight of uncertainty and guilt; she thought back to her people as though recalling the contours of a lovely landscape that was now fading away: the Village, the Little Town, the Big Chilango, all those colors, and she saw that what was happening was not a cataclysm; she understood with all her body and all of her memory, she truly understood, and when everything in the world fell silent finally said to herself I'm ready.* (107)

Not unlike the setting's "contours" and "colors" that recede from the mind's eye, the character's sense of self begins to vanish. Having been "skinned," Makina falls victim to the very abstraction that the author employs throughout, albeit here in more radicalized form that marks the end both of the novel and of the world itself. Anticipating this end "for a second—or for many seconds; she couldn't tell because she didn't have a watch, nobody had a watch" (106), Herrera's protagonist signals that all that remains is a "body" without an identity and a setting without a "landscape," not just beyond history but out of time.

The Twilight of the Future

Latin American literary history, to be sure, is replete with plotlines, characters, and settings similarly located "outside of time." One might think here of Melquiades's room in Gabriel García Márquez's *Cien años de soledad* (1967) or any of Jorge Luis Borges's countless ruminations on the nature of eternity, though other examples come readily to mind. Still, such timelessness takes on an entirely new significance not just in Herrera's border trilogy but within the contemporary Latin American novel more generally. Roberto Bolaño's *2666* (2004)—a novel known for, among other things, its apocalyptic tone and imagery—crystalizes this sense of timelessness in the Mexican Chucho Flores's description of the novel's fictional city, Santa Teresa. Flores tells the African American journalist Oscar Fate:

> *This is a big city, a real city. . . . We have everything. Factories, maquiladoras, one of the lowest unemployment rates in Mexico, a cocaine cartel, a constant flow of workers from other cities, Central American immigrants, an urban infrastructure that can't support the level of demographic growth. We have plenty of money and poverty, we have imagination and bureaucracy, we have violence and the desire to work in peace. There's just one thing we haven't got. . . . Time. . . . We haven't got any fucking time.* (286)

Chucho suggests that Santa Teresa is out of time in the sense of being in a place where time has ceased to progress and where the everyday rhythm of life itself has stalled to become part of what the novel elsewhere calls the "perpetual present" (84). But Chucho also points to another sense in which Santa Teresa is out of time: for all its factories, maquiladoras, and urban infrastructure, none of these will lead to the development of Santa Teresa, of Mexico, or of the "developing world" for that matter. Fate suggests as much when he thinks, "Time for what? . . . Time for this shithole, equal parts lost cemetery and garbage dump, to turn into a kind of Detroit?" (286). Chucho's lament, then, speaks to the loss of a conception of time long associated with the modernization projects central to the development of the Latin American nation-state throughout the nineteenth and twentieth centuries. What would have been seen, at some other moment in history, as a sign of the developing city's long march toward modernity is revealed to be nothing more than a source of frustration for a class of entrepreneurs, managers, and technocrats with nowhere to go. All that remains in the wake of this collapse of modernization is a developmentalism without development.[5]

A novel like *2666*, in this sense, maintains that *the contemporary* is not so much a question of the novel's possible global horizons as it is a product of an alteration in the global itself. As Bolaño's Chucho Flores makes clear, the novel asks how we might think of the timelessness of the present not as a cultural or existential fact but rather as a product of that model of development that neoliberalism names. Within countries like Mexico, Argentina, and Brazil, the mark of neoliberalism's success has been the virtually seamless identification of "development" with the free market—that is, with privatization, fiscal consolidation or austerity, and the elimination of restrictions on the movement of capital across borders. What some call globalization is, as Phillip McMichael puts it, the "crossing of a threshold from the national development era to a new era in which international competition and global efficiency increasingly govern and privatize national policy and growth strategies" (236). As is well known, these policies and strategies have also played a hand in the massive transfer of wealth upward that has resulted in an unequal distribution of "progress" within these same countries, to say nothing of fewer protections for workers and the environment. With no alternative in sight, however, the market prevails as the ultimate horizon of all human development—whether social, political, or economic.

Octavio Paz had already intimated something similar in his 1990 Nobel lecture, where he famously observes that, with the decline of the idea of modernity and of the modern individual's defining characteristic, historicism, "the same decline is beginning to affect our idea of Progress and, as a result, our vision of time, of history and of ourselves." "We are witnessing," Paz proclaims, "the twilight of the future." Pessimistic at first glance, the Mexican poet nonetheless believes that "the twilight of the future heralds the advent of the now" and that this is reason enough to be hopeful, because, in his words, "[t]hinking about the now implies . . . recovering . . . critical vision." The lecture subsequently directs that vision at the then nascent "triumph of the market economy," because "like all mechanisms it lacks both conscience and compassion" (37). Despite misgivings about the market's tendency to reduce "ideas, feelings, art, love, friendship and people themselves to consumer products" (37–38), Paz ultimately conceives of this critical vision as "a way of integrating [the market] into society so that it expresses the social contract and becomes an instrument of justice and

---

5   I have adapted this paragraph from Sauri, "Autonomy," which offers a full treatment of the significance of *2666*'s conception of time.

fairness." For Paz, then, such critical vision is not so much a critique of the market economy as a way of making it a better mechanism for actualizing society's potential. This also means that "to think about the now" (37) is to extend a vision of sociality that has been crucial to the success of neoliberalism throughout Latin America since the 1970s.

Nearly a quarter century after Paz's Nobel, the Brazilian philosopher Paulo Arantes offers a critical sense of what this triumph of the market has meant for the notion of progress. Reflecting on the *jornadas de junho*, the explosive strikes, marches, and riots that took place in more than one hundred cities across Brazil in June 2013, Arantes notes, "Life in Brazil has undoubtedly improved, and greatly, in these two decades of adjustment to global capitalism. And yet, no one can take it anymore" ("O futuro"). Here he reminds us that the indignation that animated the protests came into view under conditions of economic growth and low unemployment, making them something of a mixed bag of class interests and politics. Nevertheless, the protests also underlined the fact that development in Brazil has entailed significant limits on the upward mobility of millions of younger workers living in cities like São Paulo. Under the current dispensation, Arantes contends, the future promised by development turns out to be a trap, and "[t]hat trap," in his words, is the "Brazil of the future that finally arrived." A quick survey of Latin America's recent economic history confirms that the adjustment to global capitalism has brought about similar consequences throughout the region. For Arantes, then, the arrival of this future is marked more broadly by a new temporality, which, recalling Paz's "twilight of the future," he identifies elsewhere as *o novo tempo do mundo*, or new world time, in which "the very modern notion of progress—and the temporality of history that made it thinkable" have been neutralized. What follows, he continues, is a new "experience of history in an era of diminishing expectations," a form of historicity summed up in the image of the "*flat horizon*, 'without beginning, or end, or sequence'" (*O novo* 62).

But if the emphasis on abstraction that I have been tracing in the work of contemporary writers and artists like Herrera and Cartagena gives rise to similarly placeless and timeless narratives and imagery, such an emphasis is not, for all that, a product of this state of affairs alone. As we have already seen, Cartagena describes his creative process as a means to grasp "why things look and operate the way they do." And this process is easy enough to see in his earlier series *Suburbia Mexicana* (2006–9), which locates the form of historicity Arantes describes in sizable housing developments on the outskirts of Monterrey. Turning to the suburbs from which *Carpoolers'* workers hail, *Suburbia Mexicana* documents the suburban sprawl driven by the rapid expansion and deepening of the mortgage market that Mexico's national housing agencies (Infonavit and SHF) had begun in 2001 (see figures 5–8).[6] Constructed in the middle of desolate landscapes

6   In 2007, the *Financial Times* reported, "According to Fitch, the rating agency, accumulated investment in mortgages from 2001 until last year was about 850bn pesos ($78bn), which is equivalent to more than 4.3m mortgages financed by the various lending institutions. . . . Today, Infonavit is Mexico's biggest mortgage lender, with almost 60 per cent of total loans and is on course to grant 500,000 individual mortgages this year. Since 2001, the agency has granted more mortgages than it did in the previous 30 years." Meanwhile, the Sociedad Hipotecaría Federal (SHF) is "a second-tier bank that provides credit and guarantees to financial institutions offering mortgages, particularly to

Figure 5.   Alejandro Cartagena, *Apodaca*, from *Suburbia Mexicana*, 2006–9. Permission of the artist.

difficult to place, the housing developments photographed in the first part of Cartagena's series *Fragmented Cities* offer a sense of the speed and intensity with which this expansion and deepening took place. Further, the repetitive quality of the pictures that make up *Carpoolers* emerges in *Suburbia Mexicana* as a quality of the homes built during the construction boom, a uniformity made even sharper by its contrast with the natural environments in which these housing developments have cropped up.

As Cartagena puts it, this "first part of the project sheds light on the implemented neo-liberal economic strategies made by the mexican [*sic*] government since 2001 that have pushed urban growth out of the regulation of the metropolitan urban plan" ("Suburbia"). In this sense, *Suburbia Mexicana* is composed of pictures not just of housing developments on the outskirts of Monterrey but of landscapes transformed by both finance capital and the forms of deregulation and marketization that, importantly, have come to define development schemes across the globe. The total absence of any homeowners or residents in this part of Cartagena's larger project speaks to this point, inasmuch as their presence would risk making the photos about *them*, about their lives in these suburbs, and about their experience more generally. Their absence also contributes to the impression that these are landscapes abandoned to time. Cartagena's *Suburbia Mexicana*, nonetheless, seeks not to *document* the suburban sprawl of the 2000s but, more precisely, to make visible the principles of debt, financing, and deregulation, which, as abstractions, cannot simply be documented. Rather, they must be represented.[7] In this way, *Suburbia Mexicana* tries, to borrow a phrase from Fredric Jameson, "converting an encounter with history into a thought about history" (594).

Mexico's poorer classes" (Thompson). As the *FT* explains, the SHF's "main achievement has been to provide credit to so-called *sofoles*, special-purpose banks that began to finance house-building companies following the tequila crisis." The article concludes by citing Infonavit's then general director, Víctor Manuel Borrás: "The market, which used to depend on the state through the SHF, is now working on its own terms" (Thompson).

[7]   I owe this formulation to Walter Benn Michaels's *The Beauty of a Social Problem*.

To return to the novel, then, if Bolaño's Chucho Flores gives voice to this new experience of history—one that the novel evokes almost obsessively as "a desert of boredom"—*2666* also raises an important question about art more generally; namely, what happens to art when the future that developmentalism had promised to deliver to Latin America has finally arrived but in the guise of the market's triumph throughout the region? Mariano Siskind indicates why the novel is a

Figure 6.   Alejandro Cartagena, *Guadalupe*, from *Suburba Mexicana*, 2006–9. Permission of the artist.

particularly apt means to consider what the fate of art is in the "era of diminishing expectations" when he reminds us of the role it played in the late nineteenth century: "Because of the kind of experiences that the novel afforded to the readers of the colonial and semi-colonial peripheries, Latin American intellectuals immediately realized the important role that the consumption, production, and translation of novels could play in the process of socio-cultural modernization" (339). Thus if the development of the Latin American novel throughout the nineteenth and twentieth centuries was oriented largely toward imagining or achieving (or even critiquing) modernization, then the exhaustion of that process today ought to have far-reaching consequences for the genre as a whole.

One consequence would appear to be the market's more complete embrace of literature in general and of the novel in particular, confirming Paz's fears that the "triumph of the market economy" might reduce artworks to mere "consumer products," to commodities like any other. This much is suggested not just by the enlargement of the secondary market in the arts but also by the role that the visual and plastic arts, literature, and even artists and writers themselves increasingly play in the processes of valorization.[8] Herrera demonstrates an acute awareness of this state of affairs when he explains, "There is no such thing as someone who stands apart from power, that is, to the extent that he depends on the circulation of their texts, he depends on the market" ("Las palabras"). Nevertheless, he also insists, "The issue with artists is that in all periods they have to assert their autonomy, finding their spaces for autonomous creation before the different types of powers that can restrict or limit them." The novels that comprise Herrera's trilogy

---

[8]   See Sarah Brouillette and Irmgard Emmelhainz.

Figure 7.   Alejandro Cartagena, *Monterrey*, from *Suburba Mexicana*, 2006–9. Permission of the artist.

set out to prove not only that such spaces continue to exist but that the possibility of imagining an alternative to the market depends on their existence as well.

Thus Herrera's first novel, *Kingdom Cons*, conveys an equally keen attention to this situation in recounting the story of Lobo, a singer of *narcocorridos* brought to live within the Court of the King, a drug cartel in Northern Mexico. Employing the same techniques of abstraction we have already seen in *Signs*, *Kingdom Cons* allows the reader to infer the setting, but without ever mentioning words such as *Mexico*, *United States*, *drug trafficking*, or *drugs*, terms that are, according to Herrera, "already too codified, overused and that did not allow [him] to tell the story in its own words" ("Las palabras"). Lobo becomes the Artist shortly after he is brought into the Court, and this name change is significant precisely because it marks the protagonist's struggle to assert his autonomy from both the market and the very power that makes his art possible: the King. Recalling aspects of early modern patronage, the King initially provides the Artist with the means to create music at a remove from the market, here represented by the DJs' demand "to clean it up a little, write sweeter songs, less crude" (47). Instructing the Court's Manager to find another way "to move [his] music on the street," the King smiles, and the Artist thinks that his patron's "smile seemed a protective embrace that said to the Artist, Why sugarcoat the ears of those fuckers? We know what we are and we're good with it. Let them be scared, let the decent take offense. Put them to shame. Why else be an artist?" (51).

Within the context of Mexico today, such distance from market pressures is provided by cultural agencies funded by the state, particularly Conaculta, the National Council for Culture and the Arts, which subsidizes FONCA, the National Fund for Culture and Arts (itself the agency that subsidized the publication of Cartagena's *Carpoolers* as a book).[9] But these forms of state patronage exert their own kinds of pressure on writers and artists, and so, in *Kingdom Cons*, while the King's Court affords the Artist a certain distance, he is nonetheless made to understand that writing songs for his patron alone is no less a threat to his creative

[9]   For a comprehensive account of how these and other state agencies afford a kind of autonomization of the literary field, see Ignacio Sánchez Prado.

autonomy. Assuring the Artist, "what you do is art, amigo, no need to use all your words of praise on Señor," the Journalist warns him, "if one day you have to choose between your passion and your obligation, Artist, then you are truly fucked" (72). No doubt the difference between passion and obligation is, for the Journalist, the difference between an artwork conceived as an end in itself and one conceived as a means to an end, as the novel confirms later on when the King declares, "Time has come for you to make yourself useful, Artist," an order that the protagonist not only use his skills as a musician to spy on a rival cartel but also choose between his passion and his obligation (75).

Figure 8.   Alejandro Cartagena, *Santa Catarina*, from *Suburbia Mexicana*, 2006–9. Permission of the artist.

The King's injunction that an artwork be "useful," then, is another example of a demand that undermines the conception of the artwork as an end in itself. And yet the Artist eventually discovers the means necessary to assert the work's autonomy—not just from the market but from his patron as well—in a kind of intangible space. Asking himself, "Who was the King?" the Artist ultimately decides he is "[a] man with no power over the terse fabric inside the artist's head" (96). It is precisely this "terse fabric," then, that cannot be touched by the King or, more specifically, by the demand to "make yourself useful." This realization in turn allows the Artist "to feel the power of an order different from that of the Court, the skill with which he detached words from things and created his own sovereign texture and volume. A separate reality" (96) belonging to the work itself.

This also suggests that Herrera tells a rather different story about art in general and the novel's future in particular than what has become the growing consensus among critics. Josefina Ludmer, for example, considers contemporary fiction as "post-autonomous literatures," forms of writing that "cannot be read with literary criteria or categories like author, work, style, writing, text and meaning." Drawing on Ludmer, Carlos Alonso similarly argues, "Whatever we may consider to be the future of the novel, it must be understood in the context of [a] de-autonomization of the literary and cultural field" (3). What is most significant about recent novels from Latin American countries like Argentina, Colombia, and Mexico, Alonso continues, is "their indifference to being consumed as a distinct and privileged cultural discourse—in other words, as literature—as well as their ready availability to market-driven circulation" (4). Where Herrera sees possibilities for the novel, critics see confirmation of Paz's worst fears. And this is perhaps nowhere more apparent than in the "turn to affect" in Latin American studies, in which the market's triumph is marked by the rise of what Dierdra Reber characterizes as a logic that perceives society as a "feeling soma that has dispensed altogether with the need for a thinking head" (24).

Following this logic, Jon Beasley-Murray's account of "posthegemony" provides the clearest sense of what the fate of not just politics but of art might be under such circumstances. Stressing the role of habit, affect, and the multitude over against consent, opinion, and belief, Beasley-Murray argues, "What matters is how things present themselves to us, not what they may *re*present" (205). Whereas representation asks us to look beyond the sensuous immediacy of any given work to determine what it means, the emphasis on affect asks us to consider what it does to us as readers or viewers and to our bodies, raising questions about its effects. And if what matters is how things present themselves to us, the effects they provoke, then it follows that whether those things are literary in nature or not is a matter of indifference. From the perspective of affective criticism, this is precisely the point, but as critics such as Ludmer and Alonso make clear, a good deal of literary studies has arrived at a similar conclusion, albeit by different means.

Indeed, Ludmer grounds her concept of postautonomous literatures in two postulates: "The first is that everything cultural (and literary) is economic and that everything economic is cultural (and literary). And the second postulate would be that reality (if considered from the perspective of the media, which continuously constitutes it) is fiction and that fiction is reality." Thus if Beasley-Murray believes that "[w]hat matters is how things present themselves to us, not what they may *re*present," this is, from Ludmer's perspective, because in a situation where the literary and the economic are indistinguishable, there is no reality to represent. For Ludmer, this is a "reality that does not want to be represented because it already is pure representation," and so, rather than represent it, postautonomous literatures "fabricate present." But as Alonso also indicates, to grasp literature in Ludmer's terms is to treat it exclusively as a means to economic ends, to see every decision as pointing to the same "ready availability to market-driven circulation." Because the point of any commodity is to meet the demands imposed by the market, which is to say that to fulfill consumer desires and realize its value, literature's postautonomy effaces the distinction not just between literary and nonliterary works but between artworks and commodities as well.[10]

Style as a Form of Knowledge

What I have been describing as Herrera's and Cartagena's efforts to make the abstract visible in the concrete can be said to run counter to both Ludmer's notion of postautonomy and Beasley-Murray's posthegemonic emphasis on "how things

---

[10]   See Eugenio Di Stefano and Emilio Sauri for an elaboration of this reading of Ludmer and Beasley-Murray.

present themselves to us." To put the point this way is to begin to understand what Cartagena is up to in *Carpoolers* as well. For it doesn't take too much to understand that the staggering difference between the figures appearing in these pictures and the residents of San Pedro Garza García for whom they work is a product of the same model of development underlying the expansion and deepening of Mexico's mortgage market. Home to powerful conglomerates like Cemex, FEMSA, Gamesa, and Groupo Bimbo, San Pedro is not just among the richest municipalities in Mexico in terms of per capita income, it is also one of the wealthiest communities in Latin America—and in this sense it represents an inverted image of the housing developments pictured in *Suburbia Mexicana*.

Cartagena alerts us to his interest in this kind of inequality in a brief write-up of *Carpoolers* in the *New York Times*, where he notes, "There is such a big contrast between the rich and the poor here in Mexico" (McCann); and in speaking of Monterrey elsewhere, he observes, "I think precisely because it's the richest, that's why it's the most fucked up at the moment," adding, "[t]here's so much money, there are so many people wanting to have more money, there's so much ambition. The downside is there's not enough jobs to have that money, so there's a lot of poor people at the same time" ("Alejandro Cartagena Interview"). Nevertheless, it would be a mistake to view Cartagena's series of images as being about inequality. Any inequality between individuals as such is wholly absent from *Carpoolers'* pictures. For reasons I have already touched on, the uniformity of their composition cannot help but make individual differences imperceptible. This also means that Cartagena's images are not figurations of what Mezzadra and Neilson call "living labor," which is to say that *Carpoolers* remains largely indifferent to the "qualities of the container of labor power." Against the posthegemonic stress on bodies *in their immediacy*, Cartagena's photography aims to represent the abstract.

Thus, we might consider what the beholder is being asked to see in these images, though as the photographs themselves suggest, this is not quite the right question. The hidden faces and positions of the workers, along with the camera's own position, not only render the differences between them difficult to see but also have the effect of producing figures that appear wholly indifferent to the beholder's presence. Following the art historian Michael Fried, we might say that these are highly absorptive images—that is to say, photographs that create the fiction that the viewer does not exist, that he or she is not really there.[11] *Carpoolers*, then, is not asking anything of the viewer, let alone soliciting any kind of response (like empathy, indignation, or the like). But if the point of the pictures is not to solicit a response from the viewer, then how does *Carpoolers* address Cartagena's concern with "why things look the way they do"?

---

[11] For Fried, absorption emerges as a solution to a problem that the pictorial arts began to address in the mid-eighteenth century: namely, the problem of how to produce "the supreme fiction that the beholder did not exist, that he was not really there, standing before the canvas" (*Absorption* 103). Fried's art history has been largely devoted to showing how this problem has been central, first to the evolution of modernist painting; second, to the opposition between high modernism and minimalism in the mid- and late 1960s; and third, to contemporary photography since the 1970s (see Fried, *Why*).

The art historian Jessica McDonald offers one response to this question when she notes, "Resisting sentimentality, Cartagena's series operates as a typology, emphasizing the ubiquity of these carpoolers rather than telling any one of their stories." She continues: "Divested of their individuality through Cartagena's clinical approach, as well as their conflation with so many other implements of labor, the men confined to these shallow boxes become almost interchangeable." But we might make the force of McDonald's claim even clearer by emphasizing that Cartagena's absorptive images do not just resist sentimentality. They remain wholly indifferent to any response the viewer might have.[12]

The point, in other words, is not to ask what the viewer feels about these individuals, let alone what those feelings say *to* and *about* the beholder. Typology and repetition are therefore a means of achieving more absorptive pictures, marking the artwork's indifference to the beholder's experience and, in this sense, presenting an obstacle to any possible identification between the viewer and the workers. But this also means, to borrow from Herrera's description of literature, that *Carpoolers* cannot "[serve] . . . so much to denounce as it does to think about and look at reality from another place." No doubt the situation of these workers has become increasingly precarious over the course of the last two decades under the North American Free Trade Agreement. And yet if *Carpoolers* "serves not so much to denounce" as to see why this is the case, then Cartagena's series suggests that seeing why untold workers end up in the backs of pickup trucks involves not so much feeling a certain way about them as seeing the abstract principles that demand that situation—a gesture that can be said to take on increasing significance in an atmosphere defined by the postcritical refusal of abstract principles as such.

Thus, we might say that these are pictures not just of Mexican workers but also of abstract labor and that the whole point of Cartagena's procedure is to see beyond labor in its immediacy. As Marx makes clear, and as Cartagena's photographs indicate, abstract labor is not only the "substance" of value; it is also embedded in actual, concrete activities carried out by particular individuals. The presence of the workers in the photographs testifies to this fact. At the same time, however, the competitive pressures of the market demand that producers like Cemex, FEMSA, Gamesa, and Grupo Bimbo focus not on the specific or concrete qualities of any kind of labor but rather, and almost exclusively, on its productive efficiency.[13] From this perspective, the workers' bodies in *Carpoolers* function in much the same way as the appearance of the word *Mexican* does in *Signs*, when Makina encounters the builders, florists, loaders, drivers, cooks, helpers, and dishwashers on the "concrete and steel-girder plain." They are reminders of the concrete (and indexical) conditions in which *Carpoolers*, like *Signs*, aims to make abstract problems appear.

---

[12]   And this becomes even clearer when we contrast Cartagena's photography with Sebastião Salgado's photographs in *Workers* (1993) or even with a painting like Ramiro Gomez's *No Splash (after David Hockney's* A Bigger Splash, *1967)* (2013).

[13]   Or as Vivek Chibber puts it in a related context, "Capitalism forces employers to treat labor abstractly, because the market demands it" (140). Chibber adds, "abstract labor is not a distinctive kind of labor, since its content . . . cannot be specified. It is a set of formal properties, the content of which keeps changing as conditions of work change" (142).

In this way, Cartagena's creative process—to understand "why things look the way they do"—can be said to dovetail with Marx's procedure in *Capital* (1867). As Marx explains in the preface to the first edition, "individuals are dealt with here only in so far as they are the personifications of economic categories, the bearers [*Träger*] of particular class-relations and class-interests" (92). The question for Cartagena, as it was for Marx, is how to represent such economic categories. To put the point this way, however, is not only to see the irrelevance of Beasley-Murray's claim—"What matters is how things present themselves to us, not what they may *re*present"—to *Carpoolers*. It also suggests that changing the very model of development that makes the world look the way it does—and, in this sense, demands the inequality between these workers and their employers, between San Pedro Garza García and the suburbs of *Suburbia Mexicana*—involves something more than simply making the persons who appear in these photographs and their particularly concrete conditions objects of pathos. For the work of art, it requires being able to visualize the abstract.

To the extent that typology and repetition become means of achieving more absorptive pictures, marking the artwork's indifference to the viewer's experience, they also mark the possibility of imagining *Carpoolers* as something more than commodity alone. For not unlike the theatrical artwork's appeal to viewers (or readers), the commodity must appeal to consumers if it is to fetch the best price on the market. Both artwork and commodity are, on this view, means to different ends, but means all the same. To mark its distance from the commodity, the artwork must make its refusal of any such appeal legible. And it is this problem that a contemporary writer like Herrera takes up.

From this perspective, Makina's fate in the closing pages of *Signs Preceding the End of the World* looks less like a tragedy and more like the victory of the novel's abstracting tendencies over the particularity of its characters and setting. If it is true that Makina seems to perceive her fate in these terms when she sees "that what was happening was not a cataclysm," it is just as true that such tendencies leave us with a world from which history and time appear to have vanished altogether. As we have already seen, this too is our world, in which the triumph of the market economy has precipitated what Paz calls the "twilight of the future," or as Arantes puts it, a neutralization of the "very modern notion of progress—and the temporality of history that made it thinkable," which the term *contemporary* names. Herrera's style, in this sense, takes on a mimetic quality, treating objects abstractly in much the same way as the market demands.

And yet as a way of writing characteristic of a particular period, place, or person—that is, as a specific way of using language—style runs counter to the abstracting tendencies of the trilogy on the whole. The opening pages of *Signs* provides a sense of this style when a sinkhole nearly swallows Makina: "Slippery bitch of a city, she said to herself. Always about to sink back into the cellar" (11). Any translation, of course, will fail to capture Herrera's unique use of language, though the point here is that his style locates his fiction within a particular sociohistorical setting in much the same way that the appearance of *Mexican* does in the scene in which Makina encounters the workers in the Big Chilango. Herrera's language would thus appear to confirm Ian Watt's claim in *The Rise of the Novel* (1957) that the "writer's exclusive aim is to make the words bring his object home to us in all its concrete particularity, whatever the cost in repetition or parenthesis or verbosity" (29). Yet, while his style can be said to pull off this aim, Herrera nonetheless insists that such concrete particularity belongs not only to Mexico or to the border but to the novel's language as well: "I hope one can see the presence of [Mexican] reality in my novels, and of the language that is spoken on the street, but in both cases I do not pretend to reflect reality as it is . . . I am Flaubertian in that sense, I consider that the right word has to be sought. I like to say that style is not surface, style is a form of knowledge" ("Herrera, viajes" 43). This too begins to explain Herrera's extensive use of neologisms throughout the trilogy, like the noun-turned-verb "to verse" (*jarchar*) in *Signs* (which means "to leave").[14] For what such neologisms signal is not simply a refusal to document reality but, more precisely, an effort to underscore the novel's status as a particular kind of thing, what the Artist in *Kingdom Cons* calls a "separate reality."

To put the point this way, however, is already to presuppose something in the novel that makes it look and operate the way it does—to presuppose, in other words, a set of motivations or abstract principles that are neither determined by consumer demand nor a question of "how things present themselves to us." As a particular way of using language, style makes such motivations and principles visible and is therefore a "form of knowledge" not because it reflects reality but rather because it sheds light on what Herrera would describe as a space for "autonomous creation" from which "to think about and look at reality." Despite concluding with the timelessness of the market in which the future approximates the vanishing point, *Signs* is not for all that merely a mirror held up to this state of affairs. Rather, Herrera's novel indicates the degree to which his fiction departs from this perspective by taking up a version of the problem that Cartagena's photography similarly attempts to resolve—namely, how to visualize the abstract in the concrete. Mobilizing the same literary means that a critic like Ludmer believes postautonomous literatures have exhausted, Herrera's trilogy also disavows the postcritical commitment to immediacy. Makina's journey through the nine layers of Mictlán, the kingdom of the dead, insists not on *fabricating* present but on representing it, depicting *lo fronterizo* as a set of social relations governed by the same abstract laws, structures, and functions behind the concrete reality of violence and exploitation on the border and across the globe today. And in confronting such abstractions head-on, Herrera's attentiveness to form intimates the possibility of another world, making the contemporary Latin American novel a sign preceding the end of this one.

*   *   *

EMILIO SAURI is associate professor in the Department of English at the University of Massachusetts Boston. His research focuses on literature and visual art from Latin America

---

14   As Dillman points out, "The word is derived from *jarchas* (from the Arabic *kharja*, meaning exit), which were short Mozarabic verses or couplets tacked on to the end of longer Arabic or Hebrew poems written in Al-Andalus, the region we now call Spain" (112).

and the United States and reads these in relation to the development of the global economy from the end of the nineteenth century to the beginning of the twenty-first. He is coeditor of two collections, *Literature and the Global Contemporary* (2017) and *Literary Materialisms* (2013) as well as a special issue of the journal *nonsite* on Latin American literature and theory. He is currently at work on a monograph on literature and the ends of autonomy in the Americas.

Works Cited

Alonso, Carlos. "The Novel without Literature." *Novel* 44.1 (2011): 3–5.

Alworth, David. *Site Reading: Fiction, Art, Social Form*. Princeton: Princeton UP, 2015.

Arantes, Paulo. "O futuro que passou." Interview by Ivan Marsiglia. *Estadão* 22 June 2013 <http://www.estadao.com.br/noticias/geral,o-futuro-que-passou,1045705>.

———. *O novo tempo do mundo: E outros estudos sobre a era da emergência*. São Paulo: Boitempo, 2015.

Beasley-Murray, Jon. *Posthegemony: Political Theory and Latin America*. Minneapolis: U of Minnesota P, 2010.

Bolaño, Roberto. *2666*. Trans. Natasha Wimmer. New York: Picador, 2009.

Brouillette, Sarah. *Literature and the Creative Economy*. Stanford: Stanford UP, 2004.

Cartagena, Alejandro. "Alejandro Cartagena Interview." By Jonathan Blaustein. *APhoto-Editor* 26 Sept. 2012 <aphotoeditor.com/2012/09/26/alejandro-cartagena-interview/>.

———. "Beauty. Simplicity. Complexity." Interview by Kai Behrmann. *Art of Creative Photography* 9 Oct. 2016 <artofcreativephotography.com/contemporary-photography/alejandro-cartagena/>.

———. *Carpoolers*. Alejandro Cartagena, 2014 <https://alejandrocartagena.com/h/home/carpoolers/>.

———. *Suburbia Mexicana: Fragmented Cities*. Alejandro Cartagena, 2006–9 <alejandrocartagena.com/h/home/fragmented-cities/>.

Chibber, Vivek. *Postcolonial Theory and the Specter of Capital*. New York: Verso, 2013.

Cunningham, David. "'Very Abstract and Terribly Concrete': Capitalism and the Theory of the Novel." *Novel* 42.2 (2009): 311–17.

Dillman, Lisa. *Translator's Note. Signs Preceding the End of the World. By Yuri Herrera*. New York: And Other Stories, 2015.

Di Stefano, Eugenio, and Emilio Sauri. "Making It Visible: Latin Americanist Criticism, Literature, and the Question of Exploitation Today." *nonsite* 13 (2014) <http://nonsite.org/article/making-it-visible>.

Emmelhainz, Irmgard. *La tiranía del sentido común: La reconversión neoliberal en México*. Mexico City: Paradiso, 2016.

Fried, Michael. *Absorption and Theatricality: Painting and Beholder in the Age of Diderot*. Chicago: U of Chicago P, 1980.

———. *Why Photography Matters as Art as Never Before*. New Haven: Yale UP, 2008.

García Márquez, Gabriel. *One Hundred Years of Solitude*. Trans. Gregory Rabassa. New York: Harper Perennial, 1998.

Gomez, Ramiro. *No Splash (after David Hockney's "A Bigger Splash," 1967)*. 2013. Painting. Museum of Contemporary Art San Diego, San Diego, CA.

Herrera, Yuri. "Border Characters." Interview by Aaron Bady. *Nation* 2 Dec. 2015 < www.the nation.com/article/border-characters/ > .

———. *Kingdom Cons*. Trans. Lisa Dillman. New York: And Other Stories, 2017.

———. *Signs Preceding the End of the World*. Trans. Lisa Dillman. New York: And Other Stories, 2015.

———. *The Transmigration of Bodies*. Trans. Lisa Dillman. New York: And Other Stories, 2016.

———. "Yuri Herrera: 'La literatura pone problemas abstractos en una escala humana.'" Interview by Marcela Mazzei. *Revista Ñ, Clarín* 25 Oct. 2011 < www.clarin.com/rn /literatura/Entrevista_Yuri_Herrera_0_r1XwujhvQx.html > .

———. "Yuri Herrera: 'Las palabras a la que acudimos tienen historia.'" Interview by Víctor Vimos. *Telégrafo* 18 Aug. 2014 < www.eltelegrafo.com.ec/noticias/carton-piedra/34 /yuri-herrera-las-palabras-a-la-que-acudimos-tienen-historia > .

———. "Yuri Herrera, viajes hasta el final del mundo conocido." Interview by Lino González Veiguela. *Clarín* 15.85 (2010): 42–44.

Jameson, Fredric. *Valences of the Dialectic*. New York: Verso, 2009.

Knoblauch, Loring. "Alejandro Cartagena, *Carpoolers*." *Collector Daily* 20 Nov. 2014 < https: //collectordaily.com/alejandro-cartagena-carpoolers/ > .

Kornbluh, Anna. "We Have Never Been Critical: Toward the Novel as Critique." *Novel* 50.3 (2017): 397–408.

Ludmer, Josefina. "Literaturas postautónomas 2.0." *Z Cultural* 4.1 (2011) < http://revistaz cultural.pacc.ufrj.br/literaturas-postautonomas-2-0-de-josefina-ludmer/ > .

Marx, Karl. *Grundrisse*. Trans. Martin Nicolaus. New York: Penguin, 1993.

———. Preface. *Capital*. Vol. 1. Trans. Ben Fowkes. New York: Penguin, 1992. 89–93.

McCann, Matt. "Piling in a Flatbed to Get By in the Suburbs." *New York Times* 27 June 2012 < lens.blogs.nytimes.com/2012/06/27/car-poolers/ > .

McDonald, Jessica. "Power Lines." Afterword. *Carpoolers*. By Alejandro Cartagena. Mexico City: Fonca, 2014.

McMichael, Philip. *Development and Social Change: A Global Perspective*. 3rd ed. Thousand Oaks: Pine Forge, 2006.

Mezzadra, Sandro, and Brett Neilson. *Border as Method or, the Multiplication of Labor*. Durham: Duke UP, 2013.

Michaels, Walter Benn. *The Beauty of a Social Problem*. Chicago: U of Chicago P, 2015.

Paz, Octavio. "In Search of the Present." Trans. Anthony Stanton. *New Republic* 7–14 Jan. 1991, 33–38.

Reber, Dierdra. *Coming to Our Senses: Affect and an Order of Things for Global Culture*. New York: Columbia UP, 2016.

Salgado, Sebastião. *Workers: An Archaeology of the Industrial Age*. New York: Aperture, 1993.

Sánchez Prado, Ignacio. "La 'generación' como ideología cultural: El FONCA y la institucionalización de la 'narrativa joven' en México." *Explicación de textos literarios* 36.1–2 (2007–8): 8–20.

Sauri, Emilio. "Autonomy after Autonomy, or The Novel beyond Nation: Roberto Bolaño's *2666*." *Literature and the Global Contemporary*. Ed. Sarah Brouillette, Mathias Nilges and Emilio Sauri. New York: Palgrave Macmillan, 2017. 49–66.

Schwarz, Roberto. *Two Girls and Other Essays*. New York: Verso, 2013.

Siskind, Mariano. "The Globalization of the Novel and the Novelization of the Global. A Critique of World Literature." *Comparative Literature* 62.4 (2010): 336–60.

Thompson, Adam. "Mortgage Lending: Astonishing Comeback from the Tequila Crisis." *Financial Times* 11 Dec. 2007 <https://www.ft.com/content/edb8dfa4-a7c2-11dc-9485-0000779fd2ac>.

Watt, Ian. *The Rise of the Novel: Studies in Defoe, Richardson, and Fielding*. Berkeley: U of California P, 1965.

Something Extraordinary Keeps Happening:
J. G. Ballard's Enclave World

MATTHEW HART

Something extraordinary has happened at Pangbourne Village. The adult residents of this luxurious gated community have been messily slaughtered; their children have all disappeared. Scotland Yard sends a forensic psychologist, Dr. Richard Greville, to investigate. A white Englishman of middling age, he is more Lestrade than Holmes, but he eventually deduces what the reader has sensed for a while: terrorized by their perfect lives, the children have murdered their parents and run off to an existence of feral militancy. "By a grim paradox," Greville writes in his final report, "the instrument of the parents' deaths was the devoted and caring regime which they had instituted" (Ballard, *Running* 82). This is a skeletal description of *Running Wild*, a 1988 novella by the British writer J. G. Ballard.

Frank Prentice has done something inexplicable. By all accounts, he enjoyed life in Estrella de Mar, a luxury expat retirement community in southern Spain; now he has confessed to murder and looks forward only to a long stay in prison. Meanwhile, Charles Prentice, a white Englishman of middling age, has arrived in Spain to seek out the truth about his brother's crimes. More Hastings than Poirot, Charles slowly discovers that his brother has become embroiled in a bizarre psychosocial experiment in which Estrella de Mar—one link in a chain of expatriate enclaves so sleepy that, within them, time is said to have died—is being shocked back into life by the programmatic commission of criminal acts (Ballard, *Cocaine* 224). Such licensed psychopathy is, Frank's coconspirators argue, the only true defense against a slow civilizational descent into dementia. I offer here the barest outline of *Cocaine Nights*, a 1996 novel by J. G. Ballard.

Paul Sinclair is worried about his wife. A white Englishman of middling age, Paul lives in the French corporate campus of Eden-Olympia, a "luxury enclave" perched in the hills above the blue waters of the Mediterranean (Ballard, *Super-Cannes* vii). Jane Sinclair is a doctor, and she has come to France to replace her friend, David Greenwood, whose term as medic-in-residence ended when he gunned down several of the campus's finest corporate citizens. More Unnamed Narrator than Monsieur Dupin, Paul gradually begins to investigate his wife's corruption at the hands of the campus leadership, who believe that only "a voluntary and sensible psychopathy" provides the route to "a shared moral order" (64). Such are the narrative premises of J. G. Ballard's novel *Super-Cannes*, first published in the year 2000.

We often disparage plot summary as the lowest sort of criticism—but here, I hope, the exercise proves instructive, not least because this opening inventory should also include Ballard's final two novels: 2003's *Millennium People* (academics and media types rebel in a condo development) and 2006's *Kingdom Come* (petty-bourgeois rioting in a megamall). This is a programmatic novelistic project, even greater in scope than Ballard's 1970s sequence of urban dystopias, which began with *Crash* (1973), continued with *Concrete Island* (1974), and culminated in the magnificently

Novel: A Forum on Fiction 51:2   DOI 10.1215/00295132-6846120   © 2018 by Novel, Inc.

unhinged *High-Rise* (1975). For all Ballard's often-noted iconoclasm, there is arguably no contemporary British novelist with a more recognizable sensibility and
style. Reviews of his work have long emphasized, whether in approbation or condemnation, the way it reiterates a signature iconography: "birds, low-flying aircraft,
pool after empty swimming pool" (Miéville); "low-flying aircraft, wrecked auto-
mobiles, drained swimming pools, abandoned hotels" (Dirda); "empty swimming
pools, abandoned hotels, deserted runways" (Garner). But Ballard's late novels do
not only feature a repetitive sequence of symbols and images; they are also built
around an unusually restricted range of plots, characters, and—especially—settings.
Indeed, it is this combination of recursive qualities that explains why the lexicog-
raphers of the *Collins English Dictionary* thought to add "Ballardian" to their stock of
adjectives ("Ballardian"). Ballardian fiction transgresses but does not transcend; it
resists definition but ends up in the dictionary.

Since his death in 2009, Ballard's star has generally risen in academic criticism,
with that scholarly activity focused on such diverse topics as climate change (Clarke),
naturalism (Stanley), New Wave science fiction (Sykes), apocalyptic discourse
(Gomel), and the history of World War II in Asia (Kong) and Europe (Baxter).
My goal in this essay, however, is to consider how the late sequence provides a
ground for speculating about Ballard's entire oeuvre. I begin, then, with a schematic
description of the late sequence, which as a whole repeats five signature narrative
elements:

1. At the level of plot, upright citizens and ostensible innocents commit
    criminal acts. These characters may have been seduced into violence and
    larceny but they cannot usually be described as coerced.
2. A pair of interlocking themes predominate: that the millennial world is
    characterized by a suffocating blandness; and that human beings, to quote
    one of Ballard's many pronouncements on the subject, are genetically
    "violent and dangerous creatures" (Rugoff). Under such conditions,
    apparently psychopathic behaviors get figured as a kind of psycho-
    social immune response.
3. A familiar kind of questing narrator-protagonist is featured: a white
    Englishman, neither estranged from the professional bourgeoisie nor its
    representative type; not so dull that he cannot work out what is going on
    but never quite smart enough to stay ahead of the unfolding conspiracy.
4. The aesthetic development of a speculative generic hybrid combines
    elements of dystopian realism, detective fiction, and the thriller. These
    are all generic traditions in which Ballard has experimented before—so,
    in this sense, the programmatic nature of the late cycle is not just a
    matter of the qualities these five novels have in common: they also gather
    and synthesize generic characteristics otherwise scattered throughout
    his oeuvre.
5. A schematic fictional geography is created that is ostensibly realist,
    in the sense that each novel is individually committed to narrative
    verisimilitude, but that, when considered at the level of the novelistic

sequence, tends toward allegory. In this narrative geography, the gated
enclave figures as a privileged spatial agent within the diegesis. The
central quality of these enclave zones is that they are, paradoxically, at
once set off from any shared social fabric *and* representative of general
psychic and material qualities.

It is this last aspect that particularly concerns me. In what follows, I analyze Ballard's enclave settings as aesthetic and social phenomena, proceeding in that order. At
the level of method, my essay begins with critical description. This approach is as
much exegetical as analytic; it follows the grain of Ballard's writing to show how
the first four elements of his late novel sequence—criminality, social blandness, the
questing narrator-protagonist, and hybrid speculative form—coalesce within, and
might even be said to predict, the fifth element: his peculiar enclave settings.[1] I borrow
the term *critical description* from Sharon Marcus and Stephen Best, who briefly define
it as a method motivated by the belief "that texts can reveal their own truths because
texts mediate themselves; what we think theory brings to texts (form, structure,
meaning) is already present in them" (11).[2] As I shall show, Ballard's novels certainly
attempt self-mediation and self-theorization; indeed, the late sequence exemplifies
this quality. Nevertheless, any full exploration of the late novels' auto-interpretative
energies must go beyond the project of critical description, which by itself produces a
historically flat and argumentatively recursive account of Ballard's spatially fragmented narrative settings.

For this reason, the final sections of this essay take a historical turn that begins
with Ballard's own account of how his late fictions, to paraphrase Martin Amis,
give shape to the Chinese landscapes that shaped him. For Ballard, the enclave
settings of his late novels evoke nothing so much as the extraterritorial precincts
of his youth in wartime Shanghai, and especially the Lunghua Civilian Assembly
Centre, the Japanese internment camp in which he was imprisoned between 1943
and 1945. The problem for us, though, is that Ballard's account of life in Lunghua—
particularly the one given in his autobiographical novel *Empire of the Sun* (1984) but
also in more straightforwardly factual prose narratives, such as his memoir, *Miracles
of Life* (2008)—contrasts greatly with that provided by his fellow internees. How, in
the light of these discrepancies, can we better understand Ballard's claim that "a
large part of my fiction has been an attempt to evoke [Shanghai] by means other than
memory" (Ballard, *Miracles* 7)? More importantly, since I am not especially interested in just setting the record straight: how might comparing Ballard's Lunghua
with the camp described by his fellow inmates better explain the recursively programmatic nature of his late settings?

---

[1]   For reading with the grain, see Timothy Bewes, who emphasizes the way the novel, for György
Lukács, is not just "read, it *reads*" (3).

[2]   Marcus and Best have more recently collaborated with Heather Love on a special issue of
Representations, Description across the Disciplines, their introduction to which enlarges on the
term *critical description*, specifically crediting the anthropologist Anna Tsing (Marcus, Love,
and Best 3).

My goal, then, is not to dismiss Ballard's autocritical reflections. The spatial and social relations among Ballard's late fiction and nonfiction prose describe a path leading back through his body of work, showing us how to read his oeuvre as an oeuvre; they connect his novels' form and feel to their real and imagined settings; and they ultimately show how and why descriptive criticism still requires the third and fourth dimensions of historical analysis. The need for a historical perspective is, in fact, especially pressing with Ballard's late work. By the final pages of this essay, the late sequence will prove to be more grounded in the society and culture of the British mid-century than in the contemporary world it ostensibly depicts. In making these arguments, this essay covers a fair bit of ground. But it will always revert back, like the late novels themselves, to a single argumentative topos: the proposition that Ballard's work poses the problem of the ordinary extraordinary.

*   *   *

What does this mean—the ordinary extraordinary? In the first place, there is the way that speculative fiction regularly confronts the problem of making bizarre events believable. This is certainly how China Miéville, speaking in an interview, describes weird and speculative genres, which he says begin by positing "something impossible" and then grant that impossibility "its own terms and systematicity" (Gordon 366). Transposing Miéville's language to Ballard's rather differently weird fiction, we might agree that this duality makes novels like *Cocaine Nights* at once "carnivalesque" and "rationalist," for they limn social upheaval even as they ascribe predictable causes to disorderly effects (Gordon 366).

The peculiarly Ballardian version of this problem is that, while his late sequence depicts worlds blown apart by criminality, it also renders such violence ordinary. In the novel set in the French corporate campus, *Super-Cannes*, the libidinal frisson of mugging a stranger answers the dilemma of how one sustains life within "an Eden without a snake," a world denuded of temptation and thus of transgression and guilt (258). "People are like children, they need constant stimulation," claims the Dionysian tennis pro, Bobby Crawford, in *Cocaine Nights*: "Name me a time when civic pride and the arts both flourished and there wasn't extensive crime" (260–61). In this way, Bobby's criminal acts represent a kind of therapeutic antigenic assault, as in a vaccine, on the overly regulated and somnolent social body of his Spanish expat community. Crime may be extraordinary, but in these novels, it is not only performed against a backdrop of deadly ordinariness; crime only becomes meaningful for Bobby and company when set within this problem of social blandness.

But when crime becomes programmatic, it risks losing its exceptional and antigenic status. Because criminal acts are therapeutic responses to a supposedly basic psychosocial problem—"people are like children, they need constant stimulation"—each unlawful act tends toward predictability and abstraction. There is obviously a difference of kind and degree between a petty cocaine deal and a sexual assault or a murder. Still, taken as a whole—which is, after all, how both Bobby and Ballard ask us to take them—the social and affective qualities that make any particular outrage outrageous here disappear before the generalizable fact of a generic transgress. At a certain point in these novels, it no longer really matters much what anybody actually *does*, only that they *ought not to be doing it*.

Things get more ordinary still. Because the late novel cycle reiterates the same few basic elements, predictability gets baked into its very aesthetic. I have described the late cycle as systematic in nature—and it is true, Ballard's double commitment to genre fiction and the postsurrealist avant-garde clearly lends his work a recursive quality, the novels methodically working through a deliberately restricted range of formal and social types. But one could also say that, especially when reread back-to-back, in the way one does when researching an essay, the late novels are not just programmatic: they can be boring. It is not just that their protagonists tend to blur together; the same is true of their several antagonists. Wilder Penrose from *Super-Cannes* is a psychologist, while Bobby Crawford is a tennis pro, but they possess the same saturnine physicality, habit of speechmaking, and gift for divining and satisfying people's needs. Likewise, Dr. Tony Maxted, the psychiatrist figure in *Kingdom Come*, shares a muscular body with Penrose and a surname and profession with Dr. Harold Maxted, one of the adult victims in *Running Wild*—notwithstanding the fact that "Maxted" is a name familiar to Ballard readers from one of the surrogate father figures in *Empire of the Sun*. Again, this is an incomplete list, meant only to suggest that the qualities that make Ballard's late fictions unusual are the same ones that, over the course of the sequence, produce an aesthetic affect similar to that which Sianne Ngai calls *stuplimity*, "in which astonishment is paradoxically mixed with boredom" (271). So if this paragraph about novelistic form has once again devolved into the low summary of character types and relations, then that is because Ballard's late characters do not represent rare subjective states any more than they embody exquisite new possibilities in narrative point of view. Better to describe them as affectively null moves within a formal game. And it is the same game, played repeatedly across five sets, by the same men, with no tiebreaks: 6–6, 6–6, 6–6, 6–6, 6–6. Extraordinary acts with ordinary effects. How do we get to enclave settings from here?

*   *   *

The problem of extraordinary ordinariness is, at root, a variation on the question of the exception and the rule. In *Cocaine Nights*, Bobby Crawford's criminal spree shakes up Estrella de Mar and is thus a kind of diversion from the norm. And yet Bobby is not a revolutionary; he just believes criminality creates a better sort of retirement community. Ballard's antagonists do not advocate for truly revolutionary alternatives, unimaginable from within the penumbra of the present. They are more like Jean Bodin's sovereign prince, who embodies the law by standing beyond it—a figure whose authority stems from his location at once within and without the social field, marked by the power "to give law to all in general and to each in particular, and not to receive law from anyone but God" (59). This kind of decisionist political theology requires us to think of the ruler as standing at once over and apart from the ruled; it therefore produces the peculiar spatial relation that Giorgio Agamben calls the *exceptio*, in which the thing excluded proves to be constitutive of that in relation to which it stands outside (20).

This same spatial logic underlies Ballard's late settings, which are all zones of peculiar distinction: outsides within the inside of a territory. In *Millennium People*, the Chelsea Marina housing development is described as a "re-education" and "labour camp" (109); it is dubbed an "anomalous enclave" (265) and, eventually, compared to a "republic" (294). In *Kingdom Come*, we enter the Metro-Centre, a mall complex also described as a "Republic" (213) as well as "a self-contained universe" (218). Yet as much as these places stand apart, like so many Liechtensteins piercing the British body politic, they also typify what, talking in interview, Ballard descri-bed as the core geographic quality of contemporary metropolitan life, which he found especially visible in Europe since the 1970s but also evident in the Shanghai International Settlement of his youth: the way that, "for reasons of security" and economic advantage, "middle-class professionals . . . [are] subtracting themselves from the whole [arena of] civic interactions that depend on them, virtually con-ducting an internal immigration" (Sellars). Ballard's enclave settings are, in this sense, consistent with social-scientific research about the contemporary prolifera-tion of enclave settlements—for instance, Ines Gleisner and company's description of the human geography of the twenty-first century as a "territorial patchwork of introvert enclaves located side by side, each within the other." This is a phenomenon that anthropologists such as Pal Nyiri have linked to the global resurgence of extraterritorial geographies such as those that pockmarked the South China coast between the First Opium War and WWII.[3] Here, then, are isolate spaces that are at once typical of the world they exclude.

A fuller extrapolation of this argument would require evidencing the his-torical argument that extraterritorial spaces such as embassies and international zones are fundamental to the political geography of so-called globalization. They are the exceptions that prove the rule: nonnational spaces that demonstrate how key aspects of worldwide political economy are still very much projects of and for national elites and institutions.[4] Still, this essay is not about global politi-cal economy; instead, it takes up the argumentative burden of showing how the contemporary novel gives dynamic formal expression to extraterritorial space, both as it is and as it is imagined. For Ballard's enclave world cannot be explained in terms of some static homology between real and fictional spaces. Though it is possible to view Ballard's settings as what Franco Moretti calls "abstracts of social relationships" (59), they nevertheless possess a powerful semiautonomy. As formal elements in a programmatic novelistic sequence, they not only trail their generic history behind them; they possess a kind of hyperbolic unreality— a literary quality that I am describing here in the language of extraordinary

[3]   See also the work of Aihwa Ong, whose account of "graduated sovereignty" in East Asia provides a broader framework for understanding how the disaggregation of political geography allows for the "differential treatment of populations according to ethno-racial differences, and the dictates of development programs" (65).

[4]   For variations on this argument, each consistent with this article's emphasis on the extraterri-torial spatial logic of the enclave, see, in addition to those texts already cited: Mayaan Amir and Ruti Sela, Étienne Balibar, Keller Easterling, Sandro Mezzadra and Brett Neilson, Kal Raustiala, and Eyal Weizman.

ordinariness—that prevents them from being wholly absorbed within, or explained in terms of, the history of the present.[5]

To be more specific, Ballard's narrative geographies possess what Eric Hayot, in his recent theory of literary world making, calls the "anthropological" quality common to literary genres that, at the level of setting, begin by positing a "double world" (46). First, there is the special zone of the world apart. That zone might best be exemplified by the fortified postapocalyptic encampments that litter contemporary literary dystopias such as Octavia Butler's *Parable of the Sower* (1993), Margaret Atwood's *The Year of the Flood* (2009), or Chang-Rae Lee's *On Such a Full Sea* (2014). Or, to develop the example that Hayot and Ballard both cite, we might recall the "Paradise Incorporated, and Highly Restricted" of Raymond Chandler's Idle Valley, the Los Angeles subdivision at the heart of his 1953 masterpiece *The Long Goodbye* (Chandler 620; see also Hayot 43–47; and Sellars). Notwithstanding the differences between the dystopia and the noir, or between 1930s California suburbs and near-future wastelands, the same general spatial relation applies in all these examples. Against and around the exceptional zone, there exists a second world: the so-called normal world, or sociogeographic "whole," within which the extraordinary zone is contained and within which it is produced (Hayot 46–47). In this same way, Ballard's enclaves are poised between being representative microcosms and islands of peculiar perversion. The line that describes the border between the Metro-Centrer and the London suburbs, or between Estrella de Mar and the Costa del Sol, is at once the "aperture or bridge" that joins those enclaves to the world and the wall or moat that allows us to see them as distinct (Hayot 47). Herein lies their speculative generic promise: their capacity to at once imagine an extraordinary world and project it as ordinary.

*   *   *

Novel and sequence, exception and rule, enclave and territory, example and genre: working through these nested antitheses allows us to consider Ballard's settings as something more than, to quote David Alworth's recent book *Site Reading*, an impoverished and "static framework for narrative action" (19). In Ballard's late sequence, setting is more than a frame; more than the "ground" against which the "figure" of character is made visible; more than a proxy for "atmosphere" or "tone."[6] It is all of these things, of course: locale, background, atmosphere, mood—even milieu.[7] But beyond this, Ballard's late sequence does not just thematize individual spaces; in it, setting becomes the subject of the novelistic form, with the

---

[5]   For the classic attack on homological relationships between literature and society, expressed as a defense of art's semiautonomy, see Jameson 24–33.

[6]   For the figure/ground analogy as a way of conceiving of setting as a matrix for defining character, see Chatman 138–41. For the complaint that "setting . . . so readily symbolic, becomes, in some modern theories, 'atmosphere' or 'tone,'" see Wellek and Warren 224.

[7]   For the classic account of setting as milieu, in which there exists a "demonic" unity of person and place, see Auerbach 470–80.

effect that, to paraphrase Mieke Bal (139), enclaves emerge as objects of presentation within the diegesis—an acting place rather than simply a place of action.

Now, I admit, it is not a surprise to say of a novel that in it, genre, character, plot, and setting become mutually constitutive. (We are so used to that idea that our critical clichés try to encapsulate it: "Austen's Bath," "Dostoevsky's St. Petersburg," "Joyce's Dublin.") But it remains true that Ballard's late novels feature an unusually tight relation between setting and their other formal elements. And it is true that the programmatic quality of Ballard's late sequence owes a great deal to the way this tight relation is so tightly reiterated across the sequence's individual parts. What we have, here, is tightness squared. While the spatial logic of Ballard's late novels may partly be a function of their ordinary generic DNA, there is still something extraordinary about their commitment to doing the same thing repeatedly, in the same kind of space, within and among each part of the sequence.

The danger with this reading, though, is that it, too, quickly becomes generic in a bad sense, evincing a worryingly symmetrical relationship to its objects of study: crime is ordinary, exceptions are ordinary, enclaves are everywhere, and, oh, this is all a function of common generic patterns. We seem to be a long way from Alworth's account of setting as "a vibrant assemblage of human and nonhuman actors that forms a complex social unit" (14). This is what I meant earlier when I promised that, for literary scholars, Ballard's late sequence occasions an encounter with the limits of critical description as a method. If the purpose of that method is "to indicate what the text says about itself" (Marcus and Best 11), then it runs out of steam when not only Ballard's texts but, presumably, many other generic relatives are supposed to say the same things about the same kinds of spatial relations. The extraordinary truth of genre here becomes indistinguishable from the banality of the postcritical impulse. How, then, to comprehend Ballard's settings as more than generic effects?

*   *   *

In July 2015, I began some research in an attempt to do just that. The Ballard Papers in the British Library mostly comprise the author's manuscripts. The collection of personal papers is small by comparison, but does include a few boxes relating to his childhood in Shanghai's International Settlement. I was interested in those papers because Ballard himself repeatedly told us how to fix his enclave settings in space and time. The earliest version of this answer comes in a 1963 essay-manifesto, "Time, Memory, and Inner Space," in which Ballard's question—"How far do the landscapes of one's childhood . . . provide an inescapable background to all one's imaginative writing?"—prompts the answer that the future setting of his novel *The Drowned World* (1962) represents the "fusion of my childhood memories of Shanghai and those of my last ten years in London" (*User's Guide* 199). He writes of Shanghai that his earliest memories of the city all take place "during the annual long summer of floods, when the streets of the city were two or three feet deep in a brown silt-laden water, and where the surrounding countryside, in the center of the flood-table of the Yangtze, was an almost continuous mirror of drowned paddy fields and irrigation canals stirring sluggishly in the hot sunlight" (*User's Guide* 199). And, no doubt, his novels and stories make a great deal out of the symbolism of water out of place: not just drained swimming pools, but flooded fields, brackish drinking water, culverts and streams and great rivers clogged with the bodies of men and machines.

Following the critical and commercial success of *Empire of the Sun*—the publication of which was quickly followed by Stephen Spielberg's 1987 movie adaptation—Ballard began to go further, arguing that his childhood supplied him with a kind of authorial firmware. Talking to Hans Ulrich Obrist in 2003, he commented that it had become "a set of images and rhythms, dreams and expectations that are probably the basic operating formulas that govern my life to this day" (*Extreme* 384). This thesis is epitomized by his repeated use of the phrase "from Shanghai to Shepperton," which from the 1980s onward provided Ballard with the title or subtitle to two memoirs and a collection of autobiographical journalism and which was appropriated in 2006 as the title of an academic conference on his work.[8] In that sibilant phrase, the city of Ballard's youth and the London suburb in which he lived for fifty years figure as original cause and sustaining effect of his personal and literary life. As Roger Luckhurst put it in his crucial early book on Ballard, in the autobiographical narratives, Shanghai becomes "a disjunct temporal zone" that projects the "future dissolution" of both Britain's colonial past and its "neo-colonial" present (45). In this untimely chronotope, Luckhurst concludes, the borders around the Shanghai International Settlement describe "a strange loop of time [in which] memories of the past, as already future, maroon the present" (45). Ballard's settings all look the same, their creator says, because they are the same; they are allegories of Shanghai, reborn to us as the future past of a catastrophic present.

There is no gainsaying the literary affects of this autocritical gambit. The enclave zones of late novels such as *Cocaine Nights*, circumscribed by boundaries and punctuated by gatehouses, very obviously evoke the borders of the International Settlement and Lunghua camp as they are depicted in *Empire*. Beyond even this, there is the way *The Kindness of Women*, the 1991 sequel and supplement to *Empire*, takes this spatial resemblance and makes it the basis for a grand autocritical myth in which every landscape in Ballard's fiction—European or Asian, extraterrestrial or extraterritorial—is reworked into a transmuted memory of Lunghua. Thus when that novel's first-person narrator, Jim Ballard, is accused of mooning about the airfields and wetlands of East Anglia and West Canada wearing a "Lunghua look," he insists that what one person experiences as traumatic memory another reinvents as a kind of poetry: "[P]eople create their own mythologies," he says, having just described a dead Turkish aviator, his plane suspended in the waters of a Canadian

---

[8]   "From Shanghai to Shepperton" is the title of a memoir first published in the Northeast London Polytechnic review of science fiction, *Foundation* 24 (1982). In a miniature allegory of Ballardian circulation and canonization (his work moving from the para-state–funded institutions of the London underground scene, to the global traffic in cult fiction, to the academic sphere), it was then republished in a 1984 Ballard edition of the Bay Area journal *RE/Search* before being reprinted again in an academic trade anthology, *The Profession of Science Fiction* (1992). "Shanghai to Shepperton" later provided the title to the "Autobiographies" section of *A User's Guide to the Millennium* (1996) and the subtitle to the full-dress memoir, *Miracles of Life* (2008). The academic conference, organized by Jeanette Baxter (Anglia Ruskin University), was held at the University of East Anglia, May 5–6, 2006.

lake, as having flown "home" (106). Ballard has described *Kindness* as narrating "my life seen through the mirror of the fiction prompted by that life" (qtd. in *Self* 360). It is a metafictional novel, beginning in and often educing Shanghai, about a writer's impossible struggle to be "wholly done with the past" (*Kindness* 311). That struggle is "impossible" because it involves trying to move beyond, through artistic means, the original violence that stimulates the protagonist's very aesthetic imagination. This is an unlikely prospect for a Ballardian hero. After all, this is the author who insisted "psychopathology should be kept alive as a repository, probably the last repository, of the imagination" (*Extreme* 229).

Being done with the past is also impossible in another sense. If *Kindness* narrates Jim's struggle to stop turning his trauma into art, then this plotline collides directly with the novel's second metafictional aspect: the way it is constructed out of systematic allusions to the real Jim Ballard's body of fiction. Each chapter of *Kindness* is written so as to evoke one of its author's best-known works. Thus, most obviously, the opening chapters conjure, rewrite, and supplement *Empire of the Sun*. The chapter titled "The Exhibition" does not mention *Crash*, but Chris Beckett is right to describe that novel as its "invisible, radiating centre" (15). Most typically, *Kindness* will evoke a previous work without much distorting the weave of its own narrative. In "Magic World," for instance, Jim watches his children play in their new suburban home: "Water surrounded Shepperton—the river, the gravel lakes, and the reservoirs of the metropolitan water board whose high embankments formed the horizon of our lives. Once I told Miriam that we were living on the floor of a marine world that had invaded our minds, and that the people of Shepperton were a new form of aquatic mammal, creatures of a new *Water Babies*" (117).

There is nothing here too disruptively metadiagetic. Alert readers would soon notice, however, that Jim's *Water Babies* story recalls *The Drowned World*, the surreal postapocalyptic novel he would have been writing at this point in his life: a tale set in 2145, in which human survivors of planetary flooding uncover the floor (it happens to be London) beneath the tropical lagoon in which they have gathered. At the end, *The Drowned World*'s protagonist, haunted by an "ancient organic memory" (89), flees south into the sea, betting on the unfinished business of evolution and seeking rebirth as a "second Adam" (198).

All of this points back to Ballard's description of *Kindness* as "not just an autobiographical novel" but one "written with the full awareness of the fiction that that adult life generated" (qtd. in *Self* 360). What Jim experiences as a personal dilemma, *Kindness* restages at the level of an oeuvre. Ballard positions what happened in Shanghai as the tropological and topological key to a compulsively iterative literary world, including the one conjured by *Kindness* itself. That novel ends with a series of scenes that initially promise release from this cycle of repetition. Jim is in Los Angeles to attend the premiere of Stephen Spielberg's film adaptation of *Empire of the Sun*. He imagines that seeing his childhood projected onscreen has freed him "in a profound catharsis": "All the powers of modern film had come together for this therapeutic exercise. The puzzle had solved itself; the mirror, as I had promised, had been broken from within" (*Kindness* 341). Shortly before, he has finally consummated his passion for the White Russian nanny of his adolescence: "We had both been wounded and corrupted by Shanghai . . . and by making love in this California hotel we would prove to each other that the wounds had healed" (339). And yet, as this unlikely fantasy suggests, the story does not end there. Jim and his partner, Cleo, take one last trip to the Pacific coast. They witness the launching of a papyrus boat modeled on Thor Heyerdahl's *Ra*, a "replica of a replica" (342) that cannot help but remind us of Spielberg's cinematic remaking of Ballard's own fictionalization of his childhood—especially since it, too, is being filmed by an onboard cameraman. Jim again muses that he has recovered the happiness lost to him as a child: "[A]ll the murdered dead of a world war had made their peace" (342). But this happy possibility is undercut by his description of the boat, which, beset by lively winds and waves, soon escapes its handlers and is last seen "setting a course across the Pacific, with only its shanghaied cameraman as a crew" (343). At the very same moment that *Kindness* imagines an end to Jim's "Lunghua look," it restores that compulsion to us in its invocation of a "shanghaied" imagination. Even as Jim claims that his Chinese puzzle has solved itself, he is unable to conceive of any other course than that which leads "towards the China shore" (343).

*   *   *

The problem with *this* argument, though, is that its claims are self-authorizing.

I do not mean just that Ballard lends the authority of his own person to the Shanghai-to-Shepperton story but that my own argument-by-description risks tautology. I described *Kindness* so as to interpret it; or, rather, I described its own self-interpretation. In so doing, I treat that novel as at once a question and an answer, as the object of interpretation and as that interpretation itself. This methodological attitude is encouraged, of course, by the reflexive manner in which *Kindness* comments upon its own status as art, even to the point of implying that it is its own interpretation. But we, as critics, do not need to rest in that tautology. In their introduction to *Description across the Disciplines*, Marcus, Love, and Best ask: "Does knowledge have to be different from its object to *be* knowledge?" (9). The example of *Kindness* suggests that our answer should be *yes*. In the first place, to say that the meaning of *Kindness* is accessible at the level of description is to reject what we know philosophically about the nonidentical nature of objects and concepts.[9] More simply, there is just more to say about that novel than any description of it can encompass or justify. We can learn a lot about *Kindness* by describing it, but Ballard's autocritical account of his own fiction can never adequately account for its origins or affects. It is fortunate, then, that the Lunghua folders in the Ballard Papers provide plenty of evidence for the nonidentical relation between the fact of Ballard's fiction and the idea of his personal journey from China to the London suburbs.

It was not a surprise to discover that other detainees from Lunghua disputed Ballard's accounts of what it was like to live there. Ballard's readers have long

---

[9]   Adorno, in *Negative Dialectics*, calls "the thought of unity the measure of heterogeneity," for the reason that "objects do not go into their concepts without leaving a remainder . . . the concept does not exhaust the thing conceived" (5).

known that he is not a reliable witness to his past. His novels clearly reinvent the bald truth of history, most notably in the way *Empire of the Sun* writes Ballard's parents and sister out of his war story, while that novel is also clearly marred by stereotypical depictions of the Shanghainese as passive victims of a geopolitical struggle that they do not even try to direct or control. Still, the Lunghua folders contain correspondence dismissive of basic elements of *Empire*'s veracity. A letter from his fellow internee F. T. Ranson criticizes basic elements of that novel's narrative geography ("the Whangpoo [River] was not visible from the camp and anyway you say it was to the west when in fact it was to the east") and accuses Ballard of making up some events ("I never heard of any collaboration") and ignoring others: "there were escapes—Roy Scott and Louis (forget his name) made it to West China" (Ranson).[10] Above all, these correspondents dislike *Empire*'s "lurid" depiction of camp culture, in which British can-do spirit devolves into late imperial lassitude and in which the protagonist identifies strongly with the Japanese who defeated the forces of the waning British Empire: "I can't help being surprised that you should express admiration for the Japanese and at the same time report that they beat a coolie to death," writes G. S. Dunkley of Henley-on-Thames; "[m]orale in the camps was uniformly good and British internees were far from being remiss in carrying out the many menial jobs which had to be done" (Dunkley).

One can imagine Ballard disdaining these letters as the work of men inert to distinctions between fiction and history. I mention them not because they have surpassing evidentiary value—indeed, the Ballard Papers also contain letters from former internees who found the experience of reading *Empire* "oddly vindicating" and congratulate Ballard on having "caught the flavour of the place" (Reilly). The hostile letters matter because they suggest how we might be able to historicize Ballard's persistent recourse to the "anthropological" space of the *exceptio* in terms that are not reducible to a generic inheritance or autocritical mythmaking. The "Shanghai to Shepperton" tale allowed us to say what Ballard's settings mean to him that they cannot mean to an Octavia Butler or a Raymond Chandler. It pushed us beyond the idea that the programmatic settings of Ballard's late novels are the result of a merely generic compulsion and toward a history of his oeuvre that is at once implicit within the novelistic form of his autofictions and rooted in his personal history. An archival analysis allows us to go still further. By granting us a historical point of contrast outside the circle of Ballard's own life and oeuvre, the Lunghua folders provide grounds for speculation about what his enclave settings mean for the historicity of his fiction in general, including their orientation toward the extraterritorial present. When we step outside the loop of auto-interpretation, not only do we learn more about Ballard's novels; those texts also become capable of telling us more about the worlds they represent and in which they were made. The "Shanghai to Shepperton" story involves rather more than an autocritical claim; it is part of a

---

[10]   Was this F. T. Ranson, who identifies himself as a Fellow of the Royal College of Surgeons, the inspiration for the character Dr. Ransome in *Empire*? If so, it is a connection denied or repressed, for Ranson writes to Ballard: "I cant [*sic*] recognise Dr Ransome unless it is meant to be Cater." In her history of Allied internment by the Japanese military, Bernice Archer refers to a "Dr Cater" (like Ranson, she gives no first name) who taught a medical class in Lunghua (100–101).

historical argument, with its roots in the war but its ends in the present, about the meanings that can be ascribed to extraterritorial enclaves in the wartime 1940s, when the whole system of British semicolonial governance in China had just collapsed. As we shall see, the Lunghua folders supply one-half of that argument—the half that holds out hope for British business as usual on either side of the International Settlement's occupation. The shape of Ballard's Shanghai stories, by contrast, judges the imperial past to be long gone.

*   *   *

Ballard's representation of Lunghua agrees with those of his fellow internees in one crucial way: that the camp was an enclave unto itself. The Ballard Papers include the files of William Braidwood, president of the British Residents' Association of Shanghai (BRA) during the Lunghua internment and also Ballard's father's closest friend. Among Braidwood's files is a narrative history of Lunghua that refers to a Japanese mandate that the camp be self-governing and self-sufficient, even requiring that the internees must themselves punish any civilian who dares to escape from Japanese detention.[11] The Braidwood files also include much evidence of internee initiative and organizational capacity. Soon after internment began, the BRA instituted itself as a complex organism of camp government similar to the Shanghai Municipal Council in which Braidwood and many of his fellow inmates had served before the war. Far more than just distributing rations or making representations to the Japanese, the BRA organized its myriad activities under departments of "Billeting, Kitchen, Public Works, Public Health, Hospital and Clinic, Stores and Canteen, Bank, Gardening and Camp Service" (Braidwood, "Lunghua"). The ambitious nature of camp governance can perhaps be measured by the narrative history's account of how its school, "Lunghwa Academy," provided "instruction in all general subjects up to Cambridge school leaving certificates and London Matriculation standards" (Braidwood, "Lunghua").

Margaret Braidwood did not send her husband's files to Ballard until 1996, years after the publication of *Empire* and *Kindness*—though they were in his keep during the writing of *Miracles of Life*. In any case, their value for us lies in the way they show how the space of the enclave can, without disturbing our sense of its exceptionality, be identified with very different kinds of social practice and ideological value than the extraordinary ordinariness of the disjunct zones we find in Ballard's novels. In the first place, the BRA papers evidence Mark Mazower's complaint—aimed at Agamben's *Homo Sacer*—that exceptional zones, even in extrajudicial detention camps such as Lunghua, are not only characterized by the reduction of *homo politicus* to a state of bare life (Mazower 30–32). Such zones can also be more ordinarily ordinary, in the limited sense that, even in straitened circumstances, people find ways to realize their social solidarities in a manner consistent with life

[11] In the end, the Japanese did not enforce this regulation—though the worst conflicts between the Japanese, the Allied civilians, and the officers of the BRA tended to occur in the wake of detainee escapes, when the Japanese camp commandant would routinely hold the BRA responsible for discouraging and preventing escapes (Braidwood, "Escapes").

beyond or before that zone. Mazower's point is that these gradations apply even to the system of Nazi Laager; it is not hard to extend that analysis to the less deadly and less restrictive world of Lunghua.

The Braidwood memos and reports thus repeatedly affirm social continuities across time, between Lunghua now and the Shanghai International Settlement as it was; as such, they minimize the present spatial disjuncture between life in captivity and freedom outside. Braidwood's Lunghua is still the exception that proves the rule, but not in the sense that the camp represents the geographic localization of a state of affairs that is at once peculiar to the camp and general throughout society. No, for Braidwood, Lunghua is more extratemporal than extraterritorial. It is the present materialization of a *past* state of affairs: a historical bubble, filled with habits of thought and action that did not die with the International Settlement's fall and that might therefore continue after life in Lunghua also comes to an end.

Braidwood's reports are bureaucratic in nature, not introspective—and they may well give a self-serving impression of the BRA's capacity and ideals. His memos and histories nevertheless give the sense that, for this volunteer servant of empire, principles of self-governance and mutual aid were more crucial facts of war than the internees' physical or mental suffering and loss. There is obviously some measure of positive thinking going on; it helps to act as though things can and will continue to be what they were, and mean what they did, before the fall. But the Braidwood papers also contain something worth holding onto. That something is consistent with Mazower's remarks about the way some camps are more exceptional than others; but it is even more in tune with Elaine Scarry's ethical contention that the "acts of thinking" that persist even within states of exception tend not to be recognized as such (15). For Scarry, emergency zones need not be, as Agamben describes them, *kenomatic*: empty of law or reason (Agamben, *State* 6, 48). Instead, as with the kinds of routinized thought that characterize the actions of paramedics or that are enshrined in mutual aid contracts between towns vulnerable to natural disasters, the times and places of an emergency can be thick with public social and legal values. "In an emergency," Scarry writes, "the habits of ordinary life may fall away, but other habits come into play, and determine whether the action performed is fatal or benign" (14). Against extraordinary ordinariness, where the exception becomes the rule, Scarry attends to the resilience and diversity of the ordinary itself. The habits of life that persist within an emergency are still, in a sense, exterior to it. But that constitutive exteriority is temporal rather than strictly spatial, since emergency actions represent ways of acting and thinking decided upon in the part of the past that is ahead of events, before ordinary life became extraordinary.

Braidwood did not always find it easy to be sanguine. Lunghua camp was, however we conceive of it, a terrible and unpredictable place. This difficulty is epitomized in a note from his narrative history, which I found on a scrap of paper floating in a Mylar sleeve: "Barbed-wire surrounded the camp. On the whole the camp was a pleasant one with plenty of space and a number of trees." It is a strangely affecting fragment, with its paratactic swing from barbed wire to open space and the bathos of its meager "number of trees," a quality enhanced by Braidwood's uncharacteristic lapse into semiredundancy, his repetition of the noun "camp" drawing attention to the disjuncture between the fragment's apostrophes. The fragment suggests something of the strain Braidwood must have experienced in pitting his indefatigable industry against the guards' violence, his compatriots' pain and restlessness, and Britain's retreat from empire. Something of the same tone creeps into his November 1945 address to the BRA, which leavens an admission of Britain's diminished global power with the promise that "Chinese leaders have frequently stated that foreign capital will be welcome and . . . that foreign technicians [are] both necessary and welcome" ("Speech"). But it was not to be thus. After the 1949 revolution, both Braidwood and Ballard's father, James, were imprisoned by the Chinese and deported from the country. The chain of continuities that Braidwood attempts to write and administer into being—colonial, wartime, postcolonial—could not be sustained in the context of world war, Chinese revolution, and British imperial retreat across much of South and East Asia.

The art of self-government did not die in Lunghua, even if the end of the war did effectively conclude the semicolonial careers of men like Braidwood and Ballard's father. The younger Ballard, however, will have none of their claims to continuity. It is no surprise that the political geography of Lunghua depicted in *Empire of the Sun* is determined by a violent power (Japanese and, later, American) that remains—spatially, synchronically—*outside within* the camp's precincts. Likewise, that novel associates Japanese captivity not with municipal solidarities but with situations in which "anyone who sacrificed himself for the others soon died too" (119). Rather than a symbol of the temporal continuity between prewar enclave and wartime camp, Ballard's Lunghua is a heterochronic zone, at once the continuation and the demise of the extraterritorial city. Lunghua is "my new Shanghai," Jim says (77). But the space-time of the war is also described as a "peculiar space"—and here the shift to past perfect tense is important—that separates Jim from "the fifty-year-long cocktail party that had been Shanghai" (76, 82).

Ballard's Lunghua is also anything but British, unless that noun names not a nationality but a condition of unacknowledged loss. Like Estrella de Mar, Lunghua may be full of British people, but its very existence signals a loss of national authority and integrity: the "Dream of Empire" died, Ballard insists, not with Ireland in 1922 or India in 1947 but with Japan's victories in Singapore, Hong Kong, and Shanghai (*Miracles* 21). The kinds of enclave space that persist in the late sequence are still scattered about the map, but they are increasingly privatized and they have come home, colonizing European space itself. More than that, Britain's defeat by the Japanese confirmed a reality that, for Ballard, the International Settlement had itself long symbolized. As he depicts it, that enclave was always a zone apart within the British Empire as much as within the Chinese Republic. "With its newspapers in every language and scores of radio stations, Shanghai was a media city before its time," he writes: "90% Chinese" and "100% Americanised" (*Miracles* 4–5). In *Miracles of Life*, Ballard says that at Lunghua he became an American patriot (99); in *Empire*, the protagonist looks at his compatriots and realizes that "he was closer to the Japanese" (136). In his 1993 essay, "First Impressions of London," Ballard wrote of how foreign the English capital appeared to him when he first saw it in 1946: "like Bucharest with a hangover—heaps of rubble, an exhausted ferret-like people defeated by war and still deluded by Churchillian rhetoric" (*User's Guide* 185). Even in the 1990s, he insisted that such fantastic delusion was still going strong: "To understand London now one has to grasp the fact that in this city, as nowhere else in the world, World War II is still going on" (*User's Guide* 185). To insist on the spatial logic of the *exceptio* is, in this context, to insist—against Braidwood and his institutionalized optimism—that the British myth of imperial wholeness, of historical continuity and integrity, was always fractured at root. When Ballard's Shanghai fictions insist on the geography of the outside within, they protest against a symbolic national geography in which everything always "holds . . . together" (*User's Guide* 185), no matter how drearily and no matter what the cost. The *exceptio* is the spatial figure for a Britain that is no longer identical with itself and, in Shanghai, never was.

Lunghua is only ordinary—not the end of the world but just an episode to be endured—if one can first of all push back through time: back to a world more pleasant, with a number of trees, but a world that is false to Ballard. His enclave world subjects social space to an authority that stands outside: an authority that is alien, even extraordinary—but is therefore the very thing his protagonists desire or seek to be. We knew that already, of course, but the Braidwood papers let us know it differently, as part of a historical argument about the fate of British imperial spaces and values and not just as a claim about an author's psychopathology. It is not just that an archival comparison shows us new ways in which writing the "Shanghai to Shepperton" story requires the creation of new fictional truths and not the description of lines of influence among existing realities. By examining an alternate version of Lunghua, we can better understand how and why Ballard's settings so relentlessly extraterritorialize social and political space. The historical thrust of Ballard's late sequence should not be reduced to its topical subjects: drugs on the Costa, malls in the Shires. The late sequence is not about the twenty-first-century world of condo developments and research campuses—or, at least, it is not only about that world. In its narrative geography as well as in its self-conscious puncturing of bourgeois values, it is directed against the extraordinary fact that, for the people among whom Ballard lived in Lunghua and after, a lost national past still seemed to be the ordinary business of life. Ballard's late sequence is a machine for the production of settings that dislocate social space and time, settings that open out onto his version of Lunghua but close the book on another. Within and behind the production of sameness in the form of a sequence lies the rupture that was Shanghai and Lunghua. The journey "from Shanghai to Shepperton" does not just establish a repetitive relation between juvenile social cause and adult literary affect. The preposition *from* also, and more simply, describes a movement between two very different places and states. For all the contemporary glamor of millennial fictions such as *Cocaine Nights*, they are not only compelled to repeat but, in repeating, to repeatedly disavow one version of the historical past. The late novels are, in this sense, among the last extraordinary works of twentieth-century literature.

*   *   *

MATTHEW HART is an associate professor in the Department of English and Comparative Literature at Columbia University. He is the author of *Nations of Nothing but Poetry* (2010/2013) and coeditor, with David J. Alworth, of *Site Specificity without Borders,* a special issue of *ASAP/Journal* (September 2017). Hart's essay in this issue is drawn from his new book, *Extraterritorial: A Political Geography of Contemporary Fiction,* forthcoming in 2019.

Works Cited

Adorno, T. W. *Negative Dialectics*. Trans. E. B. Ashton. London: Routledge, 1973.

Agamben, Giorgio. *Homo Sacer: Sovereign Power and Bare Life*. Trans. Daniel Heller-Roazan. Stanford: Stanford UP, 1998.

———. *State of Exception*. Trans. Kevin Attell. Chicago: U Chicago P, 2005.

Alworth, David J. *Site Reading: Fiction, Art, Social Form*. Princeton: Princeton UP, 2015.

Amir, Mayaan, and Ruti Sela, eds. *Extraterritorialities in Occupied Worlds*. Earth, Milky Way: Punctum, 2016.

Amis, Martin. "Ballard's Worlds." The Terminal Collection: J. G. Ballard Firsts and Variant Editions <http://www.jgballard.ca/media/1984_sept2_observer_magazine.html> (accessed 18 May 2016).

Archer, Bernice. *The Internment of Western Civilians under the Japanese 1941–1945: A Patchwork of Internment*. London: RoutledgeCurzon, 2004.

Atwood, Margaret. *The Year of the Flood*. New York: Doubleday/Nan Talese, 2009.

Auerbach, Erich. *Mimesis: The Representation of Reality in Western Literature*. Trans. Willard R. Trask. Princeton: Princeton UP, 2003.

Balibar, Étienne. *We, the People of Europe? Reflections on Transnational Citizenship*. Trans. James Swenson. Princeton: Princeton UP, 2003.

"Ballardian." Def. 2. *Collins English Dictionary* <https://www.collinsdictionary.com/us/dictionary/english/ballardian> (accessed 18 May 2016).

Ballard, J. G. *Cocaine Nights*. Berkeley, CA: Counterpoint, 1998.

———. *Concrete Island*. London: Cape, 1974.

———. *Crash*. London: Cape, 1973.

———. *The Drowned World*. New York: Norton, 2012.

———. *Empire of the Sun*. London: Gollancz, 1984.

———. *Extreme Metaphors: Collected Interviews*. Ed. Simon Sellars and Dan O'Hara. London: Fourth Estate, 2014.

———. "From Shanghai to Shepperton." *Foundation* 24 (1982): 5–23.

———. *High-Rise*. London: Cape, 1975.

———. *The Kindness of Women*. New York: Farrar, Straus and Giroux, 1991.

———. *Kingdom Come*. London: Fourth Estate, 2006.

———. *Millennium People*. London: Harper Perennial, 2004.

———. *Miracles of Life; Shanghai to Shepperton: An Autobiography*. London: Fourth Estate, 2008.

———. *Running Wild*. New York: Farrar, Straus and Giroux, 1998.

———. *Super-Cannes*. New York: Picador, 2000.

———. *A User's Guide to the Millennium: Essays and Reviews*. New York: Picador, 1996.

Bal, Mieke. *Narratology: Introduction to the Theory of Narrative*. 3rd ed. Toronto: U of Toronto P, 2009.

Baxter, Jeannette. "Encountering the Holocaust in J. G. Ballard's Post-War Science Fictions." *Textual Practice* 26.3 (2012): 379–98.

Beckett, Chris. "The Progress of the Text: The Papers of J. G. Ballard at the British Library." *Electronic British Library Journal* 12 (2011): 1–24.

Bewes, Timothy. "Reading with the Grain: A New World in Literary Criticism." *differences* 21.3 (2010): 1–33.

Bodin, Jean. *On Sovereignty*. Ed. and trans. Julian H. Franklin. Cambridge: Cambridge UP, 1992.

Braidwood, William. "Escapes." Add. MS 88938/2/1/7/4, British Residents' Association: Minutes, Memoranda, and Reports, Papers of James Graham Ballard. Western Manuscripts Collection, British Library, London (hereafter Ballard Papers) (accessed 7 July 2015).

———. "The Lunghua Civilian Assembly Centre." Add. MS 88938/2/1/7/2, Plans of Lunghua [Lunghwa] Camp, and Documents Concerning the Construction and Condition of Its Buildings, Ballard Papers (accessed 7 July 2015).

———. "Speech to the Shanghai British Residents Association, 30 Nov. 1945." Add. MS 88938/2/1/7/4, British Residents' Association: Minutes, Memoranda, and Reports, Ballard Papers (accessed 8 July 2015).

Butler, Octavia. *Parable of the Sower*. New York: Grand Central, 2000.

Chandler, Raymond. *Later Novels and Other Writings*. New York: Penguin, 1995.

Chatman, Seymour. *Story and Discourse: Narrative Structure in Fiction and Film*. Ithaca: Cornell UP, 1978.

Clarke, Jim. "Reading Climate Change in J. G. Ballard." *Critical Survey* 25.2 (2013): 7–21.

Dirda, Michael. Rev. of *The Complete Stories of J. G. Ballard*. *Washington Post* 17 Sept. 2009.

Dunkley, G. S. Letter to J. G. Ballard. 31 Oct. 1984. Add. MS 88938/2/1/6, Letters Received from Lunghua Camp Internees Following Publication of *Empire of the Sun* (1944–91), Ballard Papers (accessed 8 July 2015).

Easterling, Keller. *Extrastatecraft: The Power of Infrastructure Space*. London: Verso, 2014.

Garner, Dwight. "His Twists and Turns, on Paper and in Life: J. G. Ballard's Memoir, *Miracles of Life*." *New York Times* 6 Feb. 2013.

Gleisner, Ines, Anselm Franke, and Eyal Weizman. "Islands: The Geography of Extraterritoriality." *Archis* no. 6 (2003): n. pag.

Gomel, Elana. "Everyday Apocalypse: J. G. Ballard and the Ethics and Aesthetics of the End of Time." *Partial Answers* 8.1 (2010): 185–208.

Gordon, Joan. "Reveling in Genre: An Interview with China Miéville." *Science Fiction Studies* 30.3 (2003): 355–73.

Hayot, Eric. *On Literary Worlds*. New York: Oxford UP, 2012.

Jameson, Fredric. *The Political Unconscious: Narrative as a Socially Symbolic Act*. London: Routledge, 1983.

Kong, Belinda. "Shanghai Biopolitans: Wartime Colonial Cosmopolis in Eileen Chang's *Love in a Fallen City* and J. G. Ballard's *Empire of the Sun*." *Journal of Narrative Theory* 39.3 (2009): 280–304.

Lee, Chang-rae. *On Such a Full Sea*. New York: Riverhead, 2014.

Luckhurst, Roger. *"The Angle between Two Walls": The Fiction of J. G. Ballard*. Liverpool: Liverpool UP, 1997.

Marcus, Sharon, and Stephen Best. "Surface Reading: An Introduction." *The Way We Read Now*. Ed. Sharon Marcus and Stephen Best. Spec. issue of *Representations* 108.1 (2009): 1–21.

Sharon Marcus, Heather Love, and Stephen Best. "Building a Better Description." *Description across Disciplines*. Ed. Sharon Marcus, Heather Love, and Stephen Best. Spec. issue of *Representations* 135.1 (2016): 1–21.

Mazower, Mark. "Foucault, Agamben: Theory and the Nazis." *boundary 2* 35.1 (2008): 23–34.

Mezzadra, Sandro, and Brett Neilson. *Border as Method, or The Multiplication of Labor*. Durham: Duke UP, 2013.

Miéville, China, et al. "J. G. Ballard: Five Years On—A Celebration." *Guardian* 4 April 2014 <https://www.theguardian.com/books/2014/apr/04/jg-ballard-celebration-five-years-writers-books-reissued>.

Moretti, Franco. *Distant Reading*. New York: Verso, 2013.

Ngai, Sianne. *Ugly Feelings*. Cambridge, MA: Harvard UP, 2005.

Nyiri, Pal. "Extraterritoriality; Foreign Concessions: The Past and Future of a Form of Shared Sovereignty." Inaugural oration. Amsterdam Free University, 19 Nov. 2009.

Ong, Aihwa. "Graduated Sovereignty in South East Asia." *Theory, Culture & Society* 17.4 (2000): 55–75.

Ranson, F. T. Letter to J. G. Ballard. 20 Oct. 1984. Add. MS 88938/2/1/6, Letters Received from Lunghua Camp Internees Following Publication of *Empire of the Sun* (1944–1991), Ballard Papers (accessed 7 July 2015).

Raustiala, Kal. *Does the Constitution Follow the Flag? The Evolution of Territoriality in American Law*. New York: Oxford UP, 2009.

Reilly, Julia. Letter to J. G. Ballard. 20 Oct. 1984. Add. MS 88938/2/1/6: Letters Received from Lunghua Camp Internees Following Publication of *Empire of the Sun* (1944–1991), Ballard Papers (accessed 7 July 2015).

Rugoff, Ralph. "Dangerous Driving: Interview with J. G. Ballard." *Frieze Magazine* 6 May 1997 <https://frieze.com/article/dangerous-driving>.

Scarry, Elaine. *Thinking in an Emergency*. New York: Norton, 2011.

Self, Will. *Junk Mail*. London: Bloomsbury, 1995.

Sellars, Simon. "J. G. Ballard Live in London." Ballardian <http://www.ballardian.com/jg-ballard-live-in-london> (accessed 18 May 2016).

Stanley, Rachael. "'The Scientist on Safari': J. G. Ballard and the Naturalist Gaze." *Textual Practice* 29.6 (2015): 1165–85.

Sykes, Tom. "Ideascape: How the British New Wave of Science Fiction Addressed the Social, Political, and Intellectual Themes of the 1960s and 1970s." *Foundation* 39.110 (2010): 73–79.

Weizman, Eyal. "On Extraterritoriality." Publicspace <http://www.publicspace.org/en/text-library/eng/b011-on-extraterritoriality> (accessed 18 May 2016).

Wellek, René, and Arthur Warren. *Theory of Literature*. New York: Harcourt, Brace, 1948.

The Contemporary Novel
and Postdemocratic Form

RACHEL GREENWALD SMITH

Is this the end of neoliberalism?

This question has percolated in the public discourse since the 2016 presidential primaries. It was raised in response to the unexpected success of Bernie Sanders. It was raised when Hillary Clinton refused to support the Trans-Pacific Partnership. It was raised when Jeb Bush's many well-funded Super PACs failed to bolster his candidacy. And in the immediate aftermath of the election of Donald Trump, the question was raised in a particularly panicked register. The question became not only, *is this the end of neoliberalism?* but also, *are we witnessing the rise of authoritarianism?*

This essay does not answer this question, but it does interrogate the assumptions that underlie the way it has been asked. In particular, it challenges the conventional wisdom about how these two concepts—neoliberalism and authoritarianism—relate to one another. While the political reality on the ground is clearly too complex to be thoroughly accounted for by either of these concepts, and while the concern that existed immediately after the election that Trump would institute an all-out authoritarian order seems to be fading, it is clear that aspects of both of these concepts are to some degree explanatory of our current moment. Neoliberal policies continue apace; indeed, privatization and deregulation are being amped up under the current administration. And certain sociopolitical features of authoritarianism—hostility toward the free press; strongman rhetoric; state-sponsored xenophobia, just to name a few—are also on the rise. How, then, to account for the convergence of these two seemingly opposed political tendencies?

The answer, I argue, can be found in the fact that neoliberalism and authoritarianism share a reliance upon the depoliticization of a citizenry, a skepticism toward the democratic notion that citizens are responsible for managing the political distribution of authority. And the dynamics of authority and democracy become clearer when set against discussions of politics and aesthetics as they have evolved from postmodernism to the present. This is because postmodernism was, in part, an experiment in what a total retreat from authority would look like in aesthetics, staged in the name of radical participatory democracy. Appearing during a period dedicated in a range of disciplines to probing the dynamics of authority and obedience, postmodernist experiments imagined themselves as opportunities to see what kind of collective freedom could emerge out of a total unleashing of each individual from authoritative structures. In the aftermath of postmodernism, then, one would imagine that we would see an effort among critics and writers to think in more nuanced ways about authority—qualitatively, quantitatively, and contextually. But this was not the dominant response to postmodernism. Instead, beginning in the 1990s and intensifying through the early twenty-first century, we see the rise of what I call *compromise aesthetics*, or the belief that all formal allegiances are unnecessary limitations to the tactical use of any and all stylistic tools for a given work. Compromise aesthetics are also suspicious of authority but not in the name of a political suspicion toward authoritarianism. Instead, compromise aesthetics envision the artist as having the freedom of the entrepreneur—radical, insofar as all formal tools are up for grabs for innovative refashioning, but not political, because collective meaning is shed from stylistic modes previously associated with ideological positions. Compromise aesthetics, I argue, are reflective of neoliberal thinking insofar as the notion of what is immediately useful and profitable overtakes any other ideological commitment.

So from the politicized experiments in total freedom of the 1960s and 1970s, we arrive at a depoliticized form of writing in the present. And this condition is not unlike the political condition of our moment, in which rather than have discussions about what forms of authority might provide opportunities for greater equality, justice, and other democratic values, the Left, we have seen, largely addresses what Francis Fukuyama calls, in his early description of what the full achievement of global capitalism would look like, "the endless solving of technical problems" (18). We have therefore overlooked the opportunity for intentional grappling with the effects of different forms of authority that might allow for the development of the fundamental values that underlie democracy: the responsibility of citizens to institute forms of collective authority and the notion that equality among individuals should be instituted and protected by the state.

The most interesting novels today, I argue, respond to this situation by offering formal forays into what forms of power are coming in to replace democratic sovereignty today. In a reading of one of these novels, Rachel Kushner's *The Flamethrowers*, I argue that the dynamics of depoliticization and authority are worked out through the figure of the novel's passive first-person narrator. While the narrator of *The Flamethrowers* fashions herself as merely a "conduit" for experience (30), the highly politicized circumstances of her environment ultimately overtake her such that she ends up being an unwitting accessory to a political murder. Tellingly, I argue, reviews of the novel espouse beliefs consistent with compromise aesthetics, praising the neutrality of the narrator's gaze while seeing the political plot of the novel as an overly heavy-handed authorial intervention. Against these positions, I argue that the dissonance that exists between the passivity of the narrator and the novelist's heavy hand is precisely the point. Just as the narrator of *The Flamethrowers* is ultimately authored by an individual, so are neoliberal subjects ultimately governed by people in power. And the abdication of decisions around who marshals that power and to what end—an abdication that arose out of the ideology of neoliberalism—has led us to a place where those figures are now becoming increasingly, and disturbingly, visible. In other words, *The Flamethrowers* shows us what a combination of invocations of individual freedom and the presence of strong-handed authority looks like: the very convergence we see in the current expression of neoliberalism.

*   *   *

The notion that neoliberalism is compatible with overt expressions of political authority suggests that neoliberalism has ideological features that are not thoroughly accounted for in one of the most foundational texts on the rise of neoliberalism in the

United States, David Harvey's *A Brief History of Neoliberalism*. Harvey argues that US citizens were amenable to the institution of neoliberal economic policies that perpetuated greater income inequality because the policies were implemented in the name of individual freedom. He writes, "The assumption that individual freedoms are guaranteed by freedom of the market and of trade is a cardinal feature of neoliberal thinking" (7). This belief in the connection between individual social freedoms and the free market was initially imagined in the context of the perceived Soviet threat, first in F. A. Hayek's *The Road to Serfdom* (1944) and later in Milton Friedman's *Capitalism and Freedom* (1962). But Harvey argues that it was not until the aftermath of the social movements of the 1960s that the ideology of individual freedom could be used to justify a program of economic changes as far-reaching as the neoliberalization that began in the 1980s. "Any political movement that holds individual freedoms to be sacrosanct," Harvey writes, "is vulnerable to incorporation into the neoliberal fold" (41). The 1960s social movements were particularly vulnerable because "[f]or almost everyone involved in the movement . . . the intrusive state was the enemy and it had to be reformed"; as a result, the institution of neoliberal policies could be "backed up by a practical strategy that emphasized the liberty of consumer choice, not only with respect to particular products but also with respect to lifestyles, modes of expression, and a wide range of cultural practices" (42). Free trade could look like an expression of free choice. Unregulated markets could appear to reflect an ethos of unregulated social expectations. Even if neoliberal policies required state-based policies and the persistence, or in some cases even the heightening, of state power, for many US citizens—particularly those insulated from the most damaging violence of the neoliberal state because of racial or class privilege—neoliberalism was justified because its economic and political tendencies seemed to correspond with greater freedom of self-expression and increased attention to the rights of the individual as opposed to the tyranny of the collective. Perversely, neoliberalism looked like the counterculture achieved by other means.

This account works as a description of how neoliberalization initially took place. But it does not account for why, with the economic crises of 2007 and 2008, we begin to see a rise in the ideological force of concepts that seem opposed to individual freedom: austerity, sacrifice, and increasingly, the notion that a powerful leader is needed to protect a vulnerable population. In *Undoing the Demos*, Wendy Brown points out that the particular form of mass sacrifice invoked to defend such practices is consistent with neoliberalism because, unlike previous authoritarian regimes, a neoliberal notion of sacrifice "relocates this classic gesture of patriotism from a political-military register to an economic one" (212). Instead of appealing to patriotic duty, individuals, she argues, "may now be legitimately sacrificed to macroeconomic imperatives" (213). Yet the rhetoric of mass sacrifice in our moment also points to the political underside of neoliberalism's imagined space of individual liberation. Brown explains that this is how "a political rationality originally born in opposition to fascism turn[s] out to mirror certain aspects of it, albeit through powers that are faceless and invisible-handed and absent an authoritarian state" (219). For Brown, neoliberalism is not fascism, but its effects can be hauntingly similar, because even if it lacks fascist content, it can take on fascist forms.

This authoritarian valence of neoliberalism is possible, Brown argues, because of what neoliberal policies do to democracy itself. As citizens are remade into economic actors and "democratic state commitments to equality, liberty, inclusion, and constitutionalism are [made] subordinate to the project of economic growth, competitive positioning, and capital enhancement," democracy looks increasingly imperiled (26). Ten years before Brown, Chantal Mouffe observed something similar, arguing that "the unchallenged hegemony of neo-liberalism represents a threat for democratic institutions" (6). But for Mouffe, neoliberalism is a symptom—albeit a significant one—of a larger problem. Liberal democracy, she argues, is based on a paradoxical alignment of two distinct political philosophies: one, liberalism, that values individual freedom and universal human rights and another, democracy, that values equality and popular sovereignty. In her view, in seeking "third way" and technocratic forms of government, the United States and Europe have become captivated by the belief that equality—one of the most important democratic values and the value that has traditionally been defended most consistently by the Left—could be superseded by individual freedom, pragmatism, and the notion of a shared universal humanity. The result of the elevation of these liberal values over other democratic values is a general abdication of politics. Arguing that "accepting that conflict and division are inherent to politics" is the only way to ensure that democracy can survive, Mouffe contends that "the blurring of the frontiers between left and right, far from being an advance in a democratic direction, is jeopardizing the future of democracy" (14, 7).

If it is hard for many individuals on the left to see liberalism as a political threat, this is in part because it was not so long ago that authoritarianism, liberalism's imagined opposite, was widely understood to be the most urgent threat to democracy. In his contribution to the 1967 Congress on the Dialectics of Liberation, a gathering characterized by "a curious pastiche of eminent scholars and political activists" including Gregory Bateson, Stokely Carmichal, and Herbert Marcuse, radical psychiatrist R. D. Laing diagnosed the root cause of domination by invoking the "simple morality tale" of the infamous shock experiments conducted by Stanley Milgram at Yale University (Cooper 7; Laing 30). The fact that a majority of Milgram's test subjects were willing to deliver what they believed to be a potentially lethal shock to an innocent victim simply because they were told to do so by an authority figure suggested, according to Laing, that most people "are prepared to do practically anything if told to do it by a sufficient authority" (29). For this reason, if one is concerned with liberation, "[i]t is particularly important to study the nature of obedience" in order to identify and combat the source of the problem: "We have all a 'reflex' towards believing and doing what we are told" (Cooper 7).

This belief—that the source of political ills stemmed from the dynamics of authority and obedience—permeated the political climate of the 1960s and 1970s, leading to a general ethos of antiauthoritarianism on the left that was also manifested in aesthetic form.[1] The result at its most extreme was the dissolution of the work of art into the "happening," an activity in which, according to Allan Kaprow,

---

[1]   For an expanded account of the relationship between 1960s literary form and the antiauthoritarian social movements of the period, see Marianne DeKoven.

"*audiences should be eliminated entirely*" in favor of a participatory event that integrates the specificity of "the particular materials and character of the environment" toward a one-time action (721). As John Barth points out in his 1967 essay "The Literature of Exhaustion," happenings and other "intermedia" arts share a "tendency to eliminate not only the traditional audience . . . but also the most traditional notion of the artist: the Aristotelian conscious agent who achieves with technique and cunning the artistic effect" (65). This is, as Barth explains, a politically motivated critique: "[T]he very idea of the controlling artist," he writes, "has been condemned as politically reactionary, authoritarian, even fascist" (65).[2]

An interest in dismantling structures of authority was at the heart of 1960s and 1970s critical theory as well. In his 1977 preface to the first volume of Gilles Deleuze and Félix Guattari's *Capitalism and Schizophrenia*, Michel Foucault praises the work for being antifascist in the most capacious definition of the term. He writes, "[T]he major enemy [of the book] is fascism. . . . And not only historical fascism, the fascism of Hitler and Mussolini . . . but also the fascism in us all, in our heads and in our everyday behavior, the fascism that causes us to love power, to desire the very thing that dominates and exploits us" (xiii). For Foucault, fascism is not merely a political threat but a subjective one. To be antifascist, then, requires rooting out fascism everywhere, including in language itself. He explains,

> Deleuze and Guattari . . . have tried to neutralize the effects of power linked to their own discourse. Hence the games and snares scattered throughout the book. . . . The book often leads one to believe it is all fun and games, when something essential is taking place, something of extreme seriousness: the tracking down of all varieties of fascism, from the enormous ones that surround and crush us to the petty ones that constitute the tyrannical bitterness of our everyday lives. (xiv)

Here Foucault describes a style that sounds very much like that of postmodern literature, with its focus on play, suspicion toward easy forms of closure, and affirmation of the political and social value of difficulty. Read this way, the peculiar stylistic qualities typical of both postmodernism and certain kinds of late-twentieth-century theory should be understood, first and foremost, as a method of "tracking down" authoritarian impulses in language. I think we are familiar enough with this argument, particularly as it pertains to literature of the period. After all, it is none other than Don DeLillo's postmodernist hero (and also, noncoincidentally, the founder of Hitler studies) Jack Gladney who finds himself plaintively musing, "May the days be aimless. Let the seasons drift. Do not advance the action according to a plan" (98). Gladney begs for formlessness in the face of the threat of literary cohesion, because, as he argues, "All plots tend to move deathward. This is the nature of plots. Political plots . . . narrative plots" (26).

But in the 1990s, we began to see increased skepticism toward precisely the kind of theoretical and aesthetic style that Foucault once saw as a necessary antidote to

---

[2]   See also Steven Belletto's contention that writers of the period waged "a critique of both totalitarian political systems and also of Cold War norms back in the States" by embracing chance over design (32).

the lurking threat of fascism as deconstructive and poststructuralist theory lost purchase. The decline of these movements occurred in part because of a growing perception that the skepticism toward authority that they performed ultimately led to a damaging reluctance to say anything of substance at all.[3] In this view, the very rejection of authoritarianism embodied in the dismantling of certain kinds of linguistic and social authority ultimately leads to a celebration of a kind of free-floating nonsensical anything-goes that, in turn, supports the logic of late capitalism. We see this perspective percolating in *White Noise*, where the alternatives to the murderous, Hitlerian plottedness of structured narratives are the diffuse "waves and radiation" of consumerism, information culture, and popular culture, which are in turn envisioned as the cultural equivalents of toxic contaminants (51).

It is in this moment that we see a significant turn in contemporary literary scholarship that aims to recuperate formal authority as something that might be productively claimed in political and aesthetic terms. The strongest recent articulation of this point has come from Walter Benn Michaels, who praises Maggie Nelson's decision to call her book of poems about her aunt's murder *Jane: A Murder* instead of *Jane: An Elegy*. Both titles, Michaels explains, "require a death, but only the murder understands the poem itself as a weapon" (6). For Michaels, this is the better choice, despite the fact that "in the wake of the deconstructive critique" any desire for an artwork to be perfect, beautiful, whole, or autonomous will be "understood as the desire also for a kind of violence" (8). This violence is necessary, he explains, because, in the context of the rise of neoliberalism, "the critique of form is the mark of a neoliberal politics" (67). The possibility that art might entail a violent imposition of perfection is preferable to the more common tendency in contemporary art, which he sees as the reduction of art to taste, individual sensibility, and the vicissitudes of attitude, a reduction that depoliticizes art at the very moment when structural inequality is growing. Better the violence of perfection, Michaels argues, than the anemia of individual experience.

We also see this interest in the recuperation of authority toward political aesthetics in Nicholas Brown's essay "The Work of Art in the Age of its Real Subsumption under Capital." Brown argues that our moment is characterized by two problems when it comes to a meaningful political aesthetic. The first is that there is no longer an "autonomous sphere" in which artists can imagine their work as outside the market. The second is that, without this autonomous sphere, there is a constant threat that all works of art can become merely commodities—that is, things that can mean anything because they mean nothing, works that are shaped only according to the preferences of a mass audience and not according to any meaningful aesthetic intention. Against this state of affairs, Brown suggests that innovative work with genre might still offer some insulation from the nonsense of the art commodity. This is because genre is at least something that is "governed by rules," something that has "requirements . . . rigid enough to pose a problem . . . a formal problem like the problem of the flatness of the canvas." Genre reinstates the authority of form and makes meaningful art possible again.

---

[3]   For one of the most incisive critiques in this vein, see Sean McCann and Michael Szalay.

These formalist positions seem to suggest that we have reached an impasse: Postmodernist play or authorial control? The slow death of toxicity or the immediacy of the gun? The incoherence of perfect freedom or the violence of total authority? Relativity or ideology? The supermarket or the camp? In this context, the pronounced rejection of high theory alongside the decline of postmodernist aesthetics could be explained by our relative distance from the threat of fascism. We may have decided that the primary enemy has shifted: from fascism to capitalism; from authoritarianism to flexibility; from what Foucault calls "sadness" on the part of the 1960s militant to the "everything is awesome" of the millennial generation.

But while many of these accounts aim their critique at the indeterminacy of postmodernism, I would argue that it is the movement that follows postmodernism that represents the most significant capitulation to the neoliberal ideology of individual freedom and entrepreneurial thinking. This movement is characterized first and foremost by its resistance to definition. Periodizing terms have proliferated— post-postmodernism; metamodernism; the new sincerity; post-irony—but none have been adopted with the kind of consistency that postmodernism enjoyed in the 1970s and 1980s. This lack of terminological consistency, however, is not merely for lack of consensus: it is symptomatic of the qualities of the aesthetic movement itself. Whatever we call our present moment, contemporary aesthetics are doggedly plural and hybrid, imagining that all forms might unproblematically coexist, blend, and merge without hierarchy. As Cole Swensen puts it, "[T]he contemporary moment is dominated by rich writings that cannot be categorized and that hybridize core attributes of previous 'camps' in diverse and unprecedented ways" (xvii). Their only exclusion is the notion of exclusion itself. For Johanna Drucker, for instance, the enemy of any real understanding of contemporary art is the "doddering scaffold of outmoded thought" that is "premised on oppositional models that are the legacy of the avant-garde" (xiv).

In other words, as efforts to define the art of the present proliferate, there are certain points of consistency within those efforts themselves. *Compromise aesthetics* is my term for the critical suspicion toward oppositionality, exclusion, and polarization that characterizes current assessments of contemporary art. Espousers of compromise aesthetics such as Swensen and Drucker see in the hybrid formal properties of contemporary art the possibility that aesthetics can be depoliticized— that is, that stylistic decisions could be rid of their ideological baggage and be made in a purely tactical fashion. It is not an accident, then, that some critics have called hybrid writing "third-way" writing, given the similarities between technocratic philosophies of politics and the technocratic approach that supporters of compromise aesthetics see as dominating contemporary art. In the political sphere, we know that the third-way approach is closely allied with neoliberalism's mandate to make all decisions based on an economic calculation. As Mouffe explains, "the so-called 'third way' . . . is no more than the justification by social democrats of their capitulation to a neo-liberal hegemony whose power relations they will not challenge" (5). In the aesthetic sphere, compromise aesthetics serve a similar function, imagining that formal choices can be made purely instrumentally, without any sense that those choices involve decisions about where one stands in terms of alliances, history, and power. In short, compromise aesthetics advocate the depoliticization of art.

Crucially, however, despite the liberal emphasis on the individual choices of artists, the political valences of compromise aesthetics are not, as postmodernist aesthetics imagined themselves, fundamentally antiauthoritarian. Formal structures that the postmodernists saw as carrying the baggage of authoritarianism—such as the maintenance of a stable, unreflexive, narrative point of view; narrative closure; and traditional plots—are acceptable within the umbrella of compromise aesthetics. This is because authoritarianism is not something that is imagined to be lurking in the background to be ferreted out, as it was for Foucault or Kaprow. The result is that forms that once may have been associated with authoritarian tendencies are allowed in, merging invisibly with styles that once signaled suspicion toward any form of authority in a text.

In other words, by depoliticizing art, compromise aesthetics provides a context for the reappearance of authority in literature, but not in the form that Michaels or Nicholas Brown would like to see. If these critics would like to see authority marshaled against the imagined freedom of the individual under neoliberalism, compromise aesthetics allow forms associated with both freedom and authority to coexist. This might look like an essentially democratic form—democracy, after all, requires the coexistence of selective forms of authority with selective freedoms—but compromise aesthetics pairs these two impulses without highlighting the choices that must be made about what kinds of authority should be allowed and what kinds should be abolished, what kinds of freedom are good for a populace and what kinds are destructive. These choices are the very core of democracy. Without them, both individual freedom *and* authority can easily become violent. While supporters of compromise aesthetics envision contemporary hybrid forms as providing an ethos of democratic inclusion, the rise of compromise aesthetics in fact signifies the rise of postdemocratic form.

*   *   *

In his review of Rachel Kushner's *The Flamethrowers*, James Wood assesses the novel in a manner consistent with compromise aesthetics. He argues that the novel's form happily elides "the long postwar argument between the rival claims of realistic and anti-realistic fiction—the seasoned triumphs of the traditional American novel on one side, and the necessary innovations of postmodern fiction on the other." For Wood, Kushner allows us to "blast through such phantom barricades" by giving us a work that offers up the feeling of emotional immediacy while providing readers with the thrill of a kind of experimentalism-lite. Wood is less enthusiastic, however, about the novel's interest in the relationship between aesthetics and politics, particularly as developed in its ending, which sees Reno, passive artist-narrator of *The Flamethrowers*, half-knowingly smuggling a member of the Red Brigades across the Alps and therefore enabling him to murder her ex-lover's brother. This part of the novel, Wood argues, is "an overloading of the novel's thematic circuits, a wrongheaded desire to make everything signify." Here, the balance between textual authority and textual freedom tips. A totalizing aesthetic-political vision emerges, revealing the author's presence too strongly.

But evidence suggests that there is a clear relationship between the novel's initial success at balancing its hybrid form and the heavy-handedness that Wood identifies in the work's final pages. In what follows, I will argue that *The Flamethrowers* is a cautionary tale about the apparent anything-goes of compromise aesthetics in the realm of art as well as the imagined individual freedom promised by neoliberalism. The novel demonstrates, both formally and thematically, how authority functions when it seems most absent, offering an account of how authoritarian and neoliberal tendencies can coexist both in politics and in art.

In a brief reflective piece on the use of photographic images in the novel, Kushner writes that when she began looking at pictures of the 1970s art scene in researching the setting of the book she found "lots of guns" and "lots of nude women." She explains, "I was faced with the pleasure and headache of somehow stitching together the pistols and the nude women as defining features of a fictional realm, and one in which the female narrator, who has the last word, and technically all words, is nevertheless continually overrun, effaced, and silenced by the very masculine world of the novel she inhabits" ("Flamethrowers"). What does it mean to be "overrun" at the same time as one has "all words"? This is a question, as Kushner intimates here, that gets at the difficulties of feminist critique after the achievements of the women's movement. How can one express the limitations put on one's expression when expression seems limitless? But this dilemma is not unique to feminism. It is also central to the difficulty of communicating the realities of racism after the end of Jim Crow and the realities of homophobia after the overturning of DOMA. Another way to put this is that this dilemma reflects a series of recent social compromises: those that see possessing and even affirming a historically marginalized identity position as essentially not in conflict with one's ability to succeed as what Foucault has called "an entrepreneur of himself" (*Biopolitics* 226). In the context of the falseness of these apparent freedoms, Kushner responds formally, creating a narrative position that reflects the continued pressure of an overwhelming authoritative structure—in this case, the structure of the novel itself and the author who crafts that structure—on individuals who feel themselves to be free—in this case, the first-person narrator.

From the beginning of the novel, Reno is represented as a neutral, passive observer. As her boyfriend, an artist deeply embedded in the New York art scene explains, "A young woman is a conduit. All she has to do is *exist*" (30). In contrast, when she meets the group of artists who will ultimately be the novel's central cast of characters, she identifies them as "[t]he people with the gun" (45). This contrast persists throughout the novel as Reno aspires to perfect passivity while her cohort possesses a kind of violent agency metaphorically connected to the presence of guns. "What occurred did so because I was open to it," she notes, in a bizarre passive construction, of her chance meeting with the people with the gun (49). She describes her experience of passing from girlhood to womanhood as entering "into the realm where you no longer questioned the notion of being trapped in one form," a state Reno feels freed from in her relationship with Sandro. "I didn't have to be recognizably one thing," she realizes, in bed next to his sleeping body. "Even his touch relayed this. It almost restored some lost innocence" (103). Reno values formlessness, shape-shifting, fluidity, and pure experience. In other words, she aspires to be a narrator so devoid of motive, specificity, and history that she can act as a vehicle for experience to directly funnel into a story. Reno, then, articulates her sense of herself in a manner that reflects the aims of compromise aesthetics: the notion that formal flexibility can be paired with narrative legibility such that a work of art can be the outcome of all of the tools—experimental and traditional—that are at a contemporary artist's disposal. And like compromise aesthetics, this position is imagined to be essentially value-free, apolitical, devoted only to the production of a quality work of art.

This narrative persona appears to provide a fictional form that would allow for a radically unrestricted form of representation. *What occurred did so.* Life streams into the narrative, unimpeded by the shaping force of the narrator, the formal element of a text that might otherwise act as the novel's executive power. The novel looks, in other words, free from external control, ideology, or prohibition: elements fall into place as they are needed, outside the censoring or encouraging force of any centralized leader. The problem with this open structure, however, as we find later in the novel, is that it paradoxically prevents the kind of engagement with politics that would be necessary for Reno's experience to avoid being governed by larger, if unseen, forms of authority.

This problem is worked out in what appears to be a strange interlude in the novel's plot, a chapter devoted to the description of a Greek marble relief that depicts a slave girl kissing a dove. In the scene, Reno is at the Metropolitan Museum of Art with Sandro, her lover, and Ronnie, her ex-lover. The two men describe their adoration of the sculpture:

> What fascinated them was a pocket of real air that flowed into and around the girl's mouth and the dove in her hand, the bird's small beak raised toward the girl's lips.
> Sandro pointed to the little recess between the bird and her mouth.
> "This is the only part of the relief that's three-dimensional. So what about the rest of her? Its flatness holds her away from us. She doesn't share our space. . . ."
> Ronnie said he loved her because she was so . . . modern. She interfered, he said, with the fantasy she was there to create. Slipping between the two, like everything in life worth lingering over. Real and false at once. (106)

In the scene, Reno identifies with the slave girl, which should not be surprising because she too is adored by both Sandro and Ronnie. But the similarities extend beyond that position. Reno, as narrator, also "doesn't share [the] space" of the characters of the novel, despite her position as a first-person narrator. In aspiring to allow experience to be channeled through her, she fashions herself as a noncharacter: simply a set of eyes, a nonperson who might allow the world around her to be recorded as it is. But like the slave girl, she has enough contact with reality to read as "real." "Real and false at once," as Ronnie suggests, anticipating Wood's analysis of the novel as "blasting through . . . the rival claims of realistic and anti-realistic fiction." Reno, as narrator, is three-dimensional enough to read as "real" but two-dimensional enough for the flow of experience to pass through her as if she were only a window onto her world and nothing more.

But this condition, according to Reno, is not merely aesthetic. As she gazes at the sculpture, she reflects: "I stared at the private space between her lips and the bird she held. I looked at the cord around her neck, adornment of the most modest sort. Every aspect of her a modesty. All I could think was, 'This is a young slave'" (106). The modesty of Reno's narrative position, through its connection to the slave girl, is cast for the first time in the novel in terms of historical and political power. The formal structure of the novel suddenly appears, in light of this connection, less like the expression of freedom and more like a form of tyranny. Even if the narrator, the conventional site of power in the novel, has willfully disempowered herself, power does not disappear from the scene. It is instead distributed elsewhere. In this case, Reno watches as increasingly it appears to be taken up by men with guns.

"You like a guy who puts a gun in his boot," a man whispers to Reno at a party soon after the slave girl scene, "*don't you*?" (168). As it turns out, she does. And it is this love of men with guns that ultimately leads Reno to be an unknowing facilitator of a political murder. But the love of guns is not just an aspect of Reno's characterization; it is the natural extension of her formal position as a first-person narrator who is, as Kushner put it, "nevertheless overrun." Wood, like Sandro and Ronnie, appreciates the novel's hybrid formal mode, a mode that relies upon the construction of a narrator who identifies herself with authorship while withdrawing herself from the power such a position entails. But Wood, like Reno, would prefer the novel to remain hovering in that narrative position, vibrating with the experience that Reno, *every aspect of her a modesty*, records. The problem, however, is that the very condition that allows for this form to occur also points precipitously toward complicity with violence. Of course the woman who embraces "the cord around her neck" as an "adornment" will "like a guy who puts a gun in his boot," we are told. The end of the novel, in which Reno, like many of the other women in the novel, is used as a tool by violent men, suggests the inevitability that an attempt to extract oneself from structures of authority and power can only result in one being used by those who traffic intentionally in authority and power. The novel therefore provides a formal model for how a populace that, in the name of liberal values of individual freedom, withdraws from participation in the intentional distribution and management of power—that is, democracy—could end up supporting the violent exercise of power—that is, authoritarianism.

*   *   *

By looking to Barth's account of the political dilemmas of postmodernist fiction, we can see precisely what kind of hybrid form Kushner employs in the construction of Reno's narrative position. In "The Literature of Exhaustion," Barth sees his moment in the late 1960s as "an age of ultimacies and 'final solutions'" (67). The best writers, he argues, "illustrate in a simple way the difference between the *fact* of aesthetic ultimacies and their artistic *use*" (68). So rather than simply participate in the perceived demise of the novel, which one might do by simply rewriting a classic work of fiction in order to undo it, the writers Barth appreciates turn the feeling of living in a moment that is seeing the end of the novel into a work of art. Jorge Luis Borges, Barth argues, is exemplary in this regard: "Borges doesn't attribute the *Quixote* to himself . . . instead, he writes a remarkable and original work of literature, the implicit theme of which is the difficulty, perhaps the unnecessity, of writing original works of literature" (69). If it is tempting to seize upon the moment of anti-authoritarianism and ultimacy to produce works of art that, in ridding themselves of the authoritarian valences of the artist, end up also ridding themselves of the capacity to make anything, writers like Borges, for Barth, are masters of "every moment throwing out the bath water without for a moment losing the baby" (70).

What this means, for Barth, is the need for writers to do something that runs against the most radical experiments in 1960s art: to retain the position of the artist as an authority. The politics of this position are explicit in "The Literature of Exhaustion." For Barth, most individuals alone are not equipped to deal with the disorientation of contemporary life. "Distressing as the fact is to us liberal democrats," he writes, "the commonality, alas, will *always* lose their way and their soul" (75). What is needed, then, are artists with "very special gifts—as extraordinary as saint- or herohood" who may "go straight through the maze to the accomplishment of [their] work" (76). Barth therefore allies himself with the hopes of liberal democracy ("us liberal democrats") but suggests that its survival depends upon a willingness to embrace forms of what he calls "aristocratic power"—power that is unabashedly opposed to the notion of perfect freedom.

Kushner's narrator does the opposite. She eagerly relinquishes her power, and violence floods in, first in the form of characters ready to take advantage of a narrator who has abdicated the authority of her position. As a result, she becomes less and less a person herself, to the point where at the end of the novel we find Reno working as a "china girl," or a model meant to help film projectionists color-correct for Caucasian skin tone. As Marvin, the man who hires her for the job, explains, she is meant to be "a reference file to reality. Like you're a reference file for Caucasian skin tones; it doesn't matter that you exist. For the technician or projectionist, you're an index for the existence of woman, flesh, flesh tones. Which brings up the question of race, unaddressed. You, as *you*, have nothing to do with it" (322). The figure of the china girl seems as if it would be a perfect metafictional image for a work of postmodernist fiction: the index for reality that cannot be real; the pure surface of color; the priority of medium over actual experience. As Wood notes, however, Reno's condition, in which "you, as *you*, have nothing to do with it," produces, in the case of *The Flamethrowers*, a work of fiction that feels like the opposite of postmodernist artificiality: it feels more real for the lack of narrative intrusion. The difference between Reno's characterization and the flat characterization typical of postmodern novels is, in part, a difference in narrative focalization. The internal focalization of *The Flamethrowers* means that Reno's flatness reads as a psychological condition rather than an artificial one. It takes a character commenting upon her to allow us to see that flatness as anything other than a manifestation of character traits like reservedness, passivity, or shyness. And in this passage, it takes the comments of a character to point out the degree to which social power inflects Reno's perspective. Reading her labeling as "woman, flesh, flesh tones . . . race, unaddressed," we see, once again, that power informs Reno's position even as she seems to eschew it.

Compare Reno's flat abstraction—flat characterization that nevertheless feels real—to the narrator of Barth's iconic story "Lost in the Funhouse." Whereas *The Flamethrowers* plays with internal focalization, obscuring the artificiality of its narrator, Barth's story plays with the problems inherent in the very act of narration by emphasizing the material circumstances of authorship. While Reno records experience with the vividness that can only come from immersion in it, Barth's narrator is obsessed with typography and semantics. We see this in the first paragraph of the story. It begins somewhat conventionally: "For whom is the funhouse fun? Perhaps for lovers. For Ambrose it is *a place of fear and confusion*" (69). But this conventional mode is quickly undermined by an extended explanation of the role of italics in fiction. The narrator explains that italics are "employed, in fiction stories especially, for 'outside,' intrusive, or artificial voices, such as radio announcements, the texts of telegrams and newspapers articles, et cetera. They should be used *sparingly.* If passages originally in roman type are italicized by someone repeating them, it's customary to acknowledge the fact. *Italics mine*" (69). If the narrator of "Lost in the Funhouse" feels "real," it is because the narrator breaks the fourth wall, talking directly to the reader about the various requirements of manuscript production and typeface manipulation. The distinction between Kushner and Barth, then, is the difference between the value of reality lying in having a body that has an identity—white woman—and that can therefore be the vessel of certain kinds of experience, as in the case of Kushner, and the value of reality lying in the ability to step outside the story and take stock of it along with the reader, assessing its mechanisms, material requirements, and assumptions. In stating *"italics mine,"* the narrator of Barth's story claims authority over it and communicates that fact directly to the reader. *I did this*, we might imagine that narrator saying. *Me. I did it. Italics mine.* Barth's text therefore signals a comfort with the fact of overt authority, as the narrator claims authorship and with it an authoritative position within the text.

Reno, of course, cannot do this because she is unaware of her own role in the novel. After being left by Sandro in Italy, hanging out with the Red Brigades, and returning to New York, she has something of an epiphany. She recognizes that the subjugation she has experienced in her relationships has something to do with her own actions. "It was something I had done to myself," she realizes (316). This could suggest a moment of real self-consciousness, of Reno's becoming something more than an empty vessel by recognizing the strange form her agency had been taking all along. But this epiphany is clearly limited. Because, of course, there is a larger force governing Reno's passivity, a force we may only identify if we remember Barth's *"Italics mine."* Reno does not abdicate power herself; it is taken from her by the author of the novel in which she is simply another character. But unlike the third-person narrator of "Lost in the Funhouse," who seems to blend with the persona of the author, Kushner, as author of *The Flamethrowers*, is sealed out of the text. The fact that Kushner would have been only seven years old when Reno first met "the people with the gun" only adds to this effect. The author of *The Flamethrowers* is entirely invisible. Until she is not.

This is one way to understand what happens when the "thematic circuits" of the novel begin to "overload." As Reno begins to be used by the characters around her, as her position as narrator begins to be called into question as a form of passivity or even exposure to violence, we might begin to feel Kushner herself pulling the strings. Recall that Kushner intended her narrator to both have "all words" and be "overrun, effaced, and silenced." Kushner's presence—in her use of photographic images throughout the text, in the gap that exists between her own generation and that of her narrator, and, perhaps most importantly, in her work negotiating between historical reality and fiction—becomes increasingly strongly felt as the novel proceeds. Returning to the key scene in which Reno contemplates the slave girl sculpture, for instance, Kushner's presence stands out in a striking moment of fictionalization. The sculpture that fascinates Sandro and Ronnie does, in actuality, exist in the collection of the Metropolitan Museum. But it does not, in fact, depict a slave girl. Instead, given the fact that the relief was part of a gravesite memorial, the girl was likely from a wealthy family. It is Kushner, then, who enslaves the girl, literally putting the cord around her neck.[4] But Kushner is, of course, invisible to Reno. Reno has to conclude, then, that she has willfully participated in her own subordination.

The Flamethrowers therefore illustrates how the depoliticization that occurs as the result of an ideological commitment to libertarian notions of individual freedom can leave a populace vulnerable to the insinuation of a more dramatic form of political authority. Democracy requires that citizens make choices about how political authority will function. The liberal notion that each individual should be entirely self-governing paradoxically undermines democracy, depriving individuals of the right and responsibility to make choices about what power structures and authorities they wish to institute. The formal equivalent to this condition can be found in works that see hybrid and plural formal qualities as allowing for the depoliticization of aesthetic choices. As Mouffe explains, "pluralism implies the permanence of conflict and antagonism." As a result, she argues, "We have therefore to abandon the very idea of a complete reabsorption of alterity into oneness and harmony" (33). The Flamethowers makes this point precisely in its aspects that supporters of compromise aesthetics, such as Wood, are likely to see as failures. When we feel Kushner's presence too strongly, when the novel's thematic force seems too heavy-handed, when the apparent transparency of Reno's narrative seems overridden, these are the moments when readers have to come to grips with the fact that art, like politics, cannot avoid the existence of power and authority.

In their 2011 manifesto, The Coming Insurrection, members of the anarchist collective the Invisible Committee write:

> The West is a civilization that has survived all the prophecies of its collapse with a singular stratagem. Just as the bourgeoisie had to deny itself as a class in order to permit the bourgeoisification of society as a whole . . . so the West has sacrificed itself as a particular civilization in order to impose itself as a universal culture. The operation can be summarized like this: an entity in its death throes sacrifices itself as a content in order to survive as a form. (91)

---

[4] See Marble Grave Stele of a Little Girl. The differences between the actual sculpture and the account of it in The Flamethrowers are noted in "Grave Stele of a Little Girl (ca. 450–440 B.C.)."

Could this be the case with democracy today? Has the content of democracy—the belief that citizens participate in the governing of their country—been sacrificed in order for individuals to feel like autonomous, liberal subjects? If so, then the formal condition of *The Flamethrowers* might be read as telling us something about our political condition today. Contrary to those who would like to see contemporary art assert formal authority against the individualism of neoliberalism, our danger today is not the thoroughgoing absence of authority. Instead, our condition is the opposite: we risk being assembled to the service of a dangerous form of meaning by forces that are unrecognizable to us because they do not announce themselves as such and rather seem to come from deep within each of us individually. Each of us individually harbors racist imaginations, sexist thoughts, violent proclivities. We perpetrate injustice and exploitation not because we are under orders; we "do it ourselves." But we forget that there are authors of those discourses. These ideas come from somewhere. And the more we fail to recognize that fact, the more the danger rises that the worst of those propensities will govern us. The reason this danger exists stems paradoxically from the ideology of freedom that initially underpinned neoliberalization. For a generation, we have aspired to empty ourselves of collective forms of political ideology and intentional forms of authority. If we have succeeded, we may need to ask what new content might come along to fill those empty forms.

*   *   *

RACHEL GREENWALD SMITH is associate professor of English at Saint Louis University and author of *Affect and American Literature in the Age of Neoliberalism* (2015). She has edited *American Literature in Transition: 2000–2010* (2017) and coedited a collection titled *Neoliberalism and Contemporary Literary Culture* (2017).

Works Cited

Barth, John. "The Literature of Exhaustion." *The Friday Book: Essays and Other Non-fiction.* Baltimore: Johns Hopkins UP, 1984. 62–76.

———. "Lost in the Funhouse." *Lost in the Funhouse: Fiction for Print, Tape, Live Voice.* New York: Bantam, 1980. 69–94.

Belletto, Steven. *No Accident, Comrade: Chance and Design in Cold War American Narratives.* Oxford: Oxford UP, 2012.

Brown, Nicholas. "The Work of Art in the Age of Its Real Subsumption under Capital." *nonsite* 13 Mar. 2012 < nonsite.org/editorial/the-work-of-art-in-the-age-of-its-real-subsumption -under-capital>

Brown, Wendy. *Undoing the Demos: Neoliberalism's Stealth Revolution.* New York: Zone, 2015.

Cooper, David. Introduction. *The Dialectics of Liberation.* Ed. David Cooper. New York: Verso, 2015.

DeKoven, Marianne. *Utopia Limited: The Sixties and the Emergence of the Postmodern*. Durham: Duke UP, 2004.

DeLillo, Don. *White Noise*. New York: Penguin, 1985.

Drucker, Johanna. *Sweet Dreams: Contemporary Art and Complicity*. Chicago: U of Chicago P, 2005.

Foucault, Michel. *The Birth of Biopolitics*. Ed. Michel Senellart, François Ewald, and Alessandro Fontana. Trans. Graham Burchell. New York: Palgrave Macmillan, 2008.

———. Preface. *Anti-Oedipus: Capitalism and Schizophrenia*. By Gilles Deleuze and Félix Guattari. Trans. Robert Hurley, Mark Seem, and Helen R. Lane. Minneapolis: U of Minnesota P, 1983.

Fukuyama, Francis. "The End of History?" *National Interest* 16 (1989): 3–18.

"*Grave Stele of a Little Girl* (ca. 450–440 B.C.)." Real Art Described in Fiction <artinfiction .tumblr.com/post/72363056541/grave-stele-of-a-little-girl-ca-450440-bc> (accessed 1 Nov. 2016).

Harvey, David. *A Brief History of Neoliberalism*. Oxford: Oxford UP, 2005.

The Invisible Committee. *The Coming Insurrection*. Cambridge: Semiotext(e), 2009.

Kaprow, Allan. "From *Assemblages, Environments, and Happenings*." *Art in Theory 1900–2000: An Anthology of Changing Ideas*. Ed. Charles Harrison and Paul Wood. 2nd ed. Malden: Blackwell, 2002. 717–21.

Kushner, Rachel. *The Flamethrowers*. New York: Scribner, 2013.

———. "The Flamethrowers." *Paris Review* no. 203 (2012) <https://www.theparisreview .org/art-photography/6197/the-flamethrowers-rachel-kushner> (accessed 5 Dec. 2016).

Laing, R. D. "The Obvious." *The Dialectics of Liberation*. Ed. David Cooper. New York: Verso, 2015. 13–33.

Marble Grave Stele of a Little Girl. Marble. Metropolitan Museum of Art, New York. <met museum.org/art/collection/search/252890> (accessed 1 Nov. 2016).

McCann, Sean, and Michael Szalay. "Do You Believe in Magic? Literary Thinking after the New Left." *Yale Journal of Criticism* 18.2 (2005): 435–68.

Michaels, Walter Benn. *The Beauty of a Social Problem*. Chicago: U of Chicago P, 2015.

Mouffe, Chantal. *The Democratic Paradox*. New York: Verso, 2005.

Swensen, Cole. Introduction. *American Hybrid: A Norton Anthology of New Poetry*. Ed. Cole Swensen and David St. John. New York: Norton, 2009.

Wood, James. "Youth in Revolt: Rachel Kushner's *The Flamethowers*." *New Yorker* 8 Apr. 2013 <newyorker.com/magazine/2013/04/08/youth-in-revolt>.

"The Freedom to See": Social Relations and Aesthetic Form in The Golden Bowl

PAUL STASI

A System of Human Relations

What might a late nineteenth-century writer like Henry James have to say about neoliberalism? At first blush the answer would seem to be quite little, as neoliberalism, according to one of its most prominent theorists, Wendy Brown, marks a distinctly modern form of governmentality, one that abandons the tenets of classical liberalism in its relentless drive to transform "every human domain and endeavor, along with humans themselves, according to a specific image of the economic" (10).[1] Reimaging human life in the image of capital, the neoliberal revolution takes place in the name of freedom but ends up destroying "freedom's grounding in sovereignty for states and subjects alike" (108). "[B]oth persons and states," Brown writes, "are expected to comport themselves in ways that maximize their capital value in the present and enhance their future value" (22). The result is the loss of a set of ideals by which liberalism—in theory if not always in practice— sought to regulate itself: "We are no longer creatures of moral autonomy, freedom, or equality. . . . We are no longer even creatures of interest relentlessly seeking to satisfy ourselves" (42). "At this point," Brown writes, "the throne of interest has vanished and at the extreme is replaced with the throne of sacrifice" (84). "At the triumphal 'end of history' in the West," Brown concludes, "most have ceased to believe in the human capacity to craft and sustain a world that is humane, free, sustainable, and, above all, modestly under human control" (221). What is sacrificed is nothing less than human agency itself.

Of course, sacrifice—the renunciation of personal interest—is one of James's great themes, found throughout his work, whether in Isabel Archer's curious return to Rome or Lambert Strether's rejection of Maria Gostrey's marriage proposal.[2]

The author would like to thank Jennifer Fleissner, Richard Godden, and, especially, Nancy Armstrong for their insightful comments on earlier drafts.

[1] Brown is, of course, not alone in finding neoliberalism a distinctly modern phenomenon. Of the many who agree with her, perhaps the most noteworthy is David Harvey, who makes a helpful distinction between neoliberalism conceived as a political project and idealist accounts that describe it as a set of governing ideologies. Harvey, in the interview "Neoliberalism Is a Political Project," defends neoliberalism's distinctiveness as a set of regulatory and governmental practices undertaken by the ruling class since the 1970s, but he agrees that idealist accounts— his example is Foucault, but Brown would certainly be in this camp as well—allow us to locate its governing ideas much further back in time.

[2] A distinguished line of critics, from Van Wyck Brooks to Dorothea Krook to, more recently, Robert Pippin have described James's ethic of sacrifice. Here is Pippin: "The moral dimension is perhaps most obvious in what appears to be James's confident insistence on the reality of moral evil . . . and by his treatment of the problem of self-sacrifice, especially the sacrifice of one's own

More to the point, James understood his homeland as similarly in sway to an all-determining economic realm. According to Collin Meissner, "America had become [for James] the embodiment of what [his] contemporary Georg Simmel called a money-culture, a culture characterized by . . . the reduction of all human relations to the language of transaction and commodity exchange, a commerce where neither the individual nor object are the mode of discourse, only the sum of money in it" (245). In support, Meissner quotes the following passage from *The American Scene*:

> It's all very well for you to look as if, since you've had no past, you're going in, as the next best thing, for a magnificent compensatory future. What are you going to make your future of, for all your airs, we want to know?—what elements of a future, as futures have gone in the great world, are at all assured to you? Do what you will, you sit here only in the lurid light of "business," and you know, without our reminding you, what guarantees, what majestic continuity and heredity, that represents. . . . No, what you are reduced to for "importance" is the present, pure and simple, squaring itself between an absent future and an absent past as solidly as it can. (James 160–61; qtd. in Meissner 244)

A culture devoted squarely to business, James suggests, is cut off from both past and future, existing in a perpetual present—another version, then, of Brown's end of history.

If, for Meissner, the late texts pursue a style that is the mirror of this all-dominant money-form, I would like to make a parallel but distinct argument, focusing as much on form as on style, and choosing, in particular, *The Golden Bowl* as my example.[3] For *The Golden Bowl*, as Edith Wharton famously remarked, seems to take place "in the void," one which, as various critics have noted, displaces historical reference in favor of a remarkably abstract and formal process that arranges and rearranges its characters' relations to one another (Wharton 191).[4] Individual interest, in this account, seems subservient to the imperatives of James's structural imagination, even as the specificity of character is subsumed by the twists and turns of that all-encompassing late style. Structure and style, that is to say, create a kind of formal equality among the characters in the text. At the same time, the actions these characters undertake are virtuosic examples of Jamesian indirection. Maggie manages to save her marriage precisely by refusing to acknowledge the wrongs that have been done to her; her efforts all take place entirely on what we might call an affective register as she time and again finds the right way to manipulate the social structure to her advantage.

---

happiness or good in recognition of some sort of requirement not relevant to one's happiness or good" (30).

[3]   Meissner writes: "[T]he prose style of the late phase shares a good deal of similarity with Simmel's explanation of money as 'nothing but the vehicle for a movement in which everything else that is not in motion is completely extinguished.' Like Simmel's money, James's late prose deploys itself 'in continuous self-alienation from any given point and thus forms the counterpart and direct negation of all being itself'" (248; quoting Georg Simmel, *Philosophy of Money*).

[4]   See, for instance, arguments by Stuart Burrows, Michael Meeuwis, and Julian Murphet.

I draw deliberately on the discourse of affect here because, as Dierdra Reber has recently suggested, affect can be read as the reigning episteme of neoliberalism's all-conquering free market. With this idea in mind, it becomes possible to read Brown's seemingly quixotic defense of the "distinctly human capacities for ethical and political freedom, creativity, unbounded reflection, or invention" (43) as a critique not only of neoliberalism's evisceration of the political but, more generally, of a scholarly moment defined by a wide range of posthumanisms, affect theory among them.[5] For Reber, however, affect is part of the long history of capitalism, whose "originary—revolutionary—self-legitimizing discourse was one rooted in the primacy of the passions" (77). The affective side of capital has always existed in dialectical tension with what she names capital's rationalizing colonial logic. What Brown describes as a new moment of capitalist governance, might, then, be better understood as an intensification of certain tendencies present within capitalism from its inception, a reading that allows us to see the relevance James's work might have for the discourse of neoliberalism.[6]

For if capital's affective mode, according to Reber, is defined fundamentally by the homeostatic movement of an impersonal system toward internal equilibrium— a set of flows that elude fixed boundaries and establish their own laws that transcend the interests of nations and subjects—we could easily read *The Golden Bowl*'s form as mirroring this impersonal drive for balance. And yet it is not quite right to say that James's texts are entirely impersonal or structural; as Omri Moses has recently argued, James consistently anchors the thoughts and experiences he explores in characters who are never quite reducible to style or form. Characters, in James, might oscillate unevenly between structural possibilities and centers of consciousness with concrete identities, but they remain characters, nonetheless, defined by the choices they make even if these choices often seem determined by a set of situational and structural pressures that stand outside them. But even here we

---

[5]   I thank Jennifer Fleissner for this insight, delivered in a talk titled "Is the Novel Neoliberal?" at the Society for Novel Studies 2016 conference.

[6]   There are many places in Marx where we might ground this understanding of neoliberalism's relationship to nineteenth-century capitalism. In the *Grundrisse*, for instance, Marx argues against the notion of rational self-interest: "The real point is not that each individual's pursuit of his private interest promotes the totality of private interest, the general interest. . . . The point is rather that private interest is itself already a socially determined interest, which can be achieved only within the conditions laid down by society and with the means provided by society. . . . The reciprocal and all-sided dependence of individuals who are indifferent to one another forms their social connection" (156–57). The pursuit of private interest is, for Marx, necessarily the pursuit of social interest, since the concept of interest is precisely the way the social order reproduces itself *through* individuals. *Interest*, we might say, is, here, another name for ideology, tethering individuals, liberal and neoliberal alike, to the accumulation of capital. In that same text, Marx describes the alienated worker as reduced to a "value-creating possibility" (453), a term that seems quite close to the neoliberal subject Brown describes above. His work, too, is filled with instances when capital is happy to sacrifice individuals in its relentless pursuit of the valorization of value. In *Capital*, Marx writes, "The mass of social wealth, overflowing with the advance of accumulation, and transformable into additional capital, thrusts itself frantically into old branches of production . . . or into newly formed branches. . . . In all such cases, there must be the possibility of throwing great masses of men suddenly into the decisive points without injury to the scale of production in other spheres. Over-population supplies these masses" (694).

must be careful, for the structural pressures that James's characters confront—as *The Golden Bowl* aptly illustrates—are most often generated by other characters. The seemingly impersonal system of James's texts is, first and foremost, a system of human relations. James, in other words, defends the agency of the subject, who is shown to act in accordance with relatively defined interests, even if those interests are often depicted in structural terms.

In contrast, then, to a neoliberalism that disguises the interest underlying its sacrifice of subjects through the seemingly impersonal logic of value production, James consistently works to reveal the human interest behind his aesthetic structures. He thus performs a curious double-move with his form, allowing it to appear self-grounding while simultaneously pointing to a set of social determinations that cannot quite make themselves felt within the world of the text itself. In this way, aesthetic form recovers history as a distinctly *human* project, precisely the understanding of history neoliberalism effaces in its subservience to the logic of capitalist exchange. To make this case, I will first turn to Walter Benn Michaels's recent argument about neoliberal aesthetics—where Michaels suggests the ways in which an autonomous form can nevertheless stage its relationship to history—before describing in greater detail what James's form represents and what it gestures to as its determining ground.

The Cracks in the Bowl

In a chapter titled "Neoliberal Aesthetics," from his 2015 book *The Beauty of a Social Problem*, Michaels makes a relatively succinct point: the "refusal of form . . . [is] at the heart of neoliberal aesthetics" (63). Michaels's argument is a complicated one—turning on a discussion of photography and drawing on the work of Michael Fried to establish the antitheatrical bias of modern aesthetic theory—but its main contours can be readily understood if we read "postmodernism" in the place of "neoliberal aesthetics." Neoliberalism's rejection of form, then, emerges from the by now familiar critique of an aesthetic autonomy associated, primarily, with modernism, a critique that, furthermore, connects form to totality and each to totalitarianism.

Michaels's discussion reaches its apex in Jacques Rancière's reading of Bartolome Murillo's *Beggar Boys Eating Grapes and Melons. Beggar Boys* represents a nearly perfect example of aesthetic autonomy: the boys seem entirely absorbed into the formal unity of the painting. "The figures," Michaels summarizes, "are thus converted into a kind of formal device for establishing the coherence of the work" (57). But for Rancière, this is exactly the problem: "What they are or do matters little," he argues, "but what is important is that they are put in their place" (Rancière 14; qtd. in Michaels 57). Rancière, in turn, offers an alternate reading of the boys' absorption. For him, they are "carefree," the noninstrumental nature of their activity suggesting an inner freedom that their condition as beggars initially belies. Michaels summarizes the point:

> [T]his doing nothing not only saves them from passive absorption but aligns them
> with an art understood, not in terms of the "project of separation" from the world
> (from nature), but in terms of its non-instrumentality, an art that is thus identified
> with the world (with nature, which has no projects at all) and with the refusal to be

put into place—whether that place is the formal space of the painting or the social space to which their position would seem to consign them. (57)

Thus an "aesthetic refusal"—of the demand for a separation from the world— becomes a social or political refusal.

Those familiar with Michaels's work can see where this argument is going, for we have here a precise instance in which the recognition of abstract equality—inner freedom—negates social inequality, the fact that these boys are beggars and thus have a specific location in the social order. Against this abstract equality, Michaels turns to Walker Evans's photographs in *Let Us Now Praise Famous Men*, which Rancière had praised for similar reasons: "Where for Rancière the photographs are an occasion for the peasants to assert their aesthetic capacities, for Agee they are a kind of demonstration of what it is to be so 'appallingly damaged' that you no longer have any such capacities" (Michaels 61). What the photographs stage, for Michaels, is the gap between the sensibility that produced them and the impoverished people they depict. It is precisely because they are beautiful, which is to say *formally conceived*, that they allow us to see the distance between our own aesthetic sensibility and the peasant's impoverishment, a distance that negates abstract equality in the name of the distinctions produced by different historical circumstances. Neoliberal aesthetics, in contrast, dissolve the boundary between aesthetics and politics. What is meant as a political critique of aesthetic form becomes, instead, an aestheticization of politics: "The political meaning of the refusal of form," Michaels writes, "is the indifference to those social structures that, not produced by how we see, cannot be overcome by seeing differently" (63). This aesthetic egalitarianism rhymes with a neoliberal egalitarianism defined as equality of access to markets: "That egalitarianism," Michaels continues, "is violated by the refusal to hire workers because of their race or sex . . . not by the inequalities generated . . . by the exploitation of labor by capital. Indeed, the very concept of 'labor' is here rendered problematic, since the worker is understood instead as a kind of capitalist—that's the meaning of the . . . concept of human capital. Thus the very concept of class disappears from the analysis" (68).[7] Neoliberalism thus unites a refusal of form with a refusal of class. The two are, in effect, the same, as each is understood to be a mode of containment.

But form and class are also ways of expressing relations—form is what connects the disparate elements of a work to each other; class, as E. P. Thompson famously argued, is not a thing but a relation—and neoliberalism, as both Michaels and Brown suggest, is relentlessly destructive of all forms of social relation. James, in contrast, is acutely aware of how his characters are placed within a larger social structure. To be sure, we would be hard pressed to find in James any overt critique of social inequality, and while this might lead us to think James has little to say about class, that would be wrong. For his books are almost entirely about class, only they are not generally about the right class: they are about the upper class, and though it is surely possible to take James to task for this almost exclusive focus and

---

[7]   Wendy Brown agrees: "[W]hen everything is capital, labor disappears as a category, as does its collective form, class" (38).

to suggest, further, that the finest of Jamesian discriminations could only exist within his world of leisure, it would be false to say that James is unaware of this. Rather, I would agree with Julian Murphet, who argues that "[i]n every case, the insurgent pleasure that erupts into these [late] novels' polite social spaces has its impetus in a private fortune built upon vulgarity and exploitation" (227). What interests me, though, is less the relationship between pleasure and vulgarity than that between economic privilege and the structural machinations of the Jamesian subject. For James's novels are entirely insistent on the remarkable wealth and privilege of the characters themselves, even as he fails, in often ostentatious ways—think, for instance, of the "little nameless object" manufactured in Woollett—to linger on its details.[8]

Indeed, the entire narrative arc of *The Golden Bowl* is dictated by the relative distinctions in wealth among its principal characters, Charlotte and Amerigo having split due to their (relative) poverty and both having been purchased by Adam Verver, who is "the representative of a force," which can only be money, defined as it is in the following, perfectly oblique late Jamesian terms: "Quantity was in the air . . . and Mr. Verver's estimable quality was almost wholly in that pervasion" (264). Having only quantity for quality, Mr. Verver, as Maggie declares, is also formless: "Father's form?" she says to the Prince. "It strikes me he hasn't got any" (30). The Prince, in contrast, is all form, which is why he can become "part of [Verver's] collection" (33). And if the Prince senses that he "cost a lot of money," Maggie, characteristically, has not "the least idea" of the price (34). Financial dependence thus undergirds the marriages in the text—the Prince having left Charlotte because "[h]e *had* to have money" (77)—but this dependence is more often presented through metaphor and perception rather than outright statement. Charlotte, for instance, is "in charge of the 'social relations' of the family," which causes Amerigo to see her as "dealing . . . with the duties of a remunerated office" (258, 260). And later, as he watches Charlotte and Adam wander the grounds of Fawns, he will produce the text's most gruesome image: "[T]he likeness of their connexion wouldn't have been wrongly figured if he had been thought of as holding in one of his pocketed hands the end of a long silken halter looped round her beautiful neck. He didn't twitch it, yet it was there; he didn't drag her, but she came" (535). This moment is curious, for it does not exactly describe the Prince's consciousness but something he would not be wrong to have seen. It is, in effect, something not seen—something that seems to emerge from the text's own consciousness, like those repeated moments of "not saying" that nevertheless elaborate the entire train of a character's thought, on which Sharon Cameron builds her argument about the autonomy of consciousness in James's work.

I find here something different, for the text's metaphorical insistence on economic metaphors and the curious way it allows but withholds this ultimate image of Charlotte's submission forces us to become aware of a set of economic relations that, while often acknowledged by the characters, are never given the full range of

---

[8] I refer, of course, to *The Ambassadors*. This object, the "vulgar" source of Chad Newsome's wealth, remains unnamed throughout the text, its obscurity the subject of a lengthy conversation between our hero Lambert Strether and his confidante Miss Gostrey (98).

determination that the text allows us to see that they have. What the late novels show us, then—and here *The Golden Bowl* is exemplary—is the way a set of affective and emotional dispositions characterized by their fluidity and openness to circumstance tend to obscure the socially determined privilege on which they depend. In this way, *The Golden Bowl* stages its relationship to a set of concerns that would seem initially to remain outside it. So while I understand why Fredric Jameson claims—making a general point about James by way of *The Wings of the Dove*—that "in the Jamesian system, we have to step outside the text altogether in order to appreciate the fact that Densher is a gigolo and Kate a designing woman," I do not agree (183). Rather, I think the text works as much to reveal as it does to conceal its dependence on what seems to stand outside its formal boundaries. One of the ways we might think about this is by focusing on what Peter Brooks long ago called James's "melodramatic imagination."[9]

For from one perspective, the details of the text would fill the pages of any contemporary bodice ripper: An Italian Prince is set to marry a wealthy American heiress. On the eve of his marriage, his old flame, herself one of the heiress's closest friends, returns to London. She marries the heiress's father, and she and the Prince resume their love affair, only to be discovered and separated for life. Of course, the novel locates itself not in these plot points, but rather in the elaborate psychological structure it is able to build upon them. In this way, the entire text mimics the action of book 2, where Maggie refuses her role in the melodrama, only to engage in a cruel, if immensely subtle, manipulation of Charlotte Stant into defeat. The novel, that is to say, is antitheatrical in form as well as in content; it tells us of characters who refuse to act melodramatically in a style that seems to endorse this refusal. But as I have already suggested, it does not simply endorse this refusal but rather stages it. So, for instance, we can read Maggie's actions in book 2 as a sacrifice of personal interest, or we can see them as a more ruthless way to promote her own interests, a pursuit aided by her heightened awareness of context.

Maggie's interests, in other words, remain consistent throughout the novel. And they are aided by class privilege, which returns in one of the most implausible moments in the text: the arrival of the bowl at Maggie's house, an implausibility underlined by the Prince, who remarks that "the coincidence is extraordinary—the sort of thing that happens mainly in novels and plays" (467). Maggie, it seems, had unwittingly stumbled upon the same bowl in the same pawnshop as Amerigo and Charlotte and, further, the shopkeeper—after having sold the bowl to her and agreed to deliver it to her house—had, for some reason, written "in a spirit of retraction, to a lady with whom he had made a most advantageous bargain" (488). James underlines this oddity with anti-Semitism—calling it "a scruple rare enough in vendors of any class and almost unprecedented in the thrifty children of Israel"

---

[9]   P. Brooks derives James's "moral manichaeism" from the conventions of melodrama, and if *The Golden Bowl* works toward their transcendence, this nevertheless displays James's continued reliance on melodramatic structures: "Nowhere more effectively than in this renunciation of melodrama did James image the melodramatic tenor of his imagination, the attraction of melodrama, the continuing need for it as a mode of consciousness and rhetorical stance, as well as the need to conquer it" (5, 195).

(488)—but the effect of the line exceeds its racism, serving to further undermine the given explanation for the bowl's return. For knowing that the bowl was "a birthday-gift to her father," is it not possible that the vendor figured out just who that father was and, perhaps, had a scruple about selling a broken object at an unfair price to one of the most famous American art collectors in London (488)? From one angle, then, the golden bowl is a symbol of Maggie's class privilege, which allows her a particular relationship to her social order, one in which shopkeepers overturn their personal interests in the service of hers.

But it is also, of course, an almost embarrassingly obvious symbol for the text's formal structure, and here we can return to Michaels's argument about form, for James would seem to be entirely in line with the "project of separation" from the world of Rancière's critique. In the preface to *The Golden Bowl*, for instance, James writes: "We see very few persons in 'The Golden Bowl,' but the scheme of the book, to make up for that, is that we shall really see about as much of them as a coherent literary form permits" (6). This coherence is built on a series of exacting parallels, two books, the first from the perspective of the Prince, the second from the perspective of the Princess, and a structure that turns on a series of exchanges, as the principal characters compose and recompose themselves in an effort to find some kind of harmony. Initially, Maggie's marriage to the Prince leaves her father open to assaults from potential suitors: "What I feel," Maggie tells him, "is that there's somehow something that used to be right and that I've made wrong" (151). And so, in due time, Charlotte Stant is brought in to right this wrong, only her arrival produces another peculiarity, for it allows Maggie and her father to carry on as they did before, which inevitably thrusts Amerigo and Charlotte into a new relation. Or, rather, an old relation rekindled: "There it all is—extraordinary beyond words," Charlotte tells the Prince just prior to the renewal of their affections. "It makes such a relation for us as, I verily believe, was never before in the world thrust upon two well-meaning creatures. Haven't we therefore to take things as we find them?" (248). The structure, it seems here, produces the relationship, which has led critics such as Leo Bersani to claim that Charlotte and the Prince "make love as a result of the arrangements contrived during the time of the novel itself. It's as if the geometry of human relations *implied* what we call human feelings into existence" (74).

This idea is supported by Maggie's actions in the novel's second half, which eschew open confrontation. "But he didn't explain—?" Fanny Assingham asks, at one point, of the Prince: "'Explain? Thank God, no!' Maggie threw back her head as with horror at the thought, then the next moment added: 'And I didn't either'" (483). Maggie, instead, opts for a set of structural machinations that attempt to put things right. These involve tiny changes in the form of their lives: Maggie remains home awaiting the Prince's arrival or shows up earlier than expected at Portland Place, and these moves, in turn, create a new set of structures whereby characters exchange places with one another. The Prince becomes Adam's partner, which forces Maggie and Charlotte into a new relation whereby Maggie can achieve her ultimate end, which is thrusting Charlotte away from her and back to Adam so that she can retain the Prince at novel's end. The novel is remarkable for the closeness it keeps to its principal characters, who seemingly exist only in a set of changing relations to one another.

And yet melodrama disrupts this version of the story as well, for the relation between Charlotte and the Prince preexists the text, and so the structures in which they find themselves do not so much create their feelings as allow those that already exist an avenue of expression.[10] Further, the basic drama of the novel rests on the difficulty a father and daughter have in handling the distance her marriage is supposed to create, a difficulty heightened by the circumstances of Maggie's past: her mother died when she was ten. We can easily enough imagine the intensity of the Ververs' relationship as a result of their shared past, but the text performs a curious maneuver with this information that is exemplary of its style: James tells us this fact but does absolutely nothing with it, refusing to offer it as an explanation for the attachment at the book's center. Not only that, James has Maggie say to her father that she does not know how she will respond to misfortune, since "I've never had the least blow" (161). James is, here, almost ostentatiously asking us to understand, at one and the same time, the conditioning power of this biographical detail *and* the way the characters almost willfully fail to see its power.

On the one hand, then, we have structure: the formal properties of the text setting loose a set of potentialities that unfold in ways determined by the manipulation of that structure. On the other hand, we have the power of the past, which the text offers us but obscures. Which returns us to the bowl. I have already suggested the way it symbolizes the aesthetic structure that governs the text, its two halves like the novel's two books and its crack like the fault line that exists in the characters' relationship. The crack, then, becomes the shared past of Charlotte and the Prince even as the bowl bridges the gap between form and history. Furthermore, its original existence is as a *ricordo*, but a *ricordo* of nothing, since it remains at first unpurchased and since, in any case, there can be no record of an event—the Prince and Charlotte's trip through London on the eve of his marriage—that must not exist. Nor can there be any record of the past in honor of which this trip was taken. The bowl, that is to say, memorializes a past it cannot represent as a crack in its seemingly pristine structure. In doing so, it represents, exactly, the form of James's text, with the crack symbolizing, all at once, the past, class privilege, and the melodramatic imagination—all those things that fracture James's seemingly hermetic form. Even the basic claim James makes about that form—that book 1 is from the Prince's perspective and book 2 is from Maggie's—is easily falsified by the fact of the Assinghams as well as by the presence of many scenes about which the supposed center of consciousness, being not present, could not know. The crack is James's hint that form can never quite attain the self-sufficiency it, simultaneously, demands.

From Economics to Affect

Neoliberalism was said to efface all notions of relation and containment, to suggest a kind of unbounded fluidity of experience that transcends the coherence of literary form and the determinations of social ground. *The Golden Bowl*, in contrast, is as

---

[10]   I thus part ways with Bersani, who argues that "their past is a weak concession on James's part to an order of psychological probability which the novel in fact dismisses" (74). In contrast, I think we should attend to the repeated movement by which the text offers plausible psychological explanations only to dismiss them.

much about relation as it is about containment. Indeed, it is as difficult to separate the two—relation and containment—from one another as it is to isolate a crucial third term: freedom. For freedom appears often in the text, almost always in connection with either relation or containment. Its first appearance occurs at the end of book 1. Charlotte and the Prince have just finished not purchasing the bowl, and he has insisted that though he cannot give her a present on this day, he will when she marries. "Well, I would marry, I think," Charlotte says as she prepares to depart, "to have something from you in all freedom" (113). The entire structure of the novel is anticipated in this line, for marriage—seemingly greater containment—will, in fact, create greater freedom for Charlotte, a connection underlined by the word's appearance in the very next sentence, which begins book 2 and describes Adam Verver, her eventual husband, opening "the door of the billiard-room with a certain freedom" (117).

Freedom soon becomes James's word of choice for describing the position in which his adulterous characters find themselves. It emerges from a clear understanding of their position—"It appeared thus that they might enjoy together extraordinary freedom, the two friends, from the moment they should understand their position aright" (237)—and is contingent on Charlotte's acting as her situation "demands" (216). "What had happened in short," James writes, "was that Charlotte and he had by a single turn of the wrist of fate . . . been placed face to face in a freedom that extraordinarily partook of ideal perfection" (244). Freedom is not, here, in opposition to structure; rather, it can take place only within its confines. Furthermore, it is within this structured freedom that the past reveals its full determining power: "The sense of the past revived for him nevertheless as it hadn't yet done: it made the other time somehow meet the future close, interlocking with it, before his watching eyes, as in a long embrace of arms and lips, and so handling and hustling the present that this poor quantity scarce retained substance enough, scarce remained sufficiently *there*, to be wounded or shocked" (244).

Freedom, that is to say, is both contextual and historical; and it is also economic, for the Prince now knows "why he had at any rate gone in, on the basis of all forms, on the basis of his having . . . sold himself, for a *situation nette*. It had all been just in order that his—well, what on earth should he call it but his freedom?—should at present be as perfect and rounded and lustrous as some huge precious pearl" (289). Initially, of course, the Prince is described as a "representative precious object" in Adam Verver's collection, and though he is purchased, in large part, for his history, he understands that this history must remain nonspecific (127). "[T]he general expectation," James tells us, "of which he was the subject . . . seemed not so much an expectation of anything in particular as a large bland blank assumption of merits almost beyond notation, of essential quality and value. It was as if he had been some old embossed coin, of a purity of gold no longer used. . . . [H]e was to constitute a possession, yet was to escape being reduced to his component parts" (41).

Just as the treasures of Europe are purchased for display in Verver's American City, so Prince Amerigo is purchased for his representative status as an aristocrat, a signifier of intrinsic value that can help prop up the quality-less quantity of Verver's money. Adam's purchase of the Prince allows him to remove the stain from "the livid vulgarity even of getting in, or getting out, first," even as James illustrates how his "years of darkness had been needed to render possible the years of light" (131).

Adam gains cultural capital, the Prince gains freedom, but freedom operates in this text as a zero-sum game. The freedom the Prince and Charlotte enjoy depends on Maggie's restriction—the "first shock of complete perception," coming when Maggie recognizes that "her husband and his colleague" were "directly interested in preventing her freedom of movement" (357). If "it was they themselves who were arranged," then "[s]he must be kept in position so as not to *dis*-arrange them" (357). What Maggie understands here is that she must now take over the arranging. At first, this rearranging seems to achieve little. Both couples remain married, and no dramatic revelations occur; the melodrama, as I have already suggested, is suppressed as James eschews the emotional intensities a melodramatic confrontation might produce for the more abstract satisfactions of formal arrangement. At the same time, though, the transformations are, within the limited space in which they occur, substantial, Charlotte's freedom metamorphosing into the image of servitude I have already quoted, even as Maggie moves herself into the "centre and core" of the Prince's affections (461). In doing so, she works to transform the economic motives underlying her marriage into affective ones, a move that simultaneously creates the gruesome image of an enslaved Charlotte, the remainder, we might say, of Maggie's affective transformations.

Moments after Fannie has smashed the bowl and left the room, we find Maggie at the melodramatic climax. The Prince is before her as she, "seeing herself finally sure, knowing everything," suddenly feels a strange "split between conviction and action" (460). James continues:

> They had begun to cease on the spot, surprisingly, to be connected; conviction, that is, budged no inch, only planting its feet the more firmly in the soil—but action began to hover like some lighter and larger but easier form, excited by its very power to keep above ground. It would be free, it would be independent, it would go in—wouldn't it?—for some prodigious and superior adventure of its own. What would condemn it, so to speak, to the responsibility of freedom . . . was the possibility, richer with every lapsing moment, that her husband would have on the whole question a new need of her, a need which was in fact being born between them in these very seconds. It struck her truly as so new that he would have felt hitherto none to compare with it at all; would indeed absolutely by this circumstance be really needing her for the first time in their whole connexion. (460–61)

Conviction and action: Maggie has never been more convinced of her husband's affair, and action, one imagines, refers to something that would expose his adultery. But in the split between the two, Maggie sees a better way to achieve her ends; hesitation will, in fact, create an attachment that action would, potentially, sunder. Her action's freedom, then, is its *seeming* separation from the knowledge of the affair, but her decision to hesitate takes shape precisely because of her conviction. Conviction, here, determines action entirely, but it does so through the transformation of *her* interest into *his* need.

Maggie thinks this need is "so new that he would have felt hitherto none to compare with it at all," which is another of the text's true yet untrue statements. For the entire novel emerges from the Prince's need, from his desire to "*make* something different" from his ancestral inheritance and the subsequent realization that "the material for the making had to be Mr. Verver's millions" (36, 36–37).[11] Need, too, was behind his inability to marry Charlotte, which, in turn, created the possibility for the affair, so what we find here is not that the Prince has, at last, discovered a need for Maggie but rather that the only need Maggie is able to recognize is an affective rather than a financial one. This is why she can refer, at novel's end, to "their freedom to be together there always," for she perceives the structure she has arranged—the banishment of Charlotte and the prevention of any confession on the Prince's part—as freedom, while the Prince, confined entirely to a world of her making, tells her, "I see nothing but *you*" (594, 595).

In the logic of the text, the Prince is here responding to his full sense of "what she so wonderfully gave," and the implication is that in disallowing the confession that would be "her proper payment," she refuses to be remunerated for the ways in which she has rearranged their social world (595). But it is difficult to understand how this arrangement is a gift for anyone other than herself, and her refusal for payment also marks a refusal of any discussion of how Charlotte has become expendable. To avoid confession, that is to say, is to disable any direct statement of why Maggie has manipulated the situation or, indeed, that she has in fact done any manipulation at all. James here links Maggie's rejection of his nevertheless insistent financial metaphors to the inability to admit that some wrong has, perhaps, been perpetrated on Charlotte. But the disclosure of this wrong is also framed, somewhat perversely, as exposing Charlotte: the Prince's "acknowledgement," James tells us, "hung there, too monstrously, at the expense of Charlotte" (595). The fiction Maggie has constructed requires that Charlotte remain "great" and "splendid," less a victim than a heroine displaying a "mastery of the greater style" (593, 595).

One way to read the ending of the text, then, is to moralize. Having already seen Charlotte at the "end of a long silken halter" and noticing, further, the "mute facial intimations" through which Adam addressed his daughter while shaking Charlotte's "twisted silken rope," we can decry the way the Ververs have treated her (535). But the novel does not allow us this easy position, for to acknowledge Charlotte's victimhood is, necessarily, to expose her affair, and though she is banished to America at text's end, she nevertheless remains fabulously wealthy and with a man she has chosen to marry. Our attempts to moralize one aspect of the text—to strike an affective posture in relation to the actions the characters undertake—push us back to structure. Which is why James offers, but ultimately withholds, the image of Charlotte enchained. James invites our sympathy for Charlotte only to displace that sympathy back to the structure of the text, a move that suggests that sympathy for the novel's "victim" is the wrong way to respond to its emotional complexities.

Michaels's discussion of neoliberal aesthetics led him to make a distinction between two modes of social differentiation. The first, tied to antidiscrimination and the politics of recognition, is defined by affect, by the attitude one takes toward the subject of discrimination. The second, tied to redistribution, is structural, and it is independent of

11   In a similar vein, Charlotte, triumphantly walking up the "'monumental' staircase," finds her own theory proved, that "materials to work with had been all she required" (205, 206).

the affects a work of art calls forth. "[T]o feel the beauty of the [social] problem," Michaels states, "is precisely not to feel the pathos of the suffering produced by the problem; it is instead to feel the structure that makes the problem" (39). The two modes of social differentiation are registered as two different responses to the work of art, which are, for Michaels, incompatible, ultimately demonstrating "the irreducibility of form to affect" (36). Our affective response to the text remains narcissistic, producing less a desire to examine the world than the feeling that we have taken the proper attitude in relation to it. Here is Michaels once again: "[T]he political meaning of the refusal of form"—and here we can read this refusal as, precisely, the desire to remain within the affective register of the work—"is the indifference to those social structures that, not produced by how we see, cannot be overcome by seeing differently" (63). James, similarly, pushes us back from affect to form, showing us not simply an autonomous structure but rather the desires that motivate that structure's seeming autonomy. *The Golden Bowl* demonstrates the work it takes to sustain life in the void. In doing so, James rejects the banal dichotomy between freedom and containment characteristic both of neoliberal economic discourse—where freedom is what transcends the nation or the subject—and of its affective counterpart in contemporary theory. Subjects remain, in James, centers of agency, even if that agency is precisely calibrated in relation to the social structures that we ourselves have built.

*   *   *

When we first find Adam Verver, he is trying to "create the sense . . . of . . . having the world to one's self" (117). Meanwhile, his "brain a strange workshop of fortune" had engendered an "acquisitive power," which finally allows him the "freedom to see" (118, 119, 135). "It came," James writes, "perhaps even too much to stand to him for *all* freedom" (135). Fortune and acquisition create an aesthetic power to see, which takes itself as the emblem of all freedom even as it has to actively create the sense of having a world to one's self. How much clearer could James possibly be?

*   *   *

PAUL STASI is associate professor of English at the University at Albany. He is the author of *Modernism, Imperialism and the Historical Sense* (2012) and the coeditor of *Ezra Pound in the Present: New Essays on Pound's Contemporaneity* (2016).

Works Cited

Bersani, Leo. "The Jamesian Lie." *Partisan Review* 36.1 (1969): 53–79.

Brooks, Peter. *The Melodramatic Imagination: Balzac, Henry James, Melodrama, and the Mode of Excess*. New Haven: Yale UP, 1976.

Brooks, Van Wyck. *The Pilgrimage of Henry James*. New York: Dutton, 1925.

Brown, Wendy. *Undoing the Demos: Neoliberalism's Stealth Revolution*. New York: Zone, 2015.

Burrows, Stuart. "The Golden Fruit: Innocence and Imperialism in *The Golden Bowl*." *Henry James Review* 21.2 (2000): 95–114.

Cameron, Sharon. *Thinking in Henry James*. Chicago: U of Chicago P, 1989.

Harvey, David. "Neoliberalism Is a Political Project." *Jacobin* 23 July 2016 < https://www.jacob inmag.com/2016/07/david-harvey-neoliberalism-capitalism-labor-crisis-resistance/ >.

James, Henry. *The Ambassadors*. New York: Penguin, 2003.

———. *The American Scene*. Bloomington: Indiana UP, 1968.

———. *The Golden Bowl*. 1904. New York: Penguin, 2009.

Jameson, Fredric. *The Antinomies of Realism*. New York: Verso, 2013.

Krook, Dorothea. *The Ordeal of Consciousness in Henry James*. Cambridge: Cambridge UP, 1967.

Marx, Karl. *Capital*. Vol. 1. Trans. Samuel Moore, Edward Aveling, and Ernest Untermann. Chicago: Kerr, 1912.

———. *Grundrisse*. Trans. Martin Nicolaus. New York: Penguin, 1973.

Meeuwis, Michael. "Living the Dream: Benjamin's *Arcades Project* and *The Golden Bowl*." *Henry James Review* 27.1 (2006): 61–74.

Meissner, Collin. "'What Ghosts Will Be Left to Walk': Mercantile Culture and the Language of Art." *Henry James Review* 21.3 (2000): 242–52.

Michaels, Walter Benn. *The Beauty of a Social Problem*. Chicago: U of Chicago P, 2015.

Moses, Omri. *Out of Character: Modernism, Vitalism, Psychic Life*. Palo Alto: Stanford UP, 2014.

Murphet, Julian. "Aesthetic Perception and 'the Flaw': Towards a Jamesonian Account of Late James." *Henry James Review* 36.3 (2015): 226–33.

Pippin, Robert. *Henry James and Modern Moral Life*. Cambridge: Cambridge UP, 2000.

Rancière, Jacques. "Notes on the Photographic Image." *Radical Philosophy* 156 (2009): 8–15.

Reber, Dierdra. "Headless Capitalism: Affect as Free-Market Episteme." *differences* 23.1 (2012): 62–101.

Simmel, Georg. *The Philosophy of Money*. Trans. Tom Bottomore and David Frisby. Ed. David Frisby. 2nd ed. London: Routledge, 1990.

Thompson, E. P. *The Making of the English Working Class*. New York: Vintage, 1966.

Wharton, Edith. *A Backward Glance*. New York: Simon and Schuster, 1987.

From a Distance:
Teju Cole, World Literature,
and the Limits of Connection

LILY SAINT

"Others are not like us . . . their forms are different from ours."

—Teju Cole, *Open City*

"Don't books come to us from a distance?"

—J. M. Coetzee

By 2011, when novelist Miguel Syjuco reviewed Teju Cole's *Open City* in the *New York Times Book Review*, "world literature" was firmly re-entrenched as a capacious and profitable classificatory term for publishers and literary scholars alike.[1] Syjuco's review draws on this discourse, praising the novel for doing "precisely what literature *should* do: it *brings together* thoughts and beliefs, and *blurs borders*. Cole suggests that we re-examine, as perhaps limited and parochial, the idea of the Great Fill-in-the-Nation Novel. Instead, we can look again at the notion of what Goethe called Weltliteratur" (emphasis added).[2] Another review similarly praises the novel's supranational backdrop, noting that "the city of [Cole's] novel is blown wide open as our world these days is blown wide open. [Its] characters are *citizens of the world*, not nations, and they contend with multiple allegiances to multiple identities" (James; emphasis added). In what has come to be a rather formulaic assessment of world literature's deontological value, with a considerably long, often overlooked history, reviewers such as these see the world literary canon as capable of fostering ethically productive, cross-cultural connections.[3]

Such claims for *world* literature echo earlier justifications for *comparative* literature that position comparativist methodologies such as multilingualism and translation as particularly suited to the instantiation of social harmony. Champions of comparative literary and world literary models frequently mobilize "linkages,"

---

[1]   David Damrosch's *What Is World Literature?* was published in 2003, and Pascale Casanova's *The World Republic of Letters* appeared in English the following year, though in French in 1999.

[2]   This theme of blurred borders is treated visually in the cover design of *Open City*'s US edition.

[3]   In 1840 Henry B. Stanton, president of the American Anti-slavery Society, called for "the literature of the world" to bring its "moral power" to bear as "our last hope." "Send us a purified and vivifying literature; a literature instinct with the principles of freedom . . . then slavery shall cease" (qtd. in Baucom 210).

Novel: A Forum on Fiction 51:2   DOI 10.1215/00295132-6846174   © 2018 by Novel, Inc.

"bridges," and a wide array of other materialist metaphors to emphasize how, in Syjuco's words, literature "brings together," or as Cole writes in another context, "how delicately connected" we are (*Known and Strange* 211). This rhetoric of connection bears an uncanny resemblance to that championed in an entirely different cultural milieu today—namely, the tech industry, where heavyweights Eric Schmidt and Jared Cohen of Google insist that "[t]he best thing anyone can do to improve the quality of life around the world is to drive connectivity" (qtd. in Cole, *Known and Strange* 183–84). Promoters of "benevolent capitalism" and world literature alike rely on this language of connection without much concern, as Zadie Smith has noted, for "[t]he quality of that connection [or] . . . the quality of the relationship that connection permits" (57).

While the meaning of world literature has been subject to considerable debate (Casanova; Damrosch; and Deckard et al.), this essay explores less a set of definitional questions (what is the world? what is literature? and so forth), instead asking: For whom is the world in world literature? Who does world literature serve? Particularly, I explore world literature's role in the libidinal economy of the global North, which desires in the Kleinian sense to "make good" or "repair" those parts of the world that have been most subject to the manifold violences accompanying "accumulation by dispossession" (Harvey 63). Does world literature really help produce such vaunted cross-border social cohesion? Can reading about suffering others somehow lead to the amelioration of that suffering through various forms of affective and material response? Or does it only work to relieve our own suffering?

While scholars such as Ian Baucom and Timothy Bewes explore the convoluted ethical negotiations necessary for writers confronting modernity's manifold forms of unethical violence, I am concerned here more with the role played by the *reader* in the production and dissemination of the discourse of world literature. For Baucom, the writer is a melancholic witness to violence, providing a "testamentary counterdiscourse" in rejoinder to the erasures operative in the dominant and one-sided histories of the victorious (178). As such, the testamentary writer, through practices of world making that constitute the writing of fictions, "bear[s] witness to the truth of what has not been (and what cannot have been) witnessed" (218). Despite "the distance of passing time or the obstacles of geographic space [that] separates the witness from the scenes of witnessing," for Baucom, the novelist's creative, fictional acts resuscitate the overwritten tragedies of modernity by bearing witness, thus serving as an ethical "counter-discourse" to those violences of historiography and archival dominion (218).[4]

But what are the ethical stakes of these alternative stories for those who are their readers or listeners? For scholars who have claimed literature's ethical merits, readers are also conscripted into a network of moral responsibility and are rendered more just, or more good, by dint of reading about other people's suffering.[5] Cole claims as much in an essay on *Wave*, Sonali Deraniyagala's memoir about the

---

[4]   Baucom's exploration of the writer's testamentary role bears considerable similarity to Toni Morrison's notion of "re-memorying" (Morrison 196).

[5]   Particularly well known examples of theories of reading that promote this ethical understanding include Wayne C. Booth, Derek Attridge, J. Hillis Miller, and Wolfgang Iser.

death of her husband and sons in the 2004 tsunami in Sri Lanka. Borrowing from the poet Anne Carson's paraphrase of Aristotle, Cole approves the "theory that watching unbearable stories about other people lost in grief and rage is good for you—may cleanse you of darkness." Furthermore, he muses, by reading such accounts of suffering, "we are in some way fortified for our own inevitable, if lesser, struggles" (*Known and Strange* 55). Admittedly, he writes, "[v]ery few of us will ever experience loss on this scale"; nonetheless, "somehow, [Deraniyagala's] having written about hers is a kind of preemptive consolation for us, too" (56). Despite the undercurrent of hesitation in Cole's claims—"in some way," "somehow," we obtain "*a kind of . . . consolation*"—the affective repair occurring in these situations moves in one direction, from the text to the reader, and there is no suggestion that it operates, or could operate, conversely, to repair the subject depicted or, indeed, in this case, the writer-victim, of the text.

Who gets repaired, then, through readerly encounters? And what "connections" are being made? Despite the claims Syjuco and others make, I argue that Cole's *Open City* juxtaposes the desire to connect with alterity through mediations like literature with evidence of a far darker hue that suggests such connective impulses are stratagems for avoiding actual responsibility rather than proof of ethico-political commitment. Figuring Julius, *Open City*'s main character, as a voracious listener, the novel neither too neatly accords ethical value to hearing other people's stories nor simply critiques listening and attending to these narratives. Instead, *Open City* makes manifest the reasons behind the global North's desire for world literature, and in the process it renders questionable any sense of moral self-righteousness that might be derived from reading these narratives. As readers of these tales of suffering—and not as their witnessing writers—the book insinuates, not only should we listen and read because certain life stories have been erased, ignored, or left out of the archives, but we should examine our urges to read and stay alert to any sense of self-righteousness such reading might produce. If distance, as I claim, provides a certain alternative to intimacy as a way of more honestly engaging with difference, that position, too, comes with its own set of troubling complicities.

*   *   *

Published in 2011, *Open City* is narrated by Julius, a Nigerian-German psychiatry student in his final residency conducting clinical research in New York City. To counteract the rigor and intensity of his work, he begins taking long picaresque walks around Manhattan.[6] The novel describes the places and people Julius encounters over the course of one year as well as those he meets during a lonely holiday in Brussels. These people are both familiar and unfamiliar to Julius, their lives and stories forming parts of the narrative, either in the first person or with Julius acting as the conduit for their histories. Within these embedded tales, Julius recounts his own responses to the encounters, responses that are sometimes deeply

---

6   The book resembles certain aspects of picaresque novels, including the constitution of plot as an episodic, *loosely connected* series of accounts sewn together by the continued presence of the central protagonist.

personal but that frequently display instead an intimidating range of esoteric knowledge from fields as disparate as biology, art history, literature, classical music, psychology, and colonial history.

With his impressive breadth of knowledge and his boundless interest in other people's stories, Julius seems driven by a sort of pathological, macrophagic cosmopolitanism. The geographic range covered in the personal histories Julius records is dizzyingly vast, including people from Nigeria, Liberia, Morocco, Belgium, Rwanda, Japan, Haiti, and Central America, all circulating in and through that quintessentially global city, New York. The span of his socioeconomic interest in others is equally catholic: Julius talks with a museum guard in a bar, a marathon runner, a detainee in an immigration center, a shoeshine man, an airplane passenger, a taxi driver, a man working in an Internet café, a college professor, his patients, and his next-door neighbor, among others.

Cole produces an entire novel at the intersections of Julius's own narration and other people's stories, suggesting, along with much recent thinking on world literature, that being "open" to alterity makes cross-cultural connection possible if one is willing to listen—or read—slowly and carefully (Brooks and Jewett; Palumbo-Liu). Julius is proud of his listening skills, recounting that his conversations with Professor Saito, his erstwhile English literature professor, taught him "the art of listening . . . and the ability to trace out a story from what was omitted" (*Open City* 9). This understanding of conversation as both revelatory and obfuscating relies on the listener's ability to string together meaning out of the not-said, an approach that informs Julius's professional activities as a psychiatrist as well.

Indeed, since so much of the narration relies on the representation of conversations, Cole's novel appears at first glance to be promoting dialogue as the linguistic form most conducive to ethical relation. Syjuco, again, writes that "[Cole's] readers will be those who understand that all stories are interconnected, that literature is not mere entertainment, and that art is nothing if not an extended conversation spanning eras, nations and languages." Viewed through this lens, dialogue is *the* form for affective-epistemological exchange, and world literature is its conduit across and through global or cosmopolitan space. Cosmopolitanism—that infamous close cousin of world literature—is, of course, also described as a "hopeful dialogue" (Sobre-Denton).

We are indeed enjoined to think explicitly about *Open City* through the lens of cosmopolitanism, since Julius sends a copy of Kwame Anthony Appiah's *Cosmopolitanism* to another of the novel's characters. Appiah's subtitle, "Ethics in a World of Strangers," positions cosmopolitanism as an ethical praxis adequate to coping with the challenges of radical difference that globalization's uneven processes have rendered quotidian. For Appiah, the sympathy and identification intrinsic to cosmopolitanism trump other, less generous, political or affective registers that may result from encounters in the "contact zone," such as those of parochialism, revulsion, distrust, or disregard (Pratt). When world literature is understood as a conduit for the dissemination of cosmopolitanism, it is thus explicitly instrumentalized, imagined as able to transform the world by promoting the spread of supranational formations that transcend cultural, linguistic, national, economic, racial, or ethnic difference.

Of course, literature itself, not just world literature, is often thought of as onto-logically cosmopolitan, thus when seen through the lens of globality, world literature might be conceived as a *doubly* connective instrument of change. At times Cole's novel subscribes to this belief in art's potential to transform the phenome-nological world, as when Julius hears Mahler's *Das Lied von der Erde*, noting that the music "fell over my activities for the entirety of the following day. There was some new intensity in even the most ordinary things all around the hospital" (17). Yet art, he is quick to point out, is not always so easy to process, understand, or absorb.[7] At a museum, Julius discovers the work of American painter John Brewster, which has, for Julius, an "air of hermeticism": "Each of the portraits was a sealed-away world, visible from without, but impossible to enter" (37). More disturbing, how-ever, than some art's apparent impenetrability, Julius concedes, is its ability to dis-tort perception irrevocably, a possibility that is foregrounded when he admits that his memory of his father's funeral was irreparably confused with his impressions of funereal paintings by El Greco and Courbet.

Given how firmly this novel lays the groundwork for thinking about literature as the site for the reproduction of ethical, cosmopolitan relation, Julius's encounters *with people*, surprisingly, affect him in even more ambivalent ways than art does. While the novel's many characters hail from a wide array of global locales, giving the narrative, in toto, a veneer of global cosmopolitanism, Julius's interactions with people most often seem to produce in him a certain callous, even opportunistic irresponsibility.[8] Artistic or mimetic forms for accessing otherness function as Julius's preferred relational modality, so that he can keep less-mediated others at a distance.[9] This closeness-in-abeyance protects Julius, of course, from vulnerabili-ties and other dangers that might arise from actual intimacies.

At a photography exhibit he visits, he stops at a glass vitrine to examine a photo featuring Hitler and Goebbels.[10] He notices a Hasidic couple standing next to him, also looking at the picture, and reflects:

I had no reasonable access to what being there, in that gallery, might mean for them; the undiluted hatred I felt for the subjects of the photo was, in the couple, transmuted into what? What was stronger than hate? I did not know and could not ask. I needed to move away, immediately, needed to rest my eye elsewhere and be absent

---

[7]   The novel trades in a deeper skepticism about the role of art than that at work in Cole's recent essay collection, *Known and Strange Things*.

[8]   Similarly, Pieter Vermeulen argues that "*Open City* exposes the limited critical purchase of the imaginative mobility and intercultural curiosity celebrated by cosmopolitan defenses of liter-ature and art" (40).

[9]   For Baucom, distance presents certain ethical possibilities for the writer by affording the time and space necessary for the contemplation and imagining of others. But for Julius, *Open City*'s reader-listener, the distance he repeatedly opts for in lieu of proximity to suffering others is char-acterized by social isolation, not imaginative connection.

[10]   Karen Jacobs argues that *Open City* is haunted by literary and theoretical responses to the Holocaust, struggling, in her estimation, to apply their analytic insights to African and African-American histories of trauma and genocide.

from this silent encounter into which I had inadvertently barged. The young couple stood close to each other, not speaking. I couldn't bear to look at them, or at what they were looking at, any longer. (154; emphasis added)

Julius's inability to engage directly with actual people's lived experience of anguish stands in marked contrast to the novel's willingness to access others' suffering through various artistic, literary, and musical mediations. His actual encounters with people in the novel thus disturb those theories that claim that intimacy with alterity—either in person *or* through reading—can be treated as equivalents that instantiate ethical relation (Attridge; Booth; Miller; Nussbaum). Instead, the urge to connect appears here as a compensatory neurosis characteristic of the cosmopolite. Through the repeated avowal of the will to connect with others, more "ugly feelings" of guilt, depression, futility, rage, disappointment, and failure—those feelings characteristic of actual intersubjective relations between subjects in the uneven global economy—are kept to a minimum (Ngai). Despite plentiful evidence that Julius seeks connections with others, rarely does this desire become manifest as anything other than fantasy, and it certainly fails to improve anyone else's lot in the novel, either affectively or materially.

For Julius, the presumed advantages of connection are repeatedly thwarted. The novel juxtaposes the urge to connect that constitutes the global cosmopolite with an equally powerful urge to escape, elude, repress, or even ignore others' suffering as well as their narratives of suffering. For Hamish Dalley, Cole's novel exposes how cosmopolitan identity depends on the cultivation of a disinterested and detached affective position, since it is only such an attitude that allows someone like Julius to be interested in all people, spaces, and times, as he, in fact, *"belongs to nowhere"* (Dalley 29). Long ago, Jean-Jacques Rousseau similarly teased that cosmopolitans "boast of loving everyone [*tout le monde*] so that they might have the right to love no one" (158), suggesting that the urge to connect often masks its very opposite desire—to avoid connection at all costs. Julius, after all, is barely capable of sustained compassion, let alone love. For where Baucom understands disinterestedness and distance as requisite to "reinvention of the human (as a type of sympathetic observer, determined to invest in and remonstrate against the sufferings of another)" (218), what Julius lacks is *prolonged* investment in others' lives—his interest in others is instead evanescent and unproductive.

In an incident that takes place early in the novel, Julius discovers that his neighbor, Carla, had died months before he knew about it. Despite the intimate proximity of shared walls, he had failed entirely to notice her absence. Realizing this, he is momentarily disturbed, reflecting:

A woman had died in the room next to mine, she had died on the other side of the wall I was leaning against, and I had known nothing of it. I had known nothing in the weeks when her husband mourned, nothing when I had nodded to him in greeting with headphones in my ears, or when I had folded clothes in the laundry room while he used the washer. I hadn't known him well enough to routinely ask how Carla was, and

I had not noticed not seeing her around. That was the worst of it. I had noticed neither her absence nor the change—there must have been a change—in [Seth's] spirit. It was not possible, even then, to go knock on his door and embrace him, or to speak with him at length. It would have been false intimacy. (21; emphasis added)

Even this guilt-ridden self-awareness on Julius's part abates a few minutes later as he puts away his groceries: "I tried to remember when, exactly, it was that [Seth] had knocked on my door to ask if I played guitar. Eventually I satisfied myself that it was before, and not after, his wife's death. I felt a certain sense of relief at this, which was taken over almost immediately by shame. But even that feeling subsided; much too quickly, now that I think of it" (*Open City* 21). Others' stories, Julius admits, may be hard to care about for more than just a moment. Cole's novel helps us to see that what often lies behind that utopian desire to feel connected, somehow, to others near and far is a marked *unwillingness* to project ourselves into the lives of others. Admitting this would acknowledge an empathetic failure profoundly antithetical to notions of literature as moral lodestar, so ethical theorists continue to repress the less salutary effects of literary engagement, insisting instead, as a sort of overcompensation, that reading helps us better know about and care for others.

Despite the grand claims used to justify the circulation and teaching of world literature, listening carefully to or reading about people in unfortunate situations may help listeners and readers to *feel* empathetically engaged while altering nothing about those lives described.[11] Indeed, Madhu Krishnan goes so far as to suggest that Julius's "consumption of otherness [functions] as a means of underwriting a fantasied self" (686). Worse than eliciting mere indifference, accounts of the pain of others may serve listeners' or readers' selfish interests rather than working toward the amelioration of suffering. In a key scene in *Open City*, Julius admits that he enjoys it when people mistakenly equate his listening ability with empathy, conceding all the while that any causal relationship between listening and fellow-feeling is tenuous at best.[12]

He recalls accompanying his former girlfriend on a church mission visit to undocumented immigrants held in a deportation center in Queens. There he meets Saidu, a handsome Liberian who recounts his persistent, if thwarted, efforts to migrate to the United States after the outbreak of war. After his mother and sister were killed; after escape from forced labor on a rubber farm; after a frightening encounter with a snake; and after lengthy treks to Guinea, Mali, and Morocco that got him to Portugal via Spain, Saidu eventually arrived in the United States only to be immediately arrested and placed in detention, where he waits to be deported. Following Saidu's story, Julius's own narration begins again: "When I got up to

[11]   At the 2017 annual Frankfurt Book Fair, literary agent Andrew Wylie delivered a keynote lecture that emphasized the importance of world literature for contemporary publishing. Suggesting that "local is global," he went on to directly articulate the perceived ethical purchase of world literature, arguing that "difference stimulates readers, sells books and resolves conflicts" (qtd. in Tivnan).

[12]   *Beautiful Animals* (2017) by Laurence Osborne is another very recent novel concerned with the superficiality of contemporary structures of benevolence.

leave, [Saidu] remained seated, and said, Come back and visit me, if I am not deported. I said that I would, but never did." Later, "I told the story to Nadège on our way back into Manhattan. . . . Perhaps she fell in love with the idea of myself that I presented in that story. I was the listener, the compassionate African who paid attention to the details of someone else's life and struggle. I had fallen in love with that idea myself" (70). If there is intimacy or connection in this section, it exists between Julius and the novel's readers, who become increasingly alert to how Julius deploys his advanced listening skills to elicit "false intimacy" and to how he capitalizes upon this to gain Nadège's love and even to propagate self-love. Julius's confessional tone builds intimacy with readers through his admission that what appears to be his care for others is often really feigned for personal advantage. By so doing, he intimates that we too, as readers who consume these stories of suffering and mistreatment in which he trades, may often do so less for the altruistic reasons we might articulate than out of a desire for moral self-regard.

It is troubling to think that Julius brings this form of detachment to his career in psychiatry. He admits: "I no longer spent much time thinking about patients, usually not until the next appointment, and often, when I was on rounds, I needed the chart to recall even the basics of a particular case" (44). While the psychiatric profession aims to "cure" patients of their affective disorders through a combination of medication and psychotherapy to diminish their sense of "disconnectedness," there is an oft-noted similarity between the ethical premises structuring psychoanalysis and those of literary engagement. Just as analysts' ethical missions may belie more personal motivations, so do the listeners-as-readers' stated incentives for caring about the stories of others frequently cloak self-interest. The vexed moral terrain constitutive of the therapeutic professions thus emphasizes *Open City*'s concern with the (un)ethics of listening to others' tragic tales.

One of Julius's patients, the Pynchonesquely named V., is a Native American history professor who is deeply troubled by New Yorkers' indifference to the genocidal trauma underwriting the city's history. While in Brussels on extended vacation, Julius uses a phone call to refill patients' prescriptions via a hospital nurse. He displays a callous disregard for his patients, an indifference made worse by his parallel admission that self-interest is his main motivation: "[The nurse] told me that V. had wanted to know how I could be reached. *I can't be reached*, I said, have her call Dr. Kim, the resident covering for me. Then, feeling the vigor of ticking things off my list, I also called Human Resources to check up on some paperwork having to do with my vacation time" (102; emphasis added). Later, however, back in New York, Julius learns from a newspaper article that V. has killed herself. Mediated through the newspaper, V.'s death enters Julius's consciousness—and even more so, ours—at a considerable remove. Julius recalls, "The *Times* had said, in the obituary I read that day, that V. wrote of atrocity without flinching. They might have said, without flinching visibly, for it had all affected her far more deeply than anyone's ability to guess" (165). For Julius, V.'s death tells a cautionary tale: she suffered, ultimately, because unlike Julius, who so agilely lunges toward and then away from endless forms of social and historical horror, V. felt all too strongly the traumas of her ancestors. V.'s overinternalization of these historical traumas so overwhelmed the borders of her self that suicide became her only escape from suffering. Seen in relation to V., distance from the pain of others emerges as a form of self-preservation. Indeed, Julius shows us again how this is accomplished in the passage immediately following his discovery of V.'s death. He reflects:

> *I could hardly imagine the kind of raw pain her family—her husband, her parents—would be experiencing. I returned to the knoll in the park, where I had come in. The dancers had started again. Many of them, I now noticed, wore red or pink. I could not remember if red was lucky in Chinese culture. The thin sound of the ehru still slithered in among the drums of the dancers' tape player, and it seemed to summon to my mind's eye the long-ago spirits that V. had been so concerned to honor in her work. Turning away from the dancers, and taking in the expanse of the bay once more, I sat on a green wooden bench. A curious junco, black on its upper half and white on the lower, hopped up to my feet. It was tiny, and soon darted away. There was another man on the bench, dressed in a linen suit, with carefully polished shoes, and a straw summer hat: summer clothes on a winter's day.* (165)

As in so many other moments in this novel, Julius's attention shifts again and again—from V. to the dancers, to the colors they are wearing, to the symbolism of those colors, to the music, back to V., "[t]urning away" again to observe a "curious" bird which "soon darted away," replaced immediately in Julius's consciousness by an oddly dressed man. This concatenation of external observations and interior reflections portrays a mind in motion, a stream of consciousness that may mimic the way minds hop about. But it also makes manifest the speed with which Julius is distracted from the tragedy of V.'s suicide by simply being in the world, by looking up or down, or by turning the page.

Yet readers are given enough information about V. to be able to linger, however momentarily, with the import of her suicide, which was a response both to the trauma of the nation's foundational genocide and to the genocide's subsequent erasure from metropolitan and national discourse. To compound the tragedy, V., who has failed to come to terms with Americans' willful amnesia, is now herself forgotten as Julius's rumination upon her death gives way almost immediately to other, unrelated thoughts. The disregard of V.'s death comes, then, in *Open* City, to function metonymically for the deaths of millions of her predecessors. If there is readerly identification at work here, it must operate in the uncomfortable realm of complicity, as we recognize how the simple concerns of our day-to-day lives so often eclipse our attention to the suffering of others. If such massive, catastrophic acts of organized violence as genocide can be wiped out of national, communal memory, then surely the cosmopolitan fantasy of literary narratives suffused with the potential to constructively transform human relation is troubled by V.'s suicidal act.

*   *   *

How much room for ethical relation can there be when Native American genocide remains largely obscured in contemporary historical consciousness, and even V.'s psychiatrist cannot find time to listen to her story? As Daniel O'Gorman notes, Julius often draws attention to the intersections between personal and historical tragedies, "us[ing] the intimate and the personal as a synecdoche for the collective and the political" (60). While the historical violences of the past and the present are not the same as the local metaphoric ones that occur, say, between Saidu and Julius, the novel seems to treat them as near equivalents. As V.'s example shows us, the two cannot be neatly separated. Her suicide, a news item that briefly registered among a multitude of other moments in Julius's consciousness, individualizes the violence of mass indigenous genocide, a violence that endures in its reincarnation as everyday disregard. The general populace's disavowal of the genocide, coupled with the passing, ephemeral treatment of V.'s suicide, repeats the repression of suffering others that recurs in Julius's many responses to others throughout the novel and emerges in its most troubling iteration at the end, to which I return below.

Yes, Cole's book tells us, the urge to care about others is real, but it is tempered by our care for ourselves and is rarely led by pure altruism or a willingness to sacrifice oneself for others, despite what Emmanuel Levinas might say about our responsibilities in the face of others. In a recent conversation between J. M. Coetzee and Arabella Kurtz, published as *The Good Story: Exchanges on Truth, Fiction, and Psychotherapy,* Coetzee writes about humans' limited ability to empathize with others: "I feel that, seen from the outside, the lives of other people almost always have a somewhat made-up, fictional quality. The capacity (which I think of as a moral capacity) to project oneself sympathetically into someone else's life is rare, *the capacity for sustained sympathetic projection even rarer*" (154; emphasis added).[13] In contrast to Julius's short-lived, fleeting form of attention to others that most frequently results in rapid forgetting, Coetzee identifies an imaginative ethics, albeit a rare one, that necessitates perseverance, commitment, and endurance, or, to use Alain Badiou's term, consistency.

In reply to Coetzee, Kurtz more optimistically posits a way of processing others' lives that eschews both the self-annihilation of the impossibly sympathetic martyr and the everyday narcissism assumed in Coetzee's assertion that "[t]he capacity . . . to project oneself sympathetically into someone else's life is rare." Drawing on Neville Symington's work, Kurtz suggests we move, or oscillate, in our attempts to better know or understand an other. This involves shifts back and forth between an affective fusion with someone else's sentiments and a "colder, keener, and altogether more separate" position of conscious reflection, which can, following that fusion, allow for a new understanding of that other (Coetzee and Kurtz 54). Kurtz's more optimistic description of the way that others' narratives come to us assumes a certain consistency or endurance, even as the approach to otherness is characterized by both a movement toward and a flight from that other.

This spatial and temporal ambivalence that defines most of our forms of relation emerges vividly in photographer Richard Renaldi's "Touching Strangers," a project that Cole discusses in *Known and Strange Things,* making visible the in-between space across which Kurtz imagines humans to constantly ricochet. For his portraits, Renaldi asks strangers to pose together, touching one another. The resulting

---

[13] Primo Levi similarly intones that "[p]erhaps the dreadful gift of pity for the many is granted only to saints . . . to all of us there remains in the best of cases, only the sporadic pity addressed to the single individual . . . within the reach of our providentially myopic senses" (39–40).

Figure 1.   Lagos 2013, Teju Cole, Instagram, @tejucole. March 9, 2016. © Teju Cole.

images highlight the way that intimacies can appear simultaneously authentic and false, awkward and consoling, and how intimacy itself may always involve all of these contradictory elements. When critics claim world literature as a mode of communication able to effect connection, they fail to recognize the very ambivalence that lies at the core of connection itself.[14]

James Wood admired Cole's novel in the *New Yorker* precisely for its depiction of Julius's shifting identifications. Wood writes: "[H]ow delicately Cole has Julius pulsate, in contradictory directions, sometimes towards [a character], in fellow feeling, and sometimes away from him, never really settling in one position." For Wood, Julius's distance from others is a sort of productive distance (Wood suggests Cole's novel thematizes "productive alienation"); similarly, Mary A. Favret's concept of a "middle distance" identifies a position that allows for that alternation between intimacy and individuality also delineated by Kurtz (Wood 68). From the middle distance, all these thinkers seem to suggest, one sees neither solely with the impartiality and abstraction characteristic of a universalist, generalizing agenda nor with an affective experience of exhaustion or anomie that can come about through too much proximity to and intimacy with suffering (figure 1). For Favret, it is literature, or art, that best embodies such a "middle distance"—it "surfaces . . . *as a poetic or aesthetic response*" to the problem of suffering others—since art's mediating forms are quintessentially good at reproducing experiences both of distance *and* of proximity (10).

In much of Cole's other writing, he shows an attraction to this understanding of art's possibilities, as it both operates to grant access to otherness and affords the distance necessary for reflection. Middle distances are given thematic and aesthetic priority, particularly in his writing about photography. In recent postings on

---

[14]   On Instagram, Cole's interest in and anxiety about proximity to others surfaces:

> *I've been thinking recently that one of the key concerns in my work is intimacy—intimate but not confessional, the distinction is vital to me. But I now wonder if any form of public emotional labor, by definition, is intimate anyway. The work is not simply "concerned" with intimacy. To work, to show your work, is to be intimate. Or rather, to insist on the work's visibility is to be political, but to permit the work's visibility is to be intimate. The traffic between these two modes. But then also patrolling the borders of the self, so that—many artists have to contend with this—so that people don't take the intimacy in the work for an invitation.* (May 12, 2016, @tejucole)

Figure 2.   Mkpuk Eba. Courtesy of Fifty One Fine Art Photography. © J. D. 'Okhai Ojeikere.

Instagram, in his 2017 book *Blind Spot* which combines photography with Cole's written musings, and through commentary in his 2016 essay collection *Known and Strange Things*, the in-between middle distance emerges as a vital analytic for Cole's work. A half distance, the profile, the fragment of a face, the back of a head—these and visions of gray tones, of the ambiguous, of "productive doubt" (*Known and*

Strange 142), where "the contours of reality 'harass' the act of drawing" (126)—all these examples from Cole's writing on art and photography coalesce to suggest a belief that one can know more, or learn more, only partially, "in the shadows," but not in the clear (148). In one essay, Cole refers to photographs by J. D. 'Okhai Ojeikere (figure 2), who "understood the expressive possibilities of women's heads, particularly those crowned with the marvelous array of hairstyles common to many Nigerian ethnic groups. These photographs, made in the years following the country's independence from Britain in 1960, record evanescent sculptures that are both performance art and temporary body modification. *Most of these heads are turned away from us*" (131; emphasis added). He asks: "Has the back of a head ever been more evocative than in these photographs?" (131).

Elsewhere, in his reflections on cinematographer Bradford Young's film, *Selma*, Cole writes of "an intensified darkness [that] makes the actors seem more private, more self-contained . . . the effect [of which] is strengthened by the many scenes in which King and the other protagonists are filmed from behind or turned away from us. We are tuned in to the eloquence of shoulders, and we hear what the hint of a profile or the fragment of a silhouette has to say" (*Known and Strange* 149–50). What is expressed in these images but the ineffable distance that is also a proximity, both linking and separating us to and from others (figure 3)?

Returning to *Open City*, it is important to emphasize that Julius's position in this middle space does *not* afford him any greater access to or understanding of others. In fact, *Open City*, unlike Cole's subsequent works, is more ambivalent about the ethical in-between position of the testamentary witness. Just as a middle distance allows for the writer to "bear witness to the truth of what has not been (and what cannot have been) witnessed," the middle distance can also allow for the relinquishing of responsibility as the subject observing moves away again from the moment of intimacy, back into an oblivion characterized by repression and denial (Baucom 218).

In the novel's final pages, Moji, a childhood acquaintance from Nigeria now living in New York, recalls a night years before when Julius raped her at a party in Nigeria. Rather than admit or deny this accusation, Julius turns inward to contemplate a passage from Nietzsche doubly mediated through an interpretation by Camus.[15] While Moji's accusation surprises the reader as much as it does Julius, and though Julius's nonresponsiveness is already well established, his moral authority is undermined, possibly beyond repair, in this final act of social disengagement. When accused of wrongdoing, Julius refuses to address the accusation directly and refers instead to other written narratives, the relevance of which is palpably abstruse. Indeed Julius's manic mental swerving toward and then away from others that we have seen in other moments in the novel begins to appear as a set of rehearsals for this final moment of blatant disconnection. In one minor earlier example, for instance, Julius boards a plane to fly from the United States to Europe (the cosmopolitan situation par excellence), reflecting: "Normally, I would have

---

[15]   O'Gorman argues that this story operates as a screen memory for Julius to further repress and avoid his own trauma (75).

Figure 3.   Teju Cole, Instagram, @tejucole. September 29, 2016. © Teju Cole.

been curious about the person in the seat next to mine, a curiosity that was almost always disappointed. I would soon afterward find myself eager to get the small talk done with and, the absence of mutual interests firmly established, to return to the book I was reading" (87). As in his response to Moji, books become the occasion for escaping human contact rather than vehicles for its inauguration. This type of withdrawal most often characterizes Julius's engagements with others, as we have seen in his reactions to both his neighbor's death and V.'s suicide. By the close of the novel, we are primed to understand Julius as a figure of social impermeability who is nonetheless self-conscious enough to recognize his own avoidance of others. At almost each moment in the text when an intersubjective encounter becomes possible, Julius overrides the invitation and returns instead to a solipsism masquerading as a superficial cosmopolitanism.

As readers of world literature, we may also be like Julius: compulsively drawn to the lives and suffering of others but ultimately unwilling to do anything about that suffering, or even, less arduously, to confront our own complicity in that suffering. Cole's work interrogates the imperative always to connect, intimating all the while certain possibilities for a middle distance as a mode of relationality. Storytelling, for Cole, is less likely to reify transnational contact zones or to imagine communities, despite what world literature's champions have to say, than it is able to caution against a facile instrumentalism that equates knowing with individual or social transformation. *Open City* thus juxtaposes the urge for harmonious cross-cultural connection with a critique of that very desire.

What does this then imply about contemporary world literature as an episte-mological exercise that seeks to grant readers access into other peoples' lives, to facilitate connection, identification, and sympathy? For Julius, such efforts can only fleetingly result in anything that comes close to knowledge of otherness or dif-ference. To accept the partiality of vision and understanding would also mean to demote the instrumentality that has been accorded world literature. This could be a kind of achievement in itself, as it would encourage readers to relinquish our enduring and grandiose fantasies about the ethical reach and impact of the literary and to champion, instead, the smaller and more humble effects of literary engagement.

But what might these more modest effects be that on occasion still engage with ethical life, albeit in muffled, diminutive, self-conscious forms? One site for this engagement inheres in *Open City*'s contradiction between Julius's propensity to forget the suffering of others and the novel's—or text's—ability to recall and con-solidate that suffering through its inscription. While Julius forgets his neighbor's death, turns the page on V.'s suicide, and evades Moji's accusation—and while reading itself mimics this temporal structure of propulsion and forgetting (we, too, turn the pages with a certain degree of forward momentum)—the novel simulta-neously renders these events static, since entextualization solidifies narrative and plot differently from how memory does. Certainly, we may return to these stories that Julius skirts, re-enlivening them and remembering them with each rereading, but whether we read the novel once or many times, its very existence as text means that each event of reading repeats and remembers these characters and their experiences of suffering.

Thus, to return to Baucom's argument about the writer as testamentary witness, we observe that the novel enacts three levels of witnessing simultaneously: it condemns Julius for his haste to forget others' pain, it alerts us to our own tendency to similarly disavow others' suffering, and yet it recalls precisely those details and experiences that are being repeatedly forgotten (and thus remembered in novel form). World literature and our engagements with it as readers, then, present noth-ing less than a training in perseverance, a Sisyphean counter-methodology to stave off contemporary modes of narcissistic distraction. Yet, as epitomized here by *Open City*, it is most successful and most honest when it produces a kind of readerly immersion kept aware of the ethical ambivalence always already structuring our efforts to connect.

*   *   *

LILY SAINT is assistant professor of English at Wesleyan and the author of *Black Cultural Life in South Africa: Reception, Apartheid, and Ethics*, forthcoming from the University of Michigan Press in November 2018. She has coedited a special issue of the *Cambridge Journal of Post-colonial Literary Inquiry* on genre in Africa (2017) and publishes in *Postcolonial Studies* and the *Journal of African Cinemas*.

Works Cited

Appiah, Kwame Anthony. *Cosmopolitanism: Ethics in a World of Strangers*. New York: Norton, 2006.

Attridge, Derek. *The Singularity of Literature*. New York: Routledge, 2004.

Badiou, Alain. *Ethics: An Essay on the Understanding of Evil*. New York: Verso, 2001.

Baucom, Ian. *Specters of the Atlantic: Finance Capital, Slavery, and the Philosophy of History*. Durham: Duke UP, 2005.

Bewes, Timothy. *The Event of Postcolonial Shame*. Princeton: Princeton UP, 2011.

Booth, Wayne C. *The Company We Keep: An Ethics of Fiction*. Berkeley: U of California P, 1988.

Brooks, Peter, and Hilary Jewett. *The Humanities and Public Life*. New York: Fordham UP, 2014.

Casanova, Pascale. *The World Republic of Letters*. Cambridge, MA: Harvard UP, 2004.

Coetzee, J. M., and Arabella Kurtz. *The Good Story: Exchanges on Truth, Fiction, and Psychotherapy*. New York: Viking, 2015.

Cole, Teju. *Known and Strange Things: Essays*. New York: Random House, 2016.

———. *Open City: A Novel*. New York: Random House, 2011.

Dalley, Hamish. "The Idea of 'Third Generation Nigerian Literature': Conceptualizing Historical Change and Territorial Affiliation in the Contemporary Nigerian Novel." *Research in African Literatures* 44.4 (2013): 15–34.

Damrosch, David. *What Is World Literature?* Princeton: Princeton UP, 2003.

Deckard, Sharae et al. *Combined and Uneven Development: Towards a New Theory of World-Literature*. Liverpool: Liverpool UP, 2015.

Favret, Mary A. *War at a Distance: Romanticism and the Making of Modern Wartime*. Princeton: Princeton UP, 2010.

Harvey, David. "The 'New' Imperialism: Accumulation by Dispossession." *Socialist Register* 40 (2004): 63–87.

Iser, Wolfgang. *The Act of Reading: A Theory of Aesthetic Response*. Baltimore: Johns Hopkins UP, 1978.

Jacobs, Karen. "Teju Cole's Photographic Afterimages." *Image Narrative* 15.2 (2014): 87–105.

James, Chantal. "Open Questions in an Open City." *Paste* 22 May 2012 < https://www.paste magazine.com/articles/2012/05/open-city-by-teju-cole.html >.

Krishnan, Madhu. "Postcoloniality, Spatiality, and Cosmopolitanism in the Open City." *Textual Practice* 29.4 (2015): 675–96.

Levi, Primo. *The Drowned and the Saved*. London: Abacus, 1988.

Miller, J. Hillis. *The Ethics of Reading: Kant, De Man, Eliot, Trollope, James, and Benjamin*. New York: Columbia UP, 1987.

Morrison, Toni. "The Site of Memory." *Inventing the Truth: The Art and Craft of Memoir*. Ed. William Zinsser. Boston: Houghton Mifflin, 1987. 185–200.

Ngai, Sianne. *Ugly Feelings*. Cambridge, MA: Harvard UP, 2004.

Nussbaum, Martha Craven. *Poetic Justice: The Literary Imagination and Public Life*. Boston: Beacon, 1995.

O'Gorman, Daniel. *Fictions of the War on Terror: Difference and the Transnational 9/11 Novel*. London: Palgrave Macmillan, 2015.

Palumbo-Liu, David. *The Deliverance of Others: Reading Literature in a Global Age*. Durham: Duke UP, 2012.

Pratt, Mary-Louise. "Arts of the Contact Zone." *Profession* 91 (1991): 33–40.

Rousseau, Jean-Jacques. *The Social Contract and Other Later Political Writings*. Trans. Victor Gourevitch. Cambridge: Cambridge UP, 1997.

Smith, Zadie. "Generation Why?" *New York Review of Books* 57.18 (2010): 57–60.

Sobre-Denton, Miriam. "Why Cosmopolitanism?" Center for Intercultural Dialogue, 12 Feb. 2014 <https://centerforinterculturaldialogue.org/2014/02/12/why-cosmopolitanism/>.

Syjuco, Miguel. "These Crowded Streets." *New York Times* 25 Feb. 2011.

Tivnan, Tom. "Wylie Blasts 'Bewildering' Global Publishing." *Bookseller* 11 Oct. 2017 <https://www.thebookseller.com/news/wylie-blasts-bewildering-global-publishing-653131>.

Vermeulen, Pieter. "Flights of Memory: Teju Cole's *Open City* and the Limits of Aesthetic Cosmopolitanism." *Journal of Modern Literature* 37.1 (2013): 40–57.

Wood, James. "The Arrival of Enigmas." *New Yorker* 28 Feb. 2011, 68–72.

Plurality in Question:
Zimbabwe and the Agonistic African Novel

JEANNE-MARIE JACKSON

Postcolonialism and the field that succeeds it—known variously in English departments as world, global, and transnational literature—struggle with the matter of categories. Globalist scholars often aim to bypass definition altogether: we tend toward dismantling the containers used to delimit cultures and identities, instead emphasizing nonreductive liminalities and flows. As Caroline Levine suggests in her recent book *Forms*, this interest in multiplicity and multivalence has led the way, in the broader critical profession, to valuing reading that seeks "places where the binary breaks down or dissolves, generating possibilities that turn the form into something more ambiguous and ill-defined—formless" (9). Categorical plurality and disbanding has no doubt been vital to the contemporary humanities, given the punishing rigidities from and against which postcolonialism emerged. At least since the publication of Edward Said's *Orientalism* in 1978, scholars of writing from the global South have pushed literary studies writ large to move past epistemologically prescriptive texts and methods. Structuralist narrative techniques, in this context, present as an insidious politics: abstract binaries like center and periphery or foreign and native are read as latent expressions of particular imperial and/or nationalist ideologies that police social distinctions.[1]

In this way, reading for an abstract kind of literary multiplicity—the epistemological and narratological endorsement of the fluid many over the demarcated one—has in many ways come to signify the progressive cosmopolitan bona fides of literary critics. This essay intends the term *plurality*, then (rather than pluralism in a clearly political sense), to mark the ongoing effacement of the novel's mediated status by a direct isomorphism of literary form and social history. African literature in particular is usually read through one of two polemical lenses that speak to the eager conflation of narrative technique and ideological persuasion: either antiessentialism, of the sort suggested above, or a countervailing assertion of collective identity. The former, more common approach holds that binaristic forms endorse social and identitarian foreclosure (who is "civilized" and who is not; who is "African

---

[1] Literary scholars often motivate their suspicion of a particular narrative structure or device based on its correspondence with historical policies and events. Mahmoud Mamdani's *Define and Rule*, for example, details the attempt to *master* a "more intimate and local understanding" of colonized cultures, which Mamdani ascribes to the nineteenth-century British jurist and indirect rule architect Henry Maine, through a legal binary that aims to "closet the native in a separate conceptual world, shut off from the world of the settler by a binary: progressive [settler] and stationary [native] societies" (13). It is not hard to make the leap from Mamdani's formulation here to the methodological corollary of structuralism in its most odious typification, as the "systematic inventories of elements and their possibilities of combination" (Culler 22) that J. Hillis Miller once attributed to "Socratic critics . . . lulled by the promise of a rational ordering of literary study" (335).

Novel: A Forum on Fiction 51:2 DOI 10.1215/00295132-6846192 © 2018 by Novel, Inc.

enough"), whereas representing transcategorical "plurality" signals a commitment to social and political inclusion.

For work on African novels to rightly transcend disciplinary silos, though, we need a more sophisticated means of asking not just what the novel *is* but what it *does*: what analytic methods do key texts structurally perform or facilitate, beyond their ostensible contexts of production? As one possible answer, I will argue here for the African novel that argues. As Levine entreats us to be bolder in moving beyond a rote preference for categorical suspension—to try, now, to "analyze the major work that forms do in our world" (9)—I want to suggest that categories are essential to narrative structures of debate, above and beyond the particular categories such structures may seem to entrench. This breaks sharply with the mantle of critique by which Africanist literary work most often proceeds in the negative, so to speak, by unpeeling so many onion layers of context to reveal an ideological core. Instead, I ask how an African novelistic tradition might technically *exceed* its individual texts' most obvious themes, permitting a more nuanced response to African narrative structures and their social significance.[2]

To this end, this essay presents the Zimbabwean novel as an aggregate case study that challenges the default and often imprecise critical virtue of plurality, or more-than-oneness. This gesture may at first seem counterprogressive: Zimbabwe is widely associated with the virulent nationalism of Robert Mugabe, the country's leader from 1980 to 2017. Humanist critics are thus wont to interpret categorical oppositions in Zimbabwean writing—for example, rural and urban, one nation versus another, or languages that just will not mix—as symptoms of the social and ideological rigidity characteristic of an autocratic state. It is no doubt true that some Zimbabwean writers have nationalist or nativist inclinations, urging international scholars of the region toward a handful of lyrical and "liminal" stylists like Yvonne Vera and Chenjerai Hove (also both well known as critics of the Mugabe regime). Departing from plurality as a post-categorical ideal, however, in favor of theorizing narrative models that *rely* on categories to argue, shows that dualistic structures do more than enforce social divisions. Key Zimbabwean works are *agonistic* in form, subjecting even plurality itself to contestation and debate. It is a tradition that privileges categorical conflict over categorical dissolution, thereby relativizing plurality to maintain sharper structures of disagreement. This, in turn, may offer an unlikely space for social plural*ism* to thrive: the agonistic novel keeps the Zimbabwean fight alive, in structural rather than obviously ideological terms.

---

[2]   The most efficient way to describe Africanist scholars' long-standing propensity for the critique of, rather than the establishment of, genres, traditions, and categories of literary analysis can be found in some outstanding previous examples of its opposite, which is to say the critique of critique. Peter Hallward's *Absolutely Postcolonial*, which he opens by decrying postcolonial theory's "own apparent resistance to distinction and classification" in its promulgation as a "general theory of the non-generalisable as such" (xi), is probably the most incisive work in this vein. More recently, the members of the Warwick Research Collective have published *Combined and Uneven Development: Towards a New Theory of World-Literature* (Deckard et al.), which argues for a forceful definition of world literature as a system, against the obfuscatory "structural" commitments of structuralism, postmodernism, and deconstruction that the authors take to undergird the adjacent fields of postcolonial and global literature.

*   *   *

I would like to begin with a brief Zimbabwean example before turning to a broad theoretical exposition. In his 2002 essay collection *Palaver Finish*, the self-exiled (and recently deceased) Zimbabwean writer Hove declares that the "beautiful dreamers" of Zimbabwe have "woken up to the ugliness of nightmare" (8). And yet one would be hard-pressed to identify the corollary dream space of the present. "Teachers, too," Hove bemoans, "have to flee the anger of the so-called [Zimbabwean Liberation] war veterans and politicians to find work in foreign cities where the education of children means providing them with the values of human dignity and the sanctity of life" (7). While few readers are likely to quibble with such values, Hove's occlusion of a specific destination here is telling. To mention the actual place *to* which the vast majority of Zimbabweans "flee"—that is, South Africa, among the most heralded democratic success stories of the postcolonial era—would invite a particularized account of democracy's own precarity.[3] As a result, Hove's invocation of a more open, dignified space is staked to geographic and conceptual vagueness. He regrets Zimbabweans' need to escape the "bad" without articulating a persuasive vision of the "good."

Hove makes a pointed criticism of the Zimbabwean state by situating its failings in an imprecise transnational frame, thereby crystallizing a brand of critical elision that is especially prevalent in Africanist literary scholarship: we are able to pick out the *absence* of complexity, but we have difficulty offering systematic, complex readings that get beyond a negative critique. The drawbacks of a postrationalist stance "against categories" in favor of more immediate, singular encounters with texts have been amply theorized in the literary field's mainstream, juxtaposing a Deleuzian plurality of amorphous design with something more like a Habermasian plural*ist* public of mutually engaged positions.[4] Walter Benn Michaels's *The*

---

[3] There has been a spate of books in political science and adjacent fields over the last ten to fifteen years debating the terms on which South Africa should or should not be considered a regional economic and democratic success story. Among them, see Patrick Bond's controversial *Elite Transition: From Apartheid to Neoliberalism in South Africa*, Michael H. Allen's *Globalization, Negotiation, and the Failure of Transformation in South Africa*, and Lawrence Hamilton's *Are South Africans Free?* The Johannesburg-based cultural theorist Achille Mbembe does not go so far as to suggest that South Africa is or is likely to become a failed state, but he noted recently in the country's major newspaper, the *Mail and Guardian*, that it now falls prey to "the mixture of clientelism, nepotism and prebendalism so prevalent in the immediate aftermath of African decolonisation."

[4] This essay makes no contribution to the postcolonial literature on Deleuze and Guattari, but the following quote on the construction of the unconscious from *A Thousand Plateaus* is helpful in both suggesting and obscuring the implications of their work for thinking about literary form's relation to political paradigms:

> The map does not reproduce an unconscious closed in upon itself; it constructs the unconscious. It fosters connections between fields, the removal of blockages on bodies without organs, the maximum opening of bodies without organs onto a plane of consistency . . . The map is open and connectable in all of its dimensions; it is detachable, reversible, susceptible to constant modification. It can be torn, reversed, adapted to any kind of mounting, reworked by an individual, group, or social formation. It can be drawn on a wall, conceived of as a work of art, constructed as a political action or as a mediation. (12)

Shape of the Signifier and Amanda Anderson's *The Way We Argue Now* are two of the best-known examples. Anderson, appositely, introduces her book by resisting "the underdeveloped and often incoherent evaluative stance of contemporary theory, its inability to clearly avow the norms and values underlying its own critical programs" (1). Benn Michaels, for his part, decries the "invention of racial identity and then of its transformation both into the pluralized form of cultural identity and into the privileging of the subject position as such" (12). But this strain of critical thought—what we might summarize as arguing for argument as a key literary domain instead of just identifying literature with subjectivity or experience—has failed to find real traction in the postcolonial arena.

In the philosopher Maria Baghramian's account, this widespread academic "preoccupation with ideas of pluralism, relativism, and multiplicity of perspectives" (44) can also be explained through the successive disciplinary afterlives of Kant's scheme-content dualism (i.e., the distinction between experience itself and the conceptual models we use to organize and make sense of experience). As Baghramian suggests, it is among the most crucial foundations of the pluralist episteme, because Kant permitted new variability in interpreting a reality that nonetheless maintained the status of true or universal. And yet scheme-content dualism, over the decades in which postcolonial and poststructuralist theory found its footing, was criticized for being *insufficiently* accountable to a plurality of experience, on account of its still being "motivated by . . . the suspect notion of a priori truth" (49). Baghramian, in good pragmatist fashion, thus indicates an irresoluble contradiction: scheme-content duality allows *both* for the existence of "reality" as such and for its conflicting organizations. In this reading, distinguishing between the real and our conceptions of the real thereby traps critics in a conceptual no-man's-land between the two poles of relativism and universality. Individualized perceptions, instead of being legitimized, are reduced to the status of mere "intermediaries between us and the world" (54), the identifying marks of what Donald Davidson calls a "featureless self" free of "distortion of the real" and "without categories and concepts" (7).

In this sense, an antiessentialist literary paradigm can be celebrated for creating an archive of particularities, valuable for its defiance of extrapolation into a larger, often violent organizing framework.[5] To again quote Davidson in "On the

---

[5]   Francoise Lionnet's 2012 address to the American Comparative Literature Association, "Shipwrecks, Slavery, and the Challenge of Global Comparison: From Fiction to Archive in the Colonial Indian Ocean," is a useful example. In it, Lionnet aims mainly to "put into crisis" (448) earlier epistemologies and uses an Amitav Ghosh novel involving Mauritius (*Sea of Poppies*) to mount "a harsh critique of the historiographic practices that tend to solidify rigid categories of academic thought, since these can then lead to artificial distinctions that justify violence and divisions" (449). South Africa, especially, has also been a key site for the development of the timely Indian Ocean studies subfield. The Centre for Indian Studies in Africa, established at Wits University in Johannesburg in 2007, has played a prominent role in bringing the field to interdisciplinary prominence, with literary studies among its chief areas of focus. Indian Ocean scholars' unifying aims are unassailable: they seek to escape the limitations of Anglo-American cultural history *and* counterhistory that a focus on either

Very Idea of a Conceptual Scheme," we might see current historicist and materialist approaches to global Southern writing as having moved usefully away from a conceptual scheme that organizes, systematizes, or divides up objects—what Davidson calls "posits" (16)—and toward the paradoxical task of accounting for, or facing, the "tribunal of experience" (14). The challenge for literary scholars with formal investments, though, who are eager to journey down this non-essentialist path, is that narrative *is*, fundamentally, an intermediary between us and the world. While an intention to find "ways in which we can be directly in touch with the world, without any further need for incorrigible or otherwise privileged and foundational epistemic items" (Baghramian 55), might make sense as a philosophical vision, it is a misconceived frame for a literary hermeneutics.

And yet the rejection of scheme/content duality—concomitant with much wishful thinking about narrative functionality's social power—remains congenial to postcolonial and more recent humanistic investments in a generalized anti-binarism. The persistent imperative of dismantling imperialist and/or nationalist epistemologies, for that matter, has also been manifest in global literature itself, as an impulse to foreground the ever-shifting "flows" behind historical and subjective construction. In this sense, many global writers, like the global critics who champion them, seek a contemporary version of what the nineteenth-century Russian novel scholar Irina Paperno once called "a model that essentially involves a lack of modeling" (9). The critical canonization of two broad schools of anglophone writing that use novels to model a nonrestrictive global Southern humanism makes the appeal of apparent nonmediation especially clear.

The first, typified by the archival anglophone Indian writer Amitav Ghosh in his novels of vast cartographic spread (particularly *Sea of Poppies* from 2008, the start of an epic trilogy about the opium trade), focuses on previously underrepresented transnational constellations to shed light on the historical vicissitudes of multidirectional commerce: Ghosh's novels are famously encyclopedic, replete with data like shipping terminology, multilingual period vernacular, and dozens of characters spread across social classes. To quote the Indian Ocean scholar Isabel Hofmeyr in a 2012 essay subtitled "The Indian Ocean as Method," anachronistic categories like "domination and resistance" or "colonizer and colonized" have given way here to a copiously detailed transnational historicism. A creole space like the Indian Ocean "requires us to take a much longer perspective, which necessarily complicates any simple binaries" (589), including the nationalist counterassertions of decolonization. It is fitting, then, that virtually every major scholar of Indian Ocean

the Atlantic or Pacific worlds tends to imply. In its place, they favor an emphasis on cosmopolitanism and circulation in "an area whose boundaries are both moveable and porous" (Moorthy and Jamal 4), aware of both the "dangers of Occidentalism and the inversion of binaries" (6). Interestingly, the ocean is also Davidson's figure of choice for discussing the difficulty of comparing conceptual or categorical schemes with experiential or sensory ones. "Someone who sets out to organize a closet arranges the things in it," he writes. "If you are told not to organize the shoes and shirts, but the closet itself, you would be bewildered. How would you organize the Pacific Ocean? Straighten out its shores, perhaps, or relocate its islands, or destroy its fish" (14).

studies, including Hofmeyr, Gaurav Desai, and Francoise Lionnet, takes Ghosh's novels as among the primary sources—and sometimes the only source—in their South-South literary archive.[6]

The other most visible transnational conjuncture of postcategorical novels and postcategorical criticism—captured ideally in the title of the essay "To Hear the Variety of Discourses" (2011) by the acclaimed South African "coloured" writer Zoë Wicomb—strives to represent representational flux on a more limited, subjective scale. In Wicomb's case, this often takes the form of a mixed-race female character in the hybridistic, littoral city of Cape Town.[7] This latter trend, in sum, valorizes subjective and cultural nonfixity by charting their interplay with equally fluid geographies, again with special focus on the Indian Ocean region through South Africa's Western Cape. Geographic spread is the hallmark strategy of most of the highest-profile recent African literary works, including Chimamanda Ngozi Adichie's *Americanah* (2013), with its many-pronged world aviation network and kaleidoscopic view of diasporic sensibilities; Taiye Selasi's *Ghana Must Go* (2013), as it charts convergences between African and diasporic families and institutions; and Binyavanga Wainaina's *One Day I Will Write about This Place* (2011), built of porous, atemporal, and synesthetic moments of self-formation. These works' many merits aside, they seem to capture what Benn Michaels describes as "the disarticulation of difference from disagreement" (30), a movement away from ideological positions in favor of a "softer" cultural and subjective orientation. Studies of the African novel, from close readings to critical movements like Afropolitanism and oceanic studies, prioritize questions of who one is and *where* one is rather than what one endorses or stands for *beyond plurality itself*. To quote again from *The Shape of the Signifier*, the field serves as the foremost critical evidence of "a movement from the universalist logic of conflict as difference of opinion to the posthistoricist logic of conflict as difference in subject position" (33).

In the instance of what I will shorthand here as the Ghosh and Wicomb variants of narrative nonfixity, international literary and academic gatekeepers have been attracted to a cosmopolitan disposition that has complicated the reception of even the most heralded Zimbabwean writers. This is because Zimbabwean novels tend to deploy a lot of dichotomous pairs, a technique that—*without* a scheme/content distinction to draw our attention to the structural effect rather than the ontology of the text (or what processes its organizing principles foster, not simply what politics they may signal)—may easily be read as discontinuous or reductive. NoViolet Bulawayo's Booker Prize–shortlisted *We Need New Names* (2013), for example, has come under fire for its rigid contrast between Bulawayo, in southern Zimbabwe, and Detroit (the main character Darling is at one point able to Skype with friends

---

[6]   See also Gaurav Desai's 2013 book *Commerce with the Universe*, winner of the 2014 Rene Wellek Prize from the American Comparative Literature Association, and, again, Lionnet's 2012 lecture "Shipwrecks, Slavery, and the Challenge of Global Comparison."

[7]   In Wicomb's 2006 novel *Playing in the Light*, for example, a Cape Town woman who is unaware of her mixed-race heritage must navigate relations with her first black employee. In *October* (2014), the main character struggles to negotiate between fraught family and social and racial relations in South Africa and those of her diasporic home of Scotland.

from home, but the connection is weak in all senses). In a thoughtful piece for the Johannesburg Workshop on Theory and Culture, the Zimbabwe-raised literary scholar Ashleigh Harris mentions "the odd structural break in the text between the sections set in Zimbabwe and those set in the US," which makes the book read like "two stories written for creative writing class: the first driven by the content demands of 'writing what you know' as the member of the group bringing the high cultural pluralism into the group," and the second "as the cinch in the deal of making this an American fiction." The most visible of the critical reviews of *We Need New Names*, though, was Nigerian novelist Helon Habila's from *The Guardian*. In a broader criticism of what is often called the "Caine Prize aesthetic" of CNN-ready depictions of African suffering for Western audiences, he notes Bulawayo's "rather free-ranging, episodic plot structure," in which "the narrator is whisked away to America."

Harris and Habila have a point: Bulawayo's novel, in its juxtaposition of Zimbabwean poverty, AIDS, and political violence with relatively secure but stultifying urban middle-class American life, depicts two very different settings. It can therefore easily be read as symptomatic of the "selling" of the African continent by a globalized publishing industry. In Habila's critique, Bulawayo shows why one might want to "escape" Zimbabwe for the United States; Harris then reads her as leveraging this escape to offer gentler but still shallow criticisms of America as well. Their shared concern is that the book's parts do not add up to a realistic whole, falling back instead on an exaggerated locational disconnection that grapples with globality at the level of trope, not structure. To summarize the critical climate surrounding African writing, then, global-pluralist scholars are urged to increase the visible range of subjective and historical positions by privileging texts that themselves foreground connectivity. The above critiques of *We Need New Names*—in which the narrator pronounces, "It's hard to explain, this feeling; it's like there's two of me" (212)—therefore suggest that Bulawayo fails to bridge multiple geographic perspectives and thus is locked within a Western structural inheritance of binary opposition. But this premium on connection is itself deeply flawed; *We Need New Names*, in narrative rather than theoretical practice, is set up to argue for the value *of* opposition in adjudicating the merits of numerous imperfect social and political options. Put differently, the novel presents *argument* as what Levine might call an "affordance" of dichotomous pairs, a term she adopts "to describe the potential uses or actions latent in materials and designs." Instead of focusing on "what forms *do*"—which, in Bulawayo's case, might be to reflect or entrench politically regressive categorical divisions—Levine suggests asking "what potentialities lie latent . . . in aesthetic and social arrangements" (6–7).

To be sure, a book that depicts life in Zimbabwe in formal disconnection from life in Detroit could be read as having failed to internalize globalized modernity. But it might also be read as a strategic contrast between two contexts—one (America) a liberal-pluralist democracy and one (Zimbabwe) for the most part not—that is stark enough to act as an alternative to either utopic plurality *or* nationalist binaries in imagining Zimbabwe.[8] If one begins from the premise that categorical ambiguity

8   I have no interest in mounting a political argument as regards Zimbabwe; there are people who are much better equipped to do so. For readers who are unfamiliar with the country's history, however, it was long marked internationally as one of the world's least pluralistic political spaces,

is of more social value than sharp debate about what categories should and do comprise, it is, admittedly, difficult to imagine how opposition might be read as structurally productive rather than just politically useful. And intolerance of ambiguity has, understandably, become the defining anxiety of Zimbabwean humanist scholarship in the years following national independence in 1980: Mugabe's thirty-seven-year reign over what many critics see as an autocratic state is a difficult thing to peer beyond.

As the novelist and vocal regime critic Stanley Nyamfukudza puts it in his 2005 lecture "To Skin a Skunk: Some Observations on Zimbabwe's Intellectual Development," Zimbabwean discourse now "operates by way of raising a selection of emotive ideas to the status of sacred cows; ideas of national unity, of sovereignty, of the sacrifices of liberation, and of patriotism and racial solidarity" (16). Likewise, Ranka Primorac, in her book *The Place of Tears: The Novel and Politics in Modern Zimbabwe*, invokes Achille Mbembe to articulate her experiences with Zimbabwe's restrictive academic culture. "Mbembe singles out two intersecting currents of thought," she writes, "which have locked African thinking about identity and freedom into oppositional mode" (8). These currents are what Mbembe calls "Afroradicalism and nativism," which impede the reinvention of a "being-together situation" (8). Scholarship on Zimbabwe, in Primorac's account, has a clear, epistemologically pluralizing mission: it can help restore literature to the status of "complex and ambivalent," to lift a description from her analysis of the internationally acclaimed novelist Vera (168). It is not, however, an endorsement of Mugabe's government to propose a more pointed conceptual apparatus for addressing the novel's relation to pluralism, growing out of a thicker conception of plurality as it attempts to cut across literary and political discourses.

This is where a return to philosophy and political theory is helpful for refining a literary method that prioritizes argument. To be clear, I am invested neither in using Zimbabwean literature to amend pluralist theory, whose authors are not literary scholars, nor in merely "applying" Western pluralist theory to Zimbabwean novels. I aim, rather, to put pluralist theory that relies heavily on figuration into conversation with literary studies' postcategorical strain under the influence of its postcolonial and/or global subfields. It goes without saying that much of this secondary material has originated from the American context, given its unusually acute preoccupation with the gap resulting from pluralism as a democratic ideal versus as an unevenly fulfilled reality.[9] This no doubt indicates a commitment on

particularly in comparison with the far more visible South Africa (whose post-apartheid democratic credentials, nonetheless, have been substantially tarnished by the Zuma presidency that began in 2009). Harare has been governed by ZANU-PF through often violent repression of minority populations (most notably of Ndebele civilians in the Gukurahundi attacks of the mid-1980s); voter rights; and impoverished communities (through Operation Murambatsvina, or "Drive Out the Rubbish," and, some would say, more recent efforts to rid the capital city of its swelling street-vendor population). The government has often been criticized abroad for its forced distribution of arable land from white "settler" families to black war veterans of the Second Chimurenga liberation war, 1966–79.

9   It need hardly be said that pluralism has been a topic of primary concern in scholarship on the American novel. See, as one recent example, Julianne Newmark's *The Pluralist Imagination: From*

my part to thinking about African national traditions in relation to broader global theoretical contexts. It is also, however, simply a matter of where and by whom plurality *as such*—which is to say, as a representational ideal—has been most thoroughly developed. The models of plurality above, which discuss Africa and Zimbabwe in particular, work jointly with more generalized work on the topic to indicate where the *design* by which pluralism is imagined becomes amorphous, untenable, and thus structurally ill-suited to argument regardless of where it occurs.

With this syncretic critical approach in mind, perhaps nowhere has the difference between plurality as an unscaled ideal and pluralism as a scalable structural practice been as lucidly articulated as in Nicholas Rescher's *Pluralism: Against the Demand for Consensus*, which lays out competing pluralisms of incommensurable shape. Right from the start, Rescher denaturalizes the assumption that plurality as such (the sort of "paradigmatic" plurality, I would suggest, that is at stake in most literary projects) is necessarily synonymous with the social good. Whereas in "much of the [philosophical] tradition consensus was viewed not just as something to be desired," he writes, "but as something whose eventual actualization is effectively assured by some principle" (e.g., rational principles, rational processes, or universal truth), "many present-day writers invest social consensus not with confidence, but with hope" (1). In response, "diversity" as a socially and institutionally manifest plurality is now often upheld as the highest order Western value.

This is a paradigmatic change perhaps still best captured by Isaiah Berlin in "The Apotheosis of the Romantic Will": "No one today is surprised by the assumption that variety is, in general, preferable to uniformity," he remarks. "Yet this has not long been so; for the notion that One is good, Many—diversity—is bad, since the truth is one, and only error is multiple is far older" (219–20). For Rescher, writing amid the identity politics of the 1990s (a moment in many ways resonant with our own), a policy of diversity without further specification by default privileges consensus over argument in how plurality, again, is figured or given discernible shape; it amounts to a question like, can't we all just get along? Instead, Rescher insists that ideologically well-intended plurality must rise to the challenge of a more proactive pluralism. He continues, "[Writers now] look upon interpersonal agreement as a substitute for the assured verities of an earlier era in whose realization they have lost faith" (1). But such mutual toleration is easily ruffled by contact with others' differing, deeper convictions. A structurally tenable pluralism, on the other hand, must inculcate social forms and practices that "make the world safe for disagreement" (5).

Such sweeping assertions nonetheless do not get us very far, and Rescher's broad pluralist paradigm of disagreement also entails taxonomy of its *types*, not all of which are created equal. He designates four ways that the general principle of pluralism can become a function of rational dispute and not just a vague commitment. The type most relevant to global literary studies is syncretism, or the "radically open-minded" view that "all the alternatives should be accepted: all those seemingly discordant positions are in fact justified; they must, somehow, be

---

East to West in American Literature, as well as now-classic studies like Walter Benn Michael's *Our America: Nativism, Modernism, and Pluralism*.

conjoined and juxtaposed" (80). This idea has particular resonance for how we discuss postcolonial literary traditions, in regard to which plurality is often pre-ordained as an interpretive goal that needs no further justification. The problem, for Rescher, is that multiplicity on its own does not necessarily equate to embarking on "the arduous but productive path of a rational choice which alone prevents our coming away empty-handed from the deliberations at issue" (96). Plurality and sustainable pluralism, that is, do not always add up to the same thing.

Championing difference (often, as for Primorac and Mbembe, through inverse condemnation of forms that do not have enough of it) should lead to debate about which structures best facilitate its cultivation. If one is interested in the relationship between narrative and political context, it is what structures *do* that counts, not what they appear to be. It is useful to note here that even in his apparent endorsement of the "consensus" pluralistic model, Zimbabwe's Nyamfukudza inadvertently indicates its limitations. "What is important is the existence of an overall consensus about what the major problems are and about what needs to be done to tackle them," he avers (18). And yet later, in his call for "a serious non-partisan forum for discussion of cultural, social, and even political and other issues," he seeks a space of "non-partisan argument" (22, 24). The meaningful question here is not whether one thinks pluralism is good but rather how it actually *looks* and operates; for Nyamfukudza it is contentious and solution-oriented rather than expressed by openness.

As concerns syncretism, considering the pluralist episteme's analogous figuration leads directly from the philosophical to the literary-political domain. What Rescher calls syncretism's "conjunctionist" program can be grasped as an approach of "conjoining" rather than synthesizing alternative positions: conjunctionism leaves all positions intact but connected to one another, whereas syncretism retains key elements from each to combine them in moving toward a new, better view. Tellingly, in light of this essay's literary focus, Rescher elects the spatial metaphor of a library's relation to the books it contains to summarize why conjunctionism is flawed. "The book should be consistent," he remarks; "it should tell its own internally coherent story. But, just as the library as a whole contains many diverse and discordant books, so reality is a complex of many different and discordant 'worlds'" (92). In effect, a "pluralist" space on this model only works because it is inanimate; it offers no insight as to how its "members" might interact.

More recently, William Connolly, the frequently cited author of *Pluralism* and *Why I Am Not a Secularist*, among other, related works, has elaborated his theory of political plurality with recourse to an imaginative structure that is similar to Rescher's "conjoining." Drawing on William James, whose intellectual contribution he takes to be that "[p]hilosophy is an art form, not a tight mode of argumentation by which necessary conclusions are drawn" (71), Connolly too is trapped in the gap between pluralist ideals and the argumentative formations required to advance them. His version of pluralism looks something like a chain that extends in all directions or perhaps an infinite Venn diagram: a centered and hierarchal sense of national belonging is replaced with "an image of interdependent minorities of different types connected through multiple lines of affiliation" (62). The quality through which the shared space of the pluralist ethos is maintained, though, is described as the "moment of mystery, abyss, rupture, openness, or difference within the faith" and then, later, "an element of mystery, rupture, or difference that evades or resists definitive interpretation" (62). Every time, in fact, that Connolly ventures to describe the payoff of what he calls "deep pluralism," he reverts to tendentious generalizations about the world. He assumes that there is a "love of difference simmering in most faiths," for example, and that this constitutes a practice that "must be *defended militantly* against this or that drive to religio-state Unitarianism" (65; emphasis added).

Connolly's commitments are sincere, but his arguments are betrayed, like those of many postcolonial scholars, by their rejection of the necessarily oppositional premise on which they rest. For Connolly, pluralism counters the threat of a black-or-white religious politics, as for those who study southern Africa a more abstract "plurality" is often meant to counter the threat of an overzealous ZANU-PF or African National Congress. But if this counterspace of complexity is a structural and descriptive "mystery" or void, meaningful more for what it rejects than for what it observes, it recreates the murky dualism of open versus closed. In other words, both Rescher's library model (which he uses as a negative illustration) and Connolly's "image of interdependent minorities" wish away the issue of "discordant theses and theories" (Rescher 95) or the logical inconsistencies that practically add up not to an all-encompassing tolerance of different positions but to positional laziness. "Syncretism's façade of openness and liberality hides from view the awesome cost of taking this sort of position," Rescher insists. "It purchases the advantage of being liberal and non-judgemental at an unacceptable price: in being over-generous, it is self-defeating" (95).

How, then, might we build toward a more robust *narrative* theory of plurality? A plurality, that is, that is structurally sustainable rather than astructural? For literary critics, the source that comes to mind is no doubt Mikhail Bakhtin and his essay "Discourse in the Novel" in particular. Its argument that has been almost ubiquitously paraphrased is, "The novel can be defined as a diversity of social speech types (sometimes even diversity of languages) and a diversity of individual voices, artistically organized" (484). The appeal here for reading the literature of Zimbabwe is clear. In their introduction to the 2005 anthology *Versions of Zimbabwe: New Approaches to Literature and Culture*, for example, Robert Muponde and Primorac identify Vera and Dambudzo Marechera, two of the country's internationally best-known writers, as "plurivocal" in contradistinction to the sometimes "xenophobic," "monologic," and "nationalist" narratives of the Third Chimurenga (xv), the popular name for ZANU-PF's fast-track 1980s land redistributions from white farmers to war veterans. This important anthology in the Zimbabwean national field, in other words, is invested primarily in undoing the "neatly symmetrical and curiously familiar" constructs of Zimbabwean "patriotic" postcolonial historiography, in which "time is conceived of as linear . . . and space as sharply divided" between rural and urban, and nation and world (xiv). In a word, Muponde and Primorac seek to restore a more expansive array of voices and shifting viewpoints to Zimbabwean writing.

If we return to Bakhtin, though, to test out the pluralizing invitation above with a more developed theory of narrative representation, the fit is in fact rather awkward.

Bakhtin also has a penchant to taxonomize, and the levels at which he does this reveal an insistence on both structural opposition and national unity that is often edited out of scholars' use of his work (albeit a far more flexible version of national unity than was then on offer in Russia). Bakhtin discusses his popular notion of dialogism as well as its partner term, *heteroglossia*, or *разноречие* (literally, diverse speech), not just as a general principle of diversity but also at three particular levels of analysis. At baseline, there are words that draw on an array of speech and language types (including the oral-folkloric Russian register of *сказ*); there are utterances that further complicate the origins and meanings of these words; and finally, there is the novel itself that binds "socially alien languages within the boundaries of one and the same national language" (499). Despite his theory of formal diversity, then, in the conviction that "language is heteroglot from top to bottom" (503), Bakhtin does not sacrifice the novel's overriding, unifying purpose or his interest in identifying "socially significant world views" as opposed to a moral achievement of inclusivity (502). Furthermore, he adheres to a belief that there is a common "movement of the theme through different languages and speech types" (485), meaning that Bakhtinian multiplicity is not mainly about individuated perspectives but is concerned with language's capacity to variously refract a shared reality. Bakhtin's capacity to accommodate something like William Connolly's hyperinclusive pluralism is thus severely limited. More to the point, he postulates the novel as an overridingly oppositional form. At its highest level of generality, it binds together utterances that "[participate] in the 'unitary languages' (in its centripetal forces and tendencies) and at the same time [partake] of social and historical heteroglossia (the centrifugal, stratifying forces)" (491). His overall theory is tinged with argument and aggression: "[T]he dialogic nature of language . . . was a struggle among socio-linguistic points of view" (491), and "[t]he word is born in a dialogue as a living rejoinder within it" (495).

A properly Bakhtinian methodology, then, centers on the relationship been a text's micro-units (words and phrases) and the text as a whole, not on the relationship between novelistic form in the broader sense of a work's structural configuration—the designs it prioritizes in moving key elements around like so many tectonic plates—and politics. To let Zimbabwean narrative truly come into its own in the critical arena, we thus need a theory that can account for the role of things like oppositionality and diversity, as they figure *in* novels, more than we need an applied Bakhtinianism that postulates such features as universal traits *of* novels. The political theorist Bonnie Honig, a recent interlocutor of William Connolly, suggests a pluralist model that I think is more germane to narrative and to Zimbabwean works especially. Whereas Connolly advocates "expansive pluralism" that heralds an unspecified proliferation of difference (48), Honig suggests an "agonistic" democratic model that privileges "dissonance, resistance, conflict or struggle" ("Political Theory" 2) as a practice instead of as a latent characteristic per Bakhtin. Her core vision of agonism is comprehensively argued in the 1993 book *Political Theory and the Displacement of Politics*, in which she pushes against the fact that political theorists typically "converge in their assumptions that success lies in . . . consolidating communities and identities" (2). For Honig, though, the aggregation of difference in the name of its advancement undermines the power of oppositional structures to refine rather than sublimate argumentative polarity.

In her essay contribution to *The New Pluralism*, a book of essays about Connolly's contributions to pluralist theory, Honig goes on to propose a more particularized version of debate and duality that emphasizes its democratic fertility ("Time of Rights"). It is one that I think has the potential to in some sense "salvage" key Zimbabwean novels from charges of ideological rigidity. In her view, the conditions of a productive democracy are conflictual and contestatory, not "pluralistic" in the immanent model of, for example, Rescher's library or endlessly Venn-diagrammatic as in Connolly's schema. Honig suggests a compatibility between oppositional structures and pluralistic goals for the lived experience of which they are part; representational strategies that might be dismissed as binaristic or reductive can then achieve a more complex result that will transcend an overly fixed politics. Hence she elsewhere favors organizing political practice into "two impulses of political life, the impulse to keep the contest going and the impulse to be finally freed of the burdens of contest" (*Political Theory* 14). In contrast to Connolly's expansiveness, Honig emphasizes the divisiveness of the public domain as the thing that preserves it.

Her next level of specificity, though, is still more promising for the Zimbabwean case, especially, and also lays the foundation for circling back to the role of South Africa in the Zimbabwean novelistic imaginary. "What democracy has always been about is fighting over the public thing," she remarks in a recent interview, before suggesting that "the state itself can be seen as an important public thing" ("Optimistic Agonist"). This lets us imagine Zimbabwe not through a vague but, too often, sanctimonious presupposition that plurality of meaning on its own can right political wrongs but through attention to what particular values and entities best symbolize and therefore shape Zimbabwean debate. Honig's public "thing"—which, unlike Connolly's more generic pluralism rooted in what Honig calls "the-right-as-symbol" despite "the myriad operations of the actual right" (*New Pluralism* 107)—insists on argument as something that addresses *real things*. This is not to say that argument for Honig is antiphilosophical: Rescher, too, sees syncretism as problematic precisely because its lack of positional clarity is "not a very promising reaction to the reality of pluralism" (940). It is simply to suggest that argument requires an object whose multivalence is temporarily suspended in order that it may catalyze an array of responses. The example that Honig uses in her interview to illustrate this difference between what she calls "symbol" and "good" is drawn from a 2012 US presidential debate, which featured the Sesame Street character Big Bird as part of a discussion of public television's defunding. Whereas the American Left, for a brief time, seized on the moment to illustrate how infantile the country's political culture had become, Honig suggests that the incident really illustrates a deep need to argue—with a clear point of focus—over "public attachments to public things" ("Optimistic Agonist"). Big Bird here is both actual and symbolic, but debate about him requires a perception of his fixity.

In the case of the canonical Zimbabwean writer Charles Mungoshi, restoring fixity and oppositionality to a productive role in narrative upsets accusations of his ideological collusion with colonial institutions, specifically the Southern Rhodesia

Literature Bureau, founded in 1954 to support indigenous literary output.[10] Read through the imperative of nonessentialism—or a moralized and politicized plurality of meaning and identity—Mungoshi's work does indeed seem symptomatic of a divisive mentality that warns Shonas against the "change" of urban centers in favor of confining them to rural lands. Frequently, as in his 1978 novel *Ndiko Kupindana Kwamazuva* (*That's How the Days Go By*, sometimes translated as *How Time Passes*), this entails a dichotomy between the contemplative and essential space of the Shona village and the acceleration of morally precarious behavior in the capital city of Harare. One line from the book, "Chimboita huro imwe yeHarare tione mukasasvika gumi" (10) (translated in an essay by Itai Muhwati as "Try to have one sip [of Harare] and see if you won't end up with ten sips"), explicitly demonizes the multiplicity of the modern. Similarly, the title of Mungoshi's other Shona novel, *Kunyarara Hakusi Kutaura?* (1983), suggests a literal emphasis on opposition if it is translated as *To Be Silent Is Not to Speak?*—a dimension that gets lost in the more idiomatic translation of *Silence Is Golden*.

The 1975 English-language Mungoshi classic *Waiting for the Rain*, with its revealing occlusion of South Africa in favor of a Shona-versus-overseas dichotomy, seems of a piece with this trend toward limiting either/ors. A child headed for an "overseas" (British) education elicits effusive pride from his father: "Why shouldn't I talk of my own son?" he exclaims. "Who has done what we—the sons of Mandengu—have done?" (59). South Africa, in contrast, is such a common and sober destination for Zimbabweans in search of jobs that another character just briefly passes over the years he spent there in the 1940s (74). The novel's range of imaginative possibility thus seems reduced to Zimbabwe and the West, a much-maligned center-periphery configuration that keeps both entities in a fixed power relation. And yet the narrative's brief gesture to South Africa here is telling, as it suggests Mungoshi's interest in arguing about a concrete thing that has paradigmatic significance because, per Honig, it fosters argument. Recalling Hove's unspecified dream space of international pluralism instead of the concrete destination of Cape Town or Johannesburg, the option of going "overseas" in *Waiting for the Rain* presents as either too threatening or too utopic, depending on which character is speaking, to be a useful object of debate. Instead, the specter of "overseas" works in tandem with South Africa's hard-knocks familiarity to figure the object of debate as nonfixity, or plurality, itself. Mungoshi stages an argument about the merits of leaving a known context in which one is able to argue. To borrow a formulation from Walter Benn Michaels, the "antagonism between two social ideals" on display in conversations *about* migration in the novel's Shona village is set to give way, with the introduction of the migratory paradigm as dominant, to "cultural difference that marks the coming of the new world" (28–29).

---

[10]   Emmanuel M. Chiwome, for example, charts the institutional and linguistic schism at the heart of modern Shona literature's "birth" with a number of key works in 1956. "The Department was based in the Ministry of Information and its task was to ensure that colonialism was given a politically correct profile," he writes, "to make it acceptable to the potentially rebellious Africans. . . . It is therefore a contradiction that novelistic practice, whose hallmark is innovation through exploration of reality, was to search for truth under the auspices of an intellectually and creatively oppressive propagandistic arm of government" (160).

Likewise, the plot of *Waiting for the Rain* concerns a contrast between the paradigms of traditional and modern, rural and urban, and African versus Westward-looking futures as elegantly marked by the brothers Lucifer and Garabha. As Lucifer accepts the patronage of a white city priest to study abroad, Garabha goes deeper into his traditional Shona drum circle; even as they jointly take over momentum from what at first seems like a wide-ranging cast of main characters, the brothers fail to connect as subjects within the narrative. At the end of the book, in a rising crest of opposition that demands a firm choice, the two literally go their separate ways. As Garabha learns to embrace his search for meaning while drumming and "singing, fading away into the bush" (165), the Eurocentric, upwardly mobile Lucifer forsakes his father's poignant gift of traditional medicine for his journey. "He staggers to the corner where the medicine bottles are, gathers them up, then carefully with a piece of rock, he smashes them one by one into very small pieces," Mungoshi writes. "Then he kneels down, locks up his two suitcases and carries them out into the waiting car" (172).

Waiting for the Rain both warrants and has received more sustained critical attention than I can offer here, but even this introduction to the text is sufficient to reinforce a larger sense of the Zimbabwean canon's pointed contrast with what Eileen Julien has theorized as the "extroverted" African novel of international acclaim, which successfully "registers in its very practice . . . the formidable imbalances and inequities that characterize Africa's place in the world" (696) by representing global circulation. The Zimbabwean traits I have identified point toward an altogether different demand in terms of our reading practices. Mungoshi, like Bulawayo, registers something more like Honig's agonism: both embed and sharpen opposing pairs in order to offer a structure in which the reader is urged not just to contemplate but perhaps to choose among competing situational options. At the very least, they are not oriented to what is often a uselessly intangible or ineffable idea of pluralism—such as Hove's "dream-space," Connolly's "ineffability," or Indian Ocean studies' priority on "complication"—which has, for Zimbabweans, most visibly been plagued by its own problems in neighboring South Africa.

My positive recasting of categorical fixity and opposition in Zimbabwean novels is no doubt open to criticism because political duality is so harmful in the country's real life: as a friend remarked upon reading an earlier draft of this essay, it made him think of the fact that Mugabe's party announces itself with a closed fist, while its main opposition, the Movement for Democratic Change (MDC) led by former Prime Minister Morgan Tsvangirai, uses an open hand. It is understandable that the modern Zimbabwean novel has provoked an ostensibly contradictory range of responses to its deep reliance on categorical demarcation. Muponde and Primorac's emphases on "plurivocality" and the like seek to complicate not just how novels are received but the entire state apparatus behind what these scholars see as a blunt and often reductive literary-critical tradition. Nonetheless, I maintain that this approach remains insufficient because, while it attends to literary complexity in writers who favor a congenial fluidity of prose style (Vera, for Primorac), it necessarily reduces other works to the status of the less complex on the basis of their relative categorical clarity.

Further exemplifying this difficult relation between analyzing novels and indicting their contexts of production and reception, Muponde and Primorac read three of the foundational Zimbabwean literature scholars from the 1980s—Musaemura Zimunya, George Kahari, and Flora Veit-Wild—as having minimized the complex relationship of key novelists like Mungoshi and Marechera to *their* social context. Zimunya, for example, is noted for his "essentialising use of 'European' as a denigrating descriptor" (xvi) and his ill-judged dismissal of Marechera as being too enmeshed in private, psychological life. Because there is general consensus that modern or "postcolonial" Zimbabwean literature—at least in terms of English prose—dates to this same decade with writers including Mungoshi, Marechera, and Stanley Samkange, among others, rising to national prominence, Muponde and Primorac's critical revision is significant. Zimunya, Kahari, and other scholars whom they assess as exhibiting a crude Afro-centrism (xvii) were not simply *re*assessing canonical novelists with a long critical history. They were instantiating, rather, a formative convergence of "reductive" modern Zimbabwean literary scholarship and reductive modern Zimbabwean writing at the moment of their co-emergence. By contrast, today's postcolonial critic must retrospectively restore the *writing* to its full complexity as a critique of its reception. I am, effectively, arguing that this is an unnecessary step if we imagine opposition as a Kantian scheme rather than as content: opposition in itself may serve the pluralist good and does not need to be critically wished away.

In this sense, Muponde and Primorac are more firmly in step with broader Africanist postnational agendas in fields like Indian Ocean studies or, perhaps, affect theory, though the centrality of land rather than sea to Zimbabwe makes the former correspondence a theoretical rather than a thematic one. Muponde begins another piece from around the same time ("Worm and the Hoe") by stating his goal of categorical expansionism outright: "The Third Chimurenga . . . is a virulent, narrowed-down version of Zimbabwean history, oversimplified and made rigid by its reliance on dualisms and binaries of insider/outsider, indigene/stranger, landed/landless, authentic/inauthentic, patriot/sell-out. The net effect of operating these binaries is the institution of othering as a permanent condition of political and cultural life where 'difference' translates unproblematically into 'foe'" (176). And yet there are inconsistencies, when one looks deeper, in his assessments of *why* such categorical rigidity is a problem. Though Muponde leads the charge to debinarize Zimbabwean literary scholarship through an enhanced understanding of Marechera in particular, he also suggests that some of Marechera's writing may indeed *be* insufficiently pluralistic. In a reading of a Marechera poem from the 1992 posthumous volume *Cemetery of Mind*, Muponde categorizes Marechera and the poet Tafataona Mahoso as people "who have continued to view their [black] victim state in terms of unresolved Manichean categories of black/white, power/powerlessness, victim/victimizer" (186).[11] The essay's immediate reversion to more discussion of Mugabe makes it clear that Marechera's skepticism about racial

---

[11]   The lines Muponde quotes are "reconciliation only works when justice is / seen to be done. / Otherwise all whites are lumped with the killers" (Marechera, qtd. in Muponde 184).

reconciliation in Zimbabwe, for Muponde, may be more plurivocal than earlier critics would allow but still falls short of the multiplicity that is commonly upheld in the postcolonial field.

I want to suggest that Muponde is right about the limitations of racialized thinking but that he and Primorac also miss the mark on what Marechera's frequent dichotomies might achieve. Marechera—who to this day inspires what the Zimbabwean writer Memory Chirere has called "Marechera-mania" among frustrated teenagers on account of his rebellious behavior against the late-colonial state (at Oxford University, especially)—is a strong case for reading the destructive effects of foreclosed possibility on and in an addled mind. At one point in *The House of Hunger*, the young male narrator stands on a hill looking down on his township with a character named Immaculate, his brother's abused lover. "She made me want to dream," he writes of his simultaneous attraction to and loathing of her, "made me believe in visions, in hope. But the rock and grit of the earth denied this" (12).

This is, from one vantage, an obvious moment of reality-induced schizophrenia, with the narrator entertaining a range of possibilities at the same time as he stamps them out because of where he lives. As the South African authority on Marechera, Annie Gagiano has written, "Fragmentation may be thought of as [*The House of Hunger's*] major theme—the disruption of human potential characteristic of so many African societies . . . in the latter part of the millennium and beyond." From another point of view, though, Marechera captures a capacity for self-argumentation that allows his groundbreaking narrative record of subjectivity to take form; indeed, his divisiveness may even constitute a more important innovation than the complex rendering of subjectivity. The indeterminate scale of "fragmentation" does not quite capture the extremity of juxtaposition in the above example: there are two options here, dreams or rocks.

As many times as the narrator says things like, "There are fragments and snatches of fragments. The momentary fingerings of a guitar" (60), he resorts to clear categorical opposition. "I was being severed from my own voice," he states about one-third of the way through the novella. "It was like this: English is my second language, Shona my first. When I talked it was in the form of an interminable argument, one side of which was always expressed in English and the other in Shona" (30). The propulsive division that the phrase "interminable argument" raises here in describing Zimbabwe's most common linguistic situation is a marked empirical *and* paradigmatic departure from, again, the oft-remarked linguistic diversity of South Africa, liberal pluralism's concrete regional representative (it has eleven official tongues, while Zimbabwe has three). While one could not push the sociolinguistic dimension too far as a literary analogy, it is worth noting that this difference in linguistic range has been a provocative literary trope. In Christopher Mlalazi's out-of-print 2009 novel *Many Rivers*, about a perilous crossing from Zimbabwe to South Africa across the Limpopo River in search of work, an Ndebele man in Johannesburg is disoriented by the combination of cultural intermingling and interpersonal violence he encounters. In this biting indictment of a common journey captured in the Shona phrase "kumhiri kwaLimpopo," which I would render idiomatically as something like "on the other side," Mlalazi uses the naïveté of his (literally) battered main character to upbraid any sense that multiplicity is a "good" on its own.

Likewise, even as Marechera introduces additional elements into the description of his mental struggle, he holds fast to their presentation as argument rather than syncretic linking. "I felt gagged by this absurd contest between Shona and English," he notes. "I knew no other language: my French and Latin were enough to make me wary of conversing in them. However, some nights I could feel the French and the Latin fighting it out in the shadowy background of the English and Shona" (30). Such nested oppositions—the escape from a choice between two socially dominant options to yet another choice between the languages of his colonial education—perfectly capture the challenge of Rescher's defining question, "how to respond to pluralism?" (97). As *The House of Hunger*'s narrator escapes his "gagging" from what seems like the local or immediate problem of English versus Shona, he finds not resolution of conflict through increased options but, instead, a second pair of languages that epitomizes Zimbabwe's colonial legacy. One opposition, then, is couched within a deeper one to generate Marechera's narrative. Even as argumentative tensions here go unresolved, they keep legible terms in play on either side.

Muponde and Primorac, in their focus on Marechera's "plurivocality," thus reflect the limitations of a far-reaching postcolonial bias toward seeing only maximal and categorically porous plurality as properly at odds with political and epistemic violence. While a reading practice set on instantiating difference would no doubt interpret Marechera's inner conflicts as evidence of his psychological entrapment within the Rhodesian legacy, we might also ask how lines in *The House of Hunger* like "The fights completely muzzled me" (30) are structurally distinctive. What, given Marechera's canonical status, do they suggest about a presciently Zimbabwean way of *keeping narrative going* amid a regional situation in which, increasingly, neither nationalism (Mugabe) nor liberal pluralism (the "new" South Africa) seems viable? And what, in this stalemate, are the most significant implications of loosening plurality's conceptual grip on our thinking about novels from this part of the world?

For starters, as Jean Comaroff and John L. Comaroff contend in their essay "Theory from the South," Africa is now at the forefront of debates about modernity and democratic practice, not just because of easy finger-pointing at "failed state(s)" but because, increasingly, theorists and citizens alike are questioning what democracy's end is meant to be. More specifically, my argument offers a new context in which to understand the challenges of creating a "transnational" critical public, given critics' persistent difficulty in reconciling what seem to be Zimbabwean writers' contradictory investments in de-essentializing nationalist narratives and narrativizing oppositional geographic relationships. To conclude, then, I want to return to Bulawayo's recent *We Need New Names*. An extended discussion of the novel's contrastive schema reveals what I think is a deliberate exaggeration of difference through, now, a global as opposed to colonial lens, which nonetheless still insists on questions of comparative value.

On the broadest formal level, Bulawayo employs virtually no "liminal" free indirect speech (just a first-person narrator and an intervening omniscient voice) and depicts sanguine racial plurality, like the "crowds and crowds of white people and black people and brown people" (158) at Barack Obama's televised inauguration, only in mediated form. Whereas *We Need New Names*, from a social rather than structural perspective, would be an obvious successor to Tsitsi Dangarembga's much-taught 1988 female coming-of-age story *Nervous Conditions* (in which an enterprising young girl from a Shona village first grows corn and later rises through the private-school system en route to her likely future migration to the United Kingdom), the competitive structure that Bulawayo's narrative and *narrator* internalize invites comparison with Marechera. "There are two homes inside my head," she says at one point, "home before [the township of] Paradise, and home in Paradise; home one and home two. Home one was best. A real house" (193). Further down the page, describing her life in Detroit, the narrator Darling expands the reference to include:

> *Home one, home two, and home three. There are four homes inside Mother of Bones's [her aunt and new guardian] head: home before the white people came to steal the country, and a king ruled; home when the white people came to steal the country, and then there was war; home when black people got our stolen country back after independence; and then the home of now. Home one, home two, home three, home four. When somebody talks about home, you have to listen carefully so you know exactly which one the person is referring to.* (193–94)

As in the example about one sip or ten from Mungoshi's *Ndiko Kupindana Kwamazuva*, such deceptively simple constructions have profound implications. A configuration of two homes offers the grounds for Darling to make a categorical evaluation and, presumably, determine what sorts of particular goods and conditions would enrich her life ("[r]adios blaring," for example, add value, whereas tin roofs detract from it [193]). The proliferation of homes both concrete and in terms of historical periodization, on the other hand, makes it difficult to even keep track of basic narrative-conversational progression.

It is fitting, therefore, that whereas the main international point of reference in *Nervous Conditions* is England, Bulawayo introduces South Africa as a key site of disenchantment. Dramatically recalling the first pages of Mlalazi's *Many Rivers* about Zimbabwean crossings to South Africa (both writers are from a close-knit community in Bulawayo, so it may indeed be an allusion), *We Need New Names* refers to a family relation who "had been eaten by a crocodile as he tried to cross the Limpopo River" (205). Even before that, Darling notes that "Mother had not wanted Father to leave for South Africa to begin with, but it was at that time when everybody was going to South Africa and other countries, some near, some far, some very, very far" (93). As in the example of concrete homes one and two as set against home's later, confusing proliferation, South Africa—an actual "good" in terms of its concrete focalization of family disagreements—here gives way to a shapeless transnationalism: South Africa is the only place that is named. South Africa is, as both Bulawayo and Mlalazi are aware, the obvious next step for the majority of aspirational or desperate Zimbabweans. But in the novel's clear representation of a more "pluralistic" liberal state, it is also the object of a targeted ambivalence that goes back to the very self-definition of the novel in Zimbabwe.

To come full circle, then, Bulawayo may well suggest an overly schematic narrative of hope's deflowering: the naive anticipation of a move from poor African township to big Western city (Detroit) is the realist inversion of the upward-mobility tale, the photonegative of cosmopolitanism's more inclusive "good" contemporaneity. At one point, the universal Zimbabwean voice that occasionally disrupts the book's first-person narration remarks, "And when we got to America we took our dreams, looked at them tenderly . . . and put them away" (243). In tension all the while, though, is a series of comparisons between another two entities, represented by Zimbabwe and South Africa, whose merits and demerits interact not as dreams turned to cynical reality but as a choice to be made between tough options in a world with no perfect cure. "All I know is that I'm certainly not clamoring to go across the borders to live where I'm called a kwerekwere" (94), says a Zimbabwean woman to her husband upon his own return from South Africa to die of AIDS. And yet even in a fairly remote part of the country, "things are now being paid for in U.S. dollars and South African rands" (205). There are two distinct forms of relation represented in this choice of currencies: the first internalizes Western powers as a locus of exaggerated and often vague hope or rejection, while the second invests in a savvier relation to a known quantity of pluralism in South Africa.

In this essay as a whole, such oppositions ultimately serve to foreground a different sort of choice in terms of an interpretive bottom line. Africanist criticism at this transitional juncture from postcolonialism to a broader transnational field still too often heralds a vague and sanctimonious plurality in the forms it seeks out or censures. On the contrary, it should now be digging deeper to grapple with locally and narratively emplaced structures of debate. In the agonistic tradition of the novel in Zimbabwe, then, I see an overdue critical intervention. The hyperpluralist alternative to structural conflict, in Connolly's words, is *straddling two or more perspectives to maintain tension between them*" (4; emphasis added). But instead of two firm hands, this model requires more legs than any writer can have.

*   *   *

JEANNE-MARIE JACKSON is assistant professor of world anglophone literature at Johns Hopkins University. Her first book, *South African Literature's Russian Soul: Narrative Forms of Global Isolation* appeared in 2015. She is currently at work on a project titled *The African Novel of Ideas: Intellection in the Age of Global Writing* (forthcoming), and she coedited a 2017 special issue of *Research in African Literatures* on religion and the (post)secular in African writing.

Works Cited

Allen, Michael H. *Globalization, Negotiation, and the Failure of Transformation in South Africa.* New York: Palgrave, 2006.

Anderson, Amanda. *The Way We Argue Now: A Study in the Cultures of Theory*. Princeton: Princeton UP, 2005.

Baghramian, Maria. "On the Plurality of Conceptual Schemes." *Pluralism: The Philosophy and Politics of Diversity*. Ed. Maria Baghramian and Attracta Ingram. London: Routledge, 2000. 44–59.

Bakhtin, Mikhail Mikhalovich. "Discourse in the Novel." *The Novel: An Anthology of Criticism and Theory 1900–2000*. Ed. Dorothy J. Hale. Malden: Blackwell, 2006. 481–509.

Benn Michaels, Walter. *Our America: Nativism, Modernism, and Pluralism*. Durham: Duke UP, 1995.

———. *The Shape of the Signifier: 1967 to the End of History*. Princeton: Princeton UP, 2004.

Berlin, Isaiah. "The Apotheosis of the Romantic Will." *The Crooked Timber of Humanity: Chapters in the History of Ideas*. Ed. Henry Hardy. Princeton: Princeton UP, 2013. 219–52.

Bond, Patrick. *Elite Transition: From Apartheid to Neoliberalism in South Africa*. London: Pluto, 2000.

Bulawayo, NoViolet. *We Need New Names*. New York: Back Bay, 2013.

Chiwome, Emmanuel M. "Modern Shona Literature as a Site of Struggle, 1956–2000." *Zimbabwean Transitions: Essays on Zimbabwean Literature in English, Ndebele, and Shona*. Ed. Mbongeni Z. Malaba and Geoffrey V. Davis. Spec. issue of *Matatu* 34.1 (2007): 159–71.

Comaroff, Jean, and John L. Comaroff. "Theory from the South; or, How Euro-America is Evolving toward Africa." *Anthropological Forum* 22.2 (2012): 113–31.

Connolly, William. *Pluralism*. Durham: Duke UP, 2005.

Culler, Jonathan. *On Deconstruction: Theory and Criticism after Structuralism*. 1982. Ithaca: Cornell UP, 2007.

Dangarembga, Tsitsi. *Nervous Conditions*. Seattle: Seal, 1988.

Davidson, Donald. "On the Very Idea of a Conceptual Scheme." *Proceedings and Addresses of the American Philosophical Association* 47 (1973–74): 5–20.

Deckard, Sharae, et al. *Combined and Uneven Development: Towards a New Theory of World-Literature*. Liverpool: Liverpool UP, 2015.

Deleuze, Gilles, and Félix Guattari. *A Thousand Plateaus: Capitalism and Schizophrenia*. Trans. Brian Massumi. Minneapolis: U of Minnesota P, 1987.

Desai, Gaurav. *Commerce with the Universe: Africa, India, and the Afrasian Imagination*. New York: Columbia UP, 2013.

Gagiano, Annie. Rev. of *The House of Hunger*, by Dambudzo Marechera. *LitNet*, African Library <http://www.oulitnet.co.za/africanlib/hunger.asp> (accessed 13 Mar. 2018).

Habila, Helon. Rev. of *We Need New Names*, by NoViolet Bulawayo. *Guardian* 20 June 2014 <https://www.theguardian.com/books/2013/jun/20/need-new-names-bulawayo -review>.

Hallward, Peter. *Absolutely Postcolonial: Writing between the Singular and the Specific*. Manchester: Manchester UP, 2002.

Hamilton, Lawrence. *Are South Africans Free?* London: Bloomsbury, 2014.

Harris, Ashleigh. "Awkward Form and Writing the African Present." JWTC: Johannesburg Workshop in Theory and Criticism, *Salon* 7 (2014) <jwtc.org.za/test/ashleigh_harris .htm>.

Hofmeyr, Isabel. "The Complicating Sea: The Indian Ocean as Method." *Comparative Studies of South Asia, Africa and the Middle East* 32.3 (2012): 584–90.

Honig, Bonnie. "The Optimistic Agonist." Interview with Nick Pearce. *OurKingdom* 7 Mar. 2013 <https://www.opendemocracy.net/ourkingdom/nick-pearce-bonnie-honig/opti mistic-agonist-interview-with-bonnie-honig>.

———. *Political Theory and the Displacement of Politics*. Ithaca: Cornell UP, 1993.

———. "The Time of Rights: Emergency Thoughts in an Emergency Setting." *The New Pluralism*. Ed. David Campbell and Morton Schoolman. Durham: Duke UP, 2008. 85–120.

Hove, Chenjerai. *Palaver Finish*. Harare: Weaver, 2002.

Julien, Eileen. "The Extroverted African Novel." *The Novel*. Ed. Franco Moretti. Vol. 1. Princeton: Princeton UP, 2006. 667–700.

Levine, Caroline. *Forms: Whole Rhythm, Hierarchy, Network*. Princeton: Princeton UP, 2015.

Lionnet, Francoise. "Shipwrecks, Slavery, and the Challenge of Global Comparison: From Fiction to Archive in the Colonial Indian Ocean." Address to the American Comparative Literature Association, 2012. *Comparative Literature* 64.4 (2012): 446–61.

Mamdani, Mahmood. *Define and Rule: Native as Political Identity*. Johannesburg: Wits UP, 2012.

Marechera, Dambudzo. *The House of Hunger*. London: Heinemann, 1978.

Mbembe, Achille. "Consumed by Our Lust for Lost Segregation." *Mail and Guardian* 28 Mar. 2013 <https://mg.co.za/article/2013-03-28-00-consumed-by-our-lust-for-lost- segregation>.

Miller, J. Hillis. "Stevens' Rock and Criticism as Cure, II." *Georgia Review* 30.2 (1976): 330–48.

Mlalazi, Christopher. *Many Rivers*. Bedford: Lion, 2009.

Moorthy, Shanti, and Ashraf Jamal, eds. *Indian Ocean Studies: Cultural, Social, and Political Perspectives*. London: Routledge, 2009.

Muhwati, Itai. "A Critical Appreciation of Victimhood in Mungoshi's Shona Novels: A Critical Study." *Zambezia* 32.1–2 (2005): 78–94.

Mushava, Stanley. "After Marechera: Subversion, Reinvention." *Herald* 7 Mar. 2016 <https://www.herald.co.zw/after-marechera-subversion-reinvention/>.

Mungoshi, Charles. *Kunyarara Hakusi Kutaura?* Harare: Zimbabwe Publishing, 1983.

———. *Ndiko Kupindana Kwamazuva.* Harare: Mambo, 1975.

———. *Waiting for the Rain.* Harare: Zimbabwe Publishing, 1975.

Muponde, Robert. "The Worm and the Hoe: Cultural Politics and Reconciliation after the Third Chimurenga." *Zimbabwe: Injustice and Political Reconciliation.* Ed. Brian Raftopoulous and Tyrone Savage. Harare: Weaver, 2005. 176–92.

Muponde, Robert, and Ranka Primorac. "Introduction: Writing against Blindness." *Versions of Zimbabwe: New Approaches to Literature and Culture.* Ed. Robert Muponde and Ranka Primorac. Harare: Weaver, 2005. xiii–xxii.

Newmark, Julianne. *The Pluralist Imagination: From East to West in American Literature.* Lincoln: U of Nebraska P, 2015.

Nyamfukudza, Stanley. "To Skin a Skunk: Some Observations on Zimbabwe's Intellectual Development." *Skinning the Skunk: Facing Zimbabwean Futures.* Ed. Mai Palmberg and Ranka Primorac. Uppsala: Nordic Africa Institute, 2005. 16–25.

Paperno, Irina. *Chernyshevsky and the Age of Realism: A Study in the Semiotics of Behavior.* Stanford: Stanford UP, 1988.

Primorac, Ranka. *The Place of Tears: The Novel and Politics in Modern Zimbabwe.* London: Tauris, 2006.

Rescher, Nicholas. *Pluralism: Against the Demand for Consensus.* Oxford: Oxford UP, 1993.

Veit-Wild, Flora. "De-silencing the Past—Challenging 'Patriotic History': New Books on Zimbabwean Literature." *Research in African Literatures* 37.3 (2006): 193–204.

———. *Teachers, Preachers, Non-believers: A Social History of Zimbabwean Literature.* London: Zell, 1992.

Wicomb, Zoë. *October.* Cape Town: Umuzi, 2014.

———. *Playing in the Light.* Johannesburg: Umuzi, 2006.

History's Happy Ending:
Bare Theory and the Novel

VAUGHN RASBERRY

In 2008, British writer Francis Spufford published *Red Plenty*, a fictionalized account of life in the Soviet Union during the early Khrushchev years. Politically and aesthetically, Spufford's achievement is to have reimagined the Soviet experiment not as a succession of failures and atrocities (though these elements lurk subtextually) but rather as the collective dreamworld of subjects who still believe in the prospect of victory over the capitalist order. By reimagining the dreamworld of Soviet citizens—who, by the early 1960s, remain chastened yet hopeful survivors of the Great Patriotic War and Stalinism—*Red Plenty* evokes a boundlessly energetic and determined social order in hot pursuit of a communist utopia just on history's horizon. Naturally, the characters of the novel do not know what setbacks and defeats history has in store. In their assessment of the international situation, Soviet citizens— buoyed by the success of *Sputnik*, the death of Stalin, and viability in the arms race, among other factors—have a long way to go but nonetheless possess a credible prospect of victory over liberal capitalism. This victory is what I am calling history's happy ending, a phrase adapted from *Red Plenty*.

The characters believe that the planned economy, a discredited project into which the novel breathes new life, is the engine capable of producing this historical triumph. Yet in a mini–morality play about racism and racial identity staged early in the novel, *Red Plenty* also signals an understated awareness that, in the communist narrative, this victory is neither complete nor feasible unless it is accompanied by another triumph: the eradication of the scourge of white supremacy and global racism—the historical phenomena that illustrate capitalist exploitation in its most naked form.

One problem the novel confronts, however, is that Soviet antiracism is underwritten by what the narrator in this scene calls *bare theory*. In what follows, I will unpack what a bare theory of race looks like in the novel, but for now I will note that this phrase appears in *Red Plenty* when one character, a student and Komsomol (Soviet youth organization) member named Galina, encounters an African American character named Roger Taylor, who is a member of a delegation to the Soviet Union promoting the democratic virtues of US capitalism. In the course of a testy exchange about the status of racial inequality in America— Galina insists the United States is irredeemably racist, whereas Roger defends the nation's racial progress—the black man gains the rhetorical upper hand, but not without a heavy toll on his dignity. This spectacle, along with the sympathy Roger

A version of this essay was presented first at Duke University's conference "Pre-Neoliberalisms and the Novel," held on April 8, 2015, and then at Stanford University's conference "Novel Institutions," held on May 19–20, 2017. The author wishes to thank audiences at both conferences for their helpful feedback on earlier versions of this essay.

garners from the Russian crowd, leads Galina to the lamentable epiphany that she had "understood only in the barest theory" why her unrelenting interrogation of Roger had left him speechless and demoralized (57).

This scene suggests that the Soviet theory and praxis of racial egalitarianism, however trenchant, nonetheless lacks sufficient sensitivity to and knowledge about the affective complexities borne from racial antagonisms that arise far outside the Soviet sphere. The problem with bare theory involves the old criticism that, as with many aspects of communism, it lacks a human dimension that reveals the theory to be flimsy if not counterproductive to egalitarian aims. In the world of this novel, which is not uncritical of the Soviet project, bare theory is one ostensibly minor but key failure in a narrative that lovingly, even euphorically, reimagines this project's successes and partial victories, its hopes and human shortcomings.

In the second half of the twentieth century and into the present, this critique—what I will call a *novelistic theory of race*—appears to have prevailed over the bare theory of race. In this key episode from Spufford's novel, the bare theory of race clearly loses out. And yet it remains a crucial element of the Soviet experiment in universal emancipation, one that I will defend against the novelistic theory. What is meant by a novelistic theory of race? There are two main components. First, it suggests a character like Roger's hard-earned right to narrate his own experience and the terms by which his relationship to the nation ought to be understood. His self-narration, in other words, ought to supersede the Soviet narrative of racial exploitation that seeks to subsume individual or particularized narratives. And second, the novelistic theory of race represents an effort among black writers, especially at mid-century, to replace caricatures of black humanity with a more complex and unmistakably modernist idiom that reflects the full range and capacity of black intellect. Historically, the novelistic theory appears to have won the day—in much the same way that democratic capitalism vanquished international communism—but in what follows I will reconsider the merits of the discarded bare theory of race.

Part of what enabled the historical victory of the novelistic theory was a persistent and persuasive literary critique of bare theories of race by some of the mid-century's most prominent novelists, including Claude McKay, Richard Wright, Ralph Ellison, and James Baldwin. Taken together, these writers assailed Soviet and communist efforts to dictate black political narratives of self-emancipation and to control the terms with which black writers describe their humanity and the nuances of racial or colonial experience.

After summarizing this literary-political critique in key novels such as Ellison's *Invisible Man* (1952) and Wright's *The Outsider* (1953), the remainder of this essay will revisit the aforementioned scene in *Red Plenty*. If the appeal to complex idioms of black subjectivity won the day historically, at least in the novel genre past and present and arguably in the wider public sphere, the contemporary political situation invites a reconsideration of just why Soviet racial ideology mobilized the African diaspora in the first place—and why the black modernist insistence on complex subjectivity and consciousness, or the novelistic theory of race, appears in retrospect like a Pyrrhic victory.

In the archive of twentieth-century African American and African diaspora literature, a certain theme dominates narratives of disaffiliation from communism: the conflict between communist master narratives and black self-narration. Like most fellow travelers, black leftists took issue with many aspects of the unfolding project of world communism, led by the Soviet Union, but above all they repudiated the pervasive tendency among communists to dictate black narratives of self-emancipation. They bristled at the idea that in their specific struggle against racial discrimination and colonial occupation, they also had to contend with new master narratives foisted upon them. A few examples from major mid-century novels illustrate this conflict.

Readers of Ralph Ellison's *Invisible Man* will recall the novel's depiction of the Brotherhood, a fictional entity whose representatives speak of the iron laws of history, the primacy of the dialectic, and the inexorable march of progress. Toward the end of the novel, the Brotherhood finally devolves into yet another malefactor among the diverse individuals and groups (northern liberals, the black bourgeoisie, black nationalists of different stripes) that seek to misdirect or manipulate Invisible Man. The author's biographer, Arnold Rampersad, credits Ellison's insistence that the Brotherhood is an invention ("no more the Communist Party than Invisible Man's college is Tuskegee Institute") but concedes that, "even so, it is the key metaphor Ellison uses to assail the totalitarian Left in its dealings with blacks. The Brotherhood, which enters the text ominously, is never defended, much less rehabilitated" (244–45). As the Brotherhood turns out to be no less pernicious than his other adversaries, Invisible is ultimately left to his own individuality and elevated if disillusioned consciousness: a narrative self that aligns with what Barbara Foley and other critics have identified as the Cold War ideological concerns motivating Ellison's composition.

Published a year after *Invisible Man*, Richard Wright's novel *The Outsider* extends this theme in a characteristically darker mode. In *The Outsider*, the protagonist, Cross Damon, once aspired to study philosophy at the University of Chicago but, after a self-incurred personal crisis, descends into murder and flees to New York under an alias, Lionel Lane. In New York, Cross encounters a communist, Hilton, who rightly suspects that Cross has killed two other characters (Gil, a communist, and Herndon, a fascist) who were themselves engaged in a life-and-death fight. In an effort to save his own life, Hilton admits that he knows about the murders but explains to Cross that he had no intention of turning him over to the police or killing him in retaliation (for the murder of his comrade Gil). After this explanation, Cross bursts out, "That's just it!" "I might forgive you if you had been going to kill me. But no; you were going to make me a slave. I would never have been able to draw a free breath as long as I lived if you had had your way. I'd have suffered, night and day. *You would have dominated my consciousness*" (437; emphasis added). Armed with this deadly secret, Hilton would be perfectly positioned to control Cross as a valuable new Party recruit—at least in the protagonist's paranoid mind. In this context, "dominated my consciousness" means subordinating Cross's self-narration—and by symbolic extension the narrative agency of all black former communists—to the will of (white) directives and the vicissitudes of party discipline. It means the denial of Cross's right to define his interpretation of history and his location within it, especially when this interpretation conflicts with Party orthodoxy. Murder seems like an excessively compensatory response to narrative domination, but part of *The Outsider*'s didactic aim is to kill the ideological pretensions of the two rival superpowers—the United States and the Soviet Union—shaping the post–World War II global order. Wright constructs a protagonist whose commitment to self-narration is so intense that it leads—not unlike the totalitarian systems he repudiates—to his self-destruction.

A few years after the publication of these novels and in the wake of Nikita Khrushchev's so-called secret speech that inventoried Stalin's crimes, Aimé Césaire submitted his "Letter to Maurice Thorez" on October 24, 1956. Khrushchev's revelations, writes Césaire, "are enough to have plunged all those who have participated in communist activity, to whatever degree, into an abyss of shock, pain, and shame (or, at least, I hope so)" (145). He includes a litany of abuses and grievous actions committed by the Soviet state and the French Communist Party: the exploitation rather than empowerment of the working class; the rise of anti-Semitism in Russia and the Eastern bloc; the asymmetrical relationships between Moscow and other communist states; the French Communist Party's progovernment position on Algeria; the antidemocratic methods of Stalin that were adopted by other communist leaders, and so on.

Pivoting to the status of the African diaspora in relation to communism, Césaire stresses the "singularity of our 'situation in the world,' which cannot be confused with any other" (147). He goes on to argue that "the struggle of colonial peoples against colonialism, the struggle of peoples of color against racism—is more complex, or better yet, of a completely different nature than the fight of the French worker against French capitalism, and it cannot in any way be considered a part, a fragment, of that struggle" (147). What I am calling the right to narrate Césaire calls the right to initiative: "If the goal of all progressive politics is to one day restore freedom to colonized peoples," Césaire concludes, "it is at least necessary that the everyday actions of progressive parties not be in contradiction with this desired end by continually destroying the very foundations, organizational as well as psychological, of this future freedom, foundations which can be reduced to a single postulate: the right to initiative" (149). Césaire's criticisms, however, did not lead him to renounce the communist idea. His hope was to reconstitute the project with blacks in a vanguard and autonomous rather than subaltern role.

Though vastly different in tone, ideological orientation, and characterization, among other formal elements, these texts exemplify a novelistic theory of race. Now I will return to *Red Plenty* in order to illustrate the novel's depiction of bare theory. In an early scene, an American delegation arrives in Moscow's Sokolniki Park as part of a tour showcasing US innovation and the "American Way of Life."[1]

---

[1] On seven gigantic screens—one screen would have been enough, even "a marvel"; seven, the narrator observes, "were a bombardment"—Russians watched attentively but could not really grasp the scenes of quotidian American life on display. "The men worked, in offices and factories. The children studied. The women, apart from the ones who were teaching the children in the schools, stayed at home, polishing and vacuuming huge rooms as uncluttered as stage sets. The camera lovingly kissed each surface" (45).

This scene fictionalizes the historic exchange between Moscow and Washington in 1959 (the year W. E. B. Du Bois was awarded the Lenin Peace Prize), when each regime set up exhibitions extolling the virtues of capitalism or communism, respectively, and sent delegations to their rival hosts. This landmark opening culminated in the famous "kitchen debate" between Nixon and Khrushchev.

Two members of the Komsomol—Galina, a Russian nursing student, and Fyodor, a factory worker—have been tasked with puncturing holes in the delegation's effusions about the innumerable advantages of the American capitalist system, in which all citizens, even members of the working class, are said to enjoy benefits typically afforded the privileged in other societies. "Now remember," Galina's supervisor instructs her, "don't miss *any* of the opportunities to put our point of view. Don't be rude to our guides, but use all of the openings that we've discussed" (42). When Galina encounters Roger Taylor of the US delegation, she is eager to unleash her rhetorical arsenal against him.

Yet there is a problem: Roger Taylor is a *Negro* American, and no one had prepared her for that fact. "The debating points they had been given," the narrator explains, "had not been devised with him in mind. . . . [T]hey [her Komsomol supervisors] must have known that some of the guides were Negroes; they might have *said*. She hurried to catch up" (47). A less canny novelist might have created a more familiar black character as an instigator of racial conflict in the narrative: a figure modeled on the numerous black American or African or West Indian radicals who sojourned to the Soviet Union in the early to mid-twentieth century, often on scholarship at the Lenin School or the Communist University of the Toilers of the East.[2] Instead, Spufford imagines a precocious and savvy African American who acts as a spokesman for the inestimable benefits of US capitalism.

In her fascinating account of the racial and gendered dimensions of the Nixon-Khrushchev debate, Kate Baldwin observes that the US government carefully calibrated the recruitment of young Russian-speaking Americans to serve as guides at the American National Exhibition in Moscow. Baldwin cites William B. Davis, a US treasury agent, who was selected as one of four black Americans among the delegation out of a total of seventy-five representatives chosen from eight hundred applicants. Spufford's character Roger Taylor could well have been modeled on Davis, who found himself in Moscow downplaying the blacklisting of Paul Robeson and questioning both Russia's commitment to racial equality and the substance of Soviet freedom. "This problematic performance of U.S. inclusion," writes Baldwin, "reflected some of the tensions between the ideals of liberal democracy as racially integrated and the appeal of Soviet internationalism as supportive of American blacks. Before they were selected by the United States Information Agency (USIA), the black American guides were fully vetted, not only regarding their Russian fluency but also as to their ideological affiliations (they were not communist sympathizers)" (xiv). Not surprisingly, black Americans who were resident or well known in the Soviet Union, and therefore unlikely to champion the American way of life, did not receive invitations to participate.

---

[2]   See, for example, *Black Bolshevik*, the autobiography of Harry Haywood, who claims to have studied in both Soviet institutions.

But Taylor, the reader is supposed to understand, is no mere puppet for US interests; he is an entrepreneurial intellectual and a student enrolled in the historically black Howard University, with a major in Russian language and literature. Roger's misidentification of Howard University as located "in Virginia, just outside of Washington," slyly signals his symbolic and spatial distance from the precincts of American power—a false statement that highlights his peripheral position vis-à-vis the US government and neutralizes the obvious fact that his mission is supported by that very government.[3]

His charismatic defense of American ingenuity and openness, embodied in his (seemingly) guileless and disarming display of American salesmanship, is obviously and powerfully reinforced by his blackness. In this moment, the novel seizes on a motif emblematic in the history of Cold War cultural diplomacy. For Taylor's Russian audience, whose skepticism wanes as his personality (if not necessarily his argument) wins them over, he is a beguiling refutation of everything the audience thinks it knows about Jim Crow. How racially hostile *is* this America they imagine only through Soviet ideology, some wonder, if the nation can produce a young Russian-speaking Negro of such refinement and sensibility?

The narrative slyly leaves some key details ambiguous. For one, readers do not know the nature of Taylor's interest in Russian culture. At the outset of his presentation, he suavely says: "Please, if I make any mistakes speaking your beautiful language, you should just sing out straight away and tell me. I'm sure I have an accent. Now, the theme of our exhibition here is the American Way of Life" (47). Here, the narrative establishes Roger's diplomatic authority by enabling him to showcase his unexpected Russian language skill at the same moment as he ingratiates himself to his audience by imploring them, in a subtle vernacular ("just sing out straight away"), to correct his mistakes.

Beyond Taylor's reference to "your beautiful language," however, the reader never learns *why* he studies Russian: was he entranced by a Turgenev or Dostoyevsky novel at a young age, upon which experience he embarked on a Russian major in order to be able to read *The Possessed* in the original? Or reading the geopolitical tea leaves at mid-century, did he intuit that the acquisition of Russian presaged a handsome career in the State Department? Did one pursuit lead to the other? These motivations are wisely left unspecified and unquestioned.

Along with a few other spectators, Galina questions the veracity of his narrative and deflects his skills of persuasion. Is it not true, they ask, that the leisure time supposedly afforded Americans is chimerical, since workers spend all their waking hours in hard labor? Is it not true that the household commodities on display are only available to the wealthy in America? Actually, Taylor replies, the selection of affordable items "was a guiding principle of the exhibition." That no luxury items were on display was a source of disappointment for some Russian viewers, including Galina, who—though she wants to disbelieve this narrative of American consumer egalitarianism—secretly envies the putative accessibility of middle-class comfort in the United States that she desires in Soviet Russia.

---

[3]   I want to acknowledge the response to my paper by Professor Anne Garetta, who encouraged me to think about this reference in the novel as symbolic rather than erroneous.

In the United States, Taylor goes on to explain,

the ordinary working guy takes it for granted that he'll own a suit to go out dancing in on a Friday night with his wife, and often he owns a car too, as we'll see when we get to the automobile exhibit outside. Maybe it takes a bit of organizing to get the life he wants, a bit of care with the money, but isn't that true everywhere in the world? The important thing is that the standard of living for ordinary Americans has risen to the level you see here, and goes on rising, year by year. (51)

Fyodor replies that Taylor seems to be referring to the *average* worker's wages and standard of living—but what about the millions surviving below this "average"? "If life is so good, Mr. Taylor, why do American steel-workers go on strike every single year?" "Because they want their lives to be even better. Because they want to earn more," Taylor replies (51).

But everyone knows, Galina chimes in, that this picture aggressively excludes black America. "Like you say," Taylor responds with exhaustion, "one of our biggest problems has been the way that our colored citizens and our white citizens get along together. We fought a whole civil war to end slavery, you know, at the same time your Tsar Alexander was ending Serfdom here. But we make progress, you know . . . and we go on getting better" (55). *So smooth, still so smooth*, Galina thinks—how will she regain the upper hand? She finds her moment in Roger's invocation of the first-person plural "we" in relation to the nation at large. "'Why do you keep saying *we*?' she interrupted. 'Why do you keep talking as if you're included?'" Do you think it's alright, she asks, "to wait, and wait, and wait?" (55). Now the exchange grows tense; the crowd perks up.

Self-satisfied but slightly panicked, Galina sees that she has upended Taylor's "lightfooted poise," forcing him now to pick "his words slowly and painfully." When he invokes the Declaration of Independence as an inviolable document guaranteeing the equality of all men, she counters that the words it contains are a lie if America's social reality so thoroughly contradicts them. Simultaneously, in the background, black and white actors in the exhibition are performing a wedding scene, but clearly, she observes, this reenactment is also a lie, since the very idea of an interracial wedding celebration (not marriage) "has been denounced as something disgusting" in the US newspapers. (As Kate Baldwin notes, in the historical exhibition, US officials actually canceled the planned interracial wedding scene, following strident objections from South Carolina senator Strom Thurmond and others [xv].) What about the dignity of his people? Where was *his* dignity? "My question, Mr. Taylor, my question is why have you betrayed your people by coming to Moscow to represent a country like that?" (56–57).

Taylor nearly succumbs to a state of shock. He wonders: *Rules? Weren't there? Some? Any?* The audience members, who had taken a liking to Taylor, turn steely, unfriendly eyes upon Galina. Encouraged now that "it was just her he had to deal with, not the whole ring of pale Muscovite faces," Taylor replies with an acid tongue that he is very glad that "my dignity means so much to you" but insists,

"I haven't betrayed anyone. And I think my opinion is the one that counts, don't you? Because the only way of telling that kind of thing is to look inside yourself, at your own conscience. And everybody has to do that. Everybody has to decide where to place their hopes, and what compromises are all right to make, and what compromises aren't OK. After all," he said, "we all do make compromises—don't we?" (58). In what looks like a manifestation of Rousseau's *volonté générale* in action, Taylor's Russian audience sides with the young American as he leads them away to another part of the exhibition.

Confused and embarrassed, Galina "understood only in the barest theory why the question had done that to him, but seeing him speechless, voiceless, she was able to glimpse for a second how important charm might have been to him, as a covering, as a defense" (57). In this scene, bare theory penetrates the illusions of US consumerism and racial democracy but misunderstands the significance of self-narration in a context when it matters most: in an encounter when this right asserts itself as insubordinate to the demands of ideology.

And yet what if bare theory is perhaps the best guarantor of meaningful racial equality? A novelistic theory of race, despite its merits and even its historical necessity, has not and probably cannot achieve this aim. Bare theory succeeds where novelistic theory falls short because it is attached to, and buttressed by, a powerful and iron-fisted state apparatus. A bare theory of race does not require understanding the complexities of black experience or the importance of narrative authority for oppressed groups. Bare theory acknowledges the following: that the construction of race and racism are entwined at every step with the emergence of many capitalist economies, at least those bound up with the Atlantic slave trade and European colonialism; that the state has both an educational and a punitive role to play in the abolition of prejudicial attitudes that flow from racial capitalism; and that no socialist utopia—or happy end of history—is possible without the state's commitment to this theory and practice.

One exemplary expression of bare theory appears in a scene from the autobiography of Harry Haywood, a prominent African American communist. "In the Soviet Union," Haywood explains in *Black Bolshevik*, "remnants of national and racial prejudices from the old society were attacked by education and law. It was a crime to give or receive direct or indirect privileges, or to exercise discrimination because of race or nationality. Any manifestation of racial or national superiority was punishable by law and regarded as a serious political offense, a social crime." He then relays an anecdote worth quoting at length:

> During my entire stay in the Soviet Union, I encountered only one incident of racial hostility. It was on a Moscow streetcar. Several of us Black students had boarded the car on our way to spend an evening with our friend MacCloud. It was after rush hour, and the car was only about half filled with Russian passengers. As usual, we were the objects of friendly curiosity. At one stop, a drunken Russian staggered aboard. Seeing us, he muttered (but loud enough for the whole car to hear) something about "Black devils in our country." A group of outraged Russian passengers thereupon seized him and ordered the motorman to stop the car. It was a citizen's arrest, the first I had ever

witnessed. "How dare you, you scum, insult people who are the guests of our country!"
What then occurred was an impromptu, on-the-spot meeting, where they debated what
to do with the man. I was to see many of this kind of "meeting" during my stay in
Russia. (170–71)

A citizen's arrest: perhaps such acts have occurred in US history, but the point of
Haywood's anecdote is to highlight the stark contrast between the Soviet and
American approaches to racial discrimination. The group decides to take the cul-
prit to the police station, where "they hustled the drunk out of the car and insisted
that we Blacks, as the injured parties, come along to make the charges." Initially
the injured parties demurred, "saying that the man was obviously drunk and not
responsible for his remarks. 'No, citizens,' said a young man (who had done most
of the talking), 'drunk or not, we don't allow this sort of thing in our country. You
must come with us to the militia (police) station and prefer [*sic*] charges against
this man.'" As he is being dragged into the station, the drunk man sobers up and
apologizes, swearing that he was angry about another matter and that he holds no
"race prejudice against those Black *gospoda* [gentlemen]." The black men take pity
on the man and accept his apology. "We didn't want to press the matter," writes
Haywood. "'No,' says the commandant, 'we'll keep him overnight. Perhaps this
will be a lesson to him'" (171). What Haywood highlights in this anecdote is what
we might call a moment of antiracist totalitarianism. As the moral of this story
makes clear, by no means can this offense be resolved in the aristocratic tradition
of an apology and a handshake: the police *must* get involved, the assailant *must*
be punished. Even if the Soviet enforcement of racial equality stretches credulity
in Haywood's account, the lesson of the drunken belligerent also presents a lesson
to American readers: a social study of diametrical contrasts in racial attitudes,
crystallized in a startling episode of Soviet-style, *citizen*-led, and state-sponsored
reeducation.

Poignantly, this scene illustrates the power of a bare theory of racial inequality.
Note that there is not much room for liberal norms of deliberation, tolerance, respect
for conflicting points of view, or the rights of the accused in Haywood's narration.
There is no room even for discussion of what has actually transpired. Every spectator knows what has happened and mobilizes accordingly. The Soviet citizens
know that their arrest is backed by the iron fist of the state. Note, also, that the
wishes of the offended party are not respected—despite their protests that the
matter could be resolved amicably, Haywood and his party are obliged to follow
through with the procedures of the citizen's arrest. The formulation of "respect
for the other" has no traction here.

Certainly genre matters in this comparison, since the contrasting racial episodes
drawn from *Red Plenty* and Haywood's *Autobiography* reflect differences in form
as much as in ideology. That said, the idea of *Red Plenty* as a *novel* is a matter of
contention among readers. Spufford refers to the narrative, appropriately, as a *fairy
tale*. Reflecting on the generic status of *Red Plenty* as a historical novel, Fredric
Jameson writes: "I think we need to return to the uniqueness, not of the form, but
of the content, and to the strangeness of the fresh start, the new age, the new

beginnings. . . . Spufford's artistry lies in his ability to make us forget, while we are reading his novel, all the things that have been left out: the areas of Soviet life as well in which people do not have renewed hope, the realities that do not fit into the fairy-tale" (120–22). The narrative entwines historical actors (Khrushchev, Henry Cabot Lodge, Averell Harriman, Alexei Nikolaevich Kosygin) and events (the Bay of Pigs, Sputnik, the space race) with fictional creations, all narrated in an ostensibly mock academic apparatus: *Red Plenty* features a bibliography, footnotes, a table of contents, a cast of characters, a learned introduction to each chapter, and so on.

This formal apparatus recalls postmodern fictions of the kind pioneered by David Foster Wallace, but it also evokes mock-academic fictions such as Borges's *A Universal History of Infamy* (*Historia universal de la infamia*, 1935) and Roberto Bolaño's *Nazi Literature in the Americas* (*La literatura Nazi en América*, 1996). Yet if *Red Plenty* plays with scholarly and fictional conventions in order to temper what might have been a scandalous dalliance with history, the novel nevertheless refuses the irony that often infuses literary works of mock scholarship. Bolaño calibrated an exquisitely ironic tone in *Nazi Literature in the Americas*, a narrative encyclopedia of fictional fascists whom history has rendered available for mockery. Yet Spufford is fictionalizing the history not of fascists but of communists. The novel insists that their collective subjectivity, bound up in an earnest sense of historical mission, is worthy of serious reconstruction. Postmodern irony and its detachments are inimical to Spufford's purpose insofar as his novel seeks to recuperate the inner lives and outward projections, the dreams and anxieties that, taken together, form a collective subject of the communist hypothesis.

On the other hand, it is easy to see an ironic element in the novel's approach to the ideas of Marxism or Soviet communism that appear, retrospectively, as devastatingly wrongheaded or outright catastrophic. In one scene, a young economist named Emil struggles to understand why the Stalinist orthodoxy and its vestigial traces in Khrushchev's reign demoted a science, economics, so patently indispensable to the success of a planned economy and thus to the viability of Soviet society itself. For Stalin, economics was easily subsumed by ideology, which dictates which economic ideas were useful (very few) and which were useless, even dangerous (all the rest). In dialogue with his colleagues, Emil discovers that everyone, even each of his fellow economists, has absorbed the Stalinist orthodoxy about their discipline, and not only, apparently, because they feared retaliation. Emil "believed that the Soviet Union was soon going to need more from its economists, because there was more to life—there was more to running an economy—than giving orders. It might do for the brute-force first stage of building an industrial base, but what came next surely had to be subtler, surely had to be adjusted to the richer and more complicated relationships in the economy, here on the threshold of plenty" (64). In Emil's mind, Stalin seemed to mock the idea that planning an economy required any intellectual effort at all, believing instead that what was important was to get "the chain of command right," "build it on the right ideological principles," and "all that was left was a few technical details" to be undertaken by the appropriate number crunchers (*not* mathematicians or economists) (64).

Before Stalin's dismissal of economic planning, Emil thinks, Marx himself "didn't say much about economics after the revolution," though "he did insistently name the state he promised was coming, at history's happy end. He called it 'consciously arranged society.' Acting together, human beings were going to construct for the world a wealth-producing apparatus that far exceeded in efficiency the apparatus that formed ad hoc, by default, when everyone chaotically scrabbled for survival" (65). This vision or *promise* of a consciously arranged society might appear in the current neoliberal moment as offered up in the text for gentle ridicule. But ridicule of so-called actually existing socialism is not what Spufford has in mind.

In this respect, the phrase "here on the threshold of plenty" is the one to focus on, for the well-known historical experience of disappointment, error, and failure in the Soviet experiment is subordinate to the characters' own sense of political possibility and faith in their ability to put the Stalinist era behind them. Like his fellow citizens portrayed in the novel, Emil believes that the Soviet Union is truly on the threshold of red plenty.

The novel's promise of red plenty, or what I am calling history's happy ending—a prosperous, consciously planned, egalitarian, and ultimately universal social order—was not only about collective striving for economic plenitude. For the promise of history's happy ending, to reiterate, was attainable only with the concurrent elimination of racial oppression and colonial exploitation. No vision or revision of the communist hypothesis, it seems to me, can afford to ignore this epochal but surprisingly understated legacy of the communist version of the end of history.

Yet as proponents of the communist hypothesis contemplate the roads not taken in history's experiments in communism—the path of subtraction rather than destruction, in Alain Badiou's terms—seldom have contemporary critics probed this antiracist legacy for historical lessons (54). Rarely, for example, have they considered the consequences of communism's slow severance with the global anticolonial movement, whether the relationship in question is the negritude movement's friction with the French Communist Party, the Sino-Soviet Split, or the alienation of African Americans from the Communist Party USA.

Finally, it is important to acknowledge the importance of the novelistic theory of race and its attendant emphasis on the right to narrate. This scene from *Red Plenty* hinges precisely on this right, which Homi K. Bhabha describes as "the authority to tell stories, recount or recast histories, that create the web of social life and change the direction of its flow. The right to narrate is not simply a linguistic act; it is also a metaphor for the fundamental human interest in freedom itself, the right to be heard—to be recognized and represented." Arguably, this right matters most when the narration in question collides with one's own ideological disposition or even with the putative self-interests of the enunciator (as in the example of Roger Taylor). And yet I have argued that the novel also underscores, in the exchange of Galina and Roger, a more politically salient vision of a road constructed but not traveled in the twentieth century—one that might not have led to history's happy ending but that could have precipitated what appears then and now as a hopelessly utopian prospect: a colorblind world order.

*   *   *

VAUGHN RASBERRY is associate professor of English at Stanford University, affiliated with both the Center for Comparative Studies in Race and Ethnicity and the Program in Modern Thought and Literature. His first book, *Race and the Totalitarian Century: Geopolitics in the Black Literary Imagination*, appeared in 2016 and received the American Political Science Association's 2017 Ralph Bunche Award as well as the Before Columbus Foundation's 2017 American Book Award.

Works Cited

Badiou, Alain. *The Century.* Cambridge: Polity, 2007.

Baldwin, Kate A. *The Racial Imaginary of the Cold War Kitchen: From Sokol'niki Park to Chicago's South Side.* Hanover: Dartmouth College P, 2016.

Bhabha, Homi K. "The Right to Narrate." *Harvard Design Magazine* 38 (2014) <http://www .harvarddesignmagazine.org/issues/38/the-right-to-narrate>.

Césaire, Aimé. "Letter to Maurice Thorez." *Social Text* 28.2 (2010): 145–52.

Ellison, Ralph. *Invisible Man.* New York: Random House, 1952.

Foley, Barbara. *Wrestling with the Left: The Making of Ralph Ellison's Invisible Man.* Durham: Duke UP, 2010.

Haywood, Harry. *Black Bolshevik: Autobiography of an Afro-American Communist.* Chicago: Liberator, 1978.

Jameson, Fredric. "In Soviet Arcadia." *New Left Review* 75 (2012): 119–27.

Rampersad, Arnold. *Ralph Ellison: A Biography.* New York: Knopf, 2007.

Spufford, Francis. *Red Plenty.* Minneapolis: Graywolf, 2010.

Wright, Richard. *The Outsider.* New York: Harper Perennial, 2008.

Keep up to date on new scholarship

Issue alerts are a great way to stay current on all the cutting-edge scholarship from your favorite Duke University Press journals. This free service delivers tables of contents directly to your inbox, informing you of the latest groundbreaking work as soon as it is published.

To sign up for issue alerts:

1. Visit **dukeu.press/register** and register for an account. You do not need to provide a customer number.

2. After registering, visit **dukeu.press/alerts**.

3. Go to "Latest Issue Alerts" and click on "Add Alerts."

4. Select as many publications as you would like from the pop-up window and click "Add Alerts."

read.dukeupress.edu/journals　

Printed and bound by CPI Group (UK) Ltd, Croydon, CR0 4YY

13/04/2025

14656479-0004